Heretics in the Temple

Heretics in the Temple

*Americans Who Reject
the Nation's Legal Faith*

David Ray Papke

NEW YORK UNIVERSITY PRESS
New York and London

NEW YORK UNIVERSITY PRESS
New York and London

Copyright © 1998 by New York University
All rights reserved

Library of Congress Cataloging-in-Publication Data

Papke, David Ray, 1947–
Heretics in the temple : Americans who reject the nation's legal
faith / David Ray Papke.
p. cm. — (Critical America)
Includes bibliographical references and index.
ISBN 0-8147-6632-3 (alk. paper)
1. Law—United Sates—Philosophy—History. 2. Effectiveness and
validity of law—United States—History. 3. Critical legal studies—
United States. 4. Culture and law. I. Title. II. Series.
KF379.P37 1998
349.73'01—dc21   98-15987
CIP

New York University Press books are printed on acid-free paper,
and their binding materials are chosen for strength and durability.

Manufactured in the United States of America

10 9 8 7 6 5 4 3 2 1

For Nora, My Feather

Contents

Acknowledgments

I began seriously considering the American legal faith neither during my days in graduate school nor in my first years as a professor. Instead, it was a 1987 Fulbright year in Taiwan that piqued my curiosity. Time and again my graduate students at Tamkang University underscored the tremendous emphasis Americans place on law, the way the American dominant culture was in their opinion the most legalistic in the world. I carried this sensitivity back with me to the United States, and in subsequent years grew especially intrigued by those Americans who somehow rejected the nation's legal faith.

While writing this book, I have been fortunate to hold a joint appointment in the School of Law and the School of Liberal Arts at Indiana University-Purdue University at Indianapolis (IUPUI). Students and colleagues stationed on "both sides of the street" sharpened my thinking and improved my work. In particular, colleagues Minde Browning, Daniel Cole, Michael Heise, Elise Papke, June Starr, and Danaya Wright critiqued parts of my manuscript draft. I benefited as well from summer research support from the School of Law and from the assistance of many IUPUI librarians, especially Beverly Bryant, who processed and pursued countless books I needed from other libraries. Jean Armin, James Irwin, and Darlene Phillips kindly typed parts of the manuscript and dealt with a range of computer problems well beyond my ken, managing in the midst of it all to encourage me in my work.

Beyond IUPUI, I welcomed the comments of Michael Grossberg, Mark Pittinger, and Norman Rosenberg on early drafts of parts of the manuscript. I also received valuable comments from audience members when I presented related papers at meetings of the American Culture Association, American Studies Association, Association of American

Law Schools, and Organization of American Historians. Different versions of parts of chapters 1, 4, and 5 appeared, respectively, in the *Journal of American Culture,* the *University of Cincinnati Law Review,* and the *Vermont Law Review.* I thank the editors of those journals for their help and their permission to republish.

Finally, my work greatly benefited from the input and editorial suggestions of Richard Delgado, Jean Stefancic, and Niko Pfund. Prolific scholars and critically engaged citizens, Richard and Jean thoughtfully made my book part of the Critical America series. Niko, my editor at New York University Press, was enthusiastic and frank at every turn. One could not hope for better collegial support.

1

A Legal Faith for the
New Republic

Thomas Paine's life prior to arriving in the American colonies in 1774 hardly augured for success. His uncirculated vita included a bankruptcy, two unsuccessful marriages, and false career starts as a tobacconist, grocer, and corset maker. But Paine's thought and writing had a sharp political edge, and his publication in 1776 of *Common Sense* produced thunderous approval. The pamphlet sold a remarkable one hundred thousand copies in only three months and became the most influential tract of the independence movement. In the midst of his fiery call for revolution, Paine paused to admit that many of the Englishmen in the colonies would be anxious about establishing a nation without a king. We have an alternative, he suggested. Americans could solemnly set aside a day to honor the governmental charter. More specifically, Paine said, bring forth the charter itself, place it on top of the Bible, and then place a crown on top of the charter. The whole world would then know, Paine said, "that in America the law is king."[1]

A century and a half earlier, when Europeans began settling in North America, such glorification of the law would have had little appeal. Many colonists had carried a respect for the British law and legal institutions with them on the Atlantic crossing, but up and down the colonial seaboard legal systems were idiosyncratic and less important than community, status, religion, and race in providing social order. Only in the eighteenth century did colonists begin truly to rely on law and legal institutions to settle their disputes and chart their social course. To be sure, there was no shortage of grousing about individual judicial rulings and also more collective protests by the poor and disenchanted along the Hudson, in Virginia, and in the western Carolinas. However, even these collective complaints were indicators that law and legal institutions had taken on increased importance in colonial society.

What explains this development? The answer is complex and cannot be reduced to simply the drive for independence. Within the law itself, lawyering became more profitable, and the legal profession attracted more sons of the elite. More lawyers meant more lawsuits and larger, more refined colonial courts. On the grander social level, landowners, merchants, and financiers found the law increasingly useful in asserting their claims and resolving their disputes, and even craftsmen, farmers, and simple "mechanicks," exposed to the vicissitudes of the market, came increasingly to believe in the utility of legal rules, actions, and officials. Most abstractly, a grand change was taking place, one including the growth of cities, improved communication and transport, and the formation of new social groups. This "modernization," as scholars sometimes dub it, included an increased reliance on rational-legal systems of authority as opposed to older charismatic and traditional ones. The changes did not occur overnight, but colonial Americans came to see legal rights and duties as the keys to relationships, legal institutions as devices to avoid chaos and preserve liberty, and law-abiding conduct as something highly ethical.[2]

Ironically, even the Declaration of Independence—the chief revolutionary document—shows the extent to which confidence in law had taken hold at the founding of the Republic. The chief author was Thomas Jefferson, a thirty-four-year-old member of the Virginia planter class and most decidedly a lawyer. While other prominent members of the Virginia bar such as Patrick Henry and John Marshall became lawyers after only a few months of study, Jefferson had devoted five years to his legal studies at the College of William and Mary and in George Wythe's prestigious law office. He even at one point taught himself Anglo-Saxon in hopes of better understanding the origins and nuances of the English common law. Later, he assembled a law library so extensive that Virginia courts relied on it.[3]

Most commentary on the Declaration of Independence centers on the preamble's stirring invocation of natural rights. Several of the legal heretics who will growl later in this text were enamored with the preamble, and today schoolchildren asked to memorize the preamble might assume it is the whole document. But the Declaration of Independence is much lengthier and more complex than the preamble, and, reflecting the background of its chief author, much of it is legalistic. Its form is that of a bill in equity, complete with a statement regarding jurisdiction, the identification of parties, a list of wrongs, an explanation of why other remedies would not suffice, a request for remedy, and even the typical concluding oath.[4] Had Jefferson not been presenting his claim for independence to the court of world opinion, he might have used the very same form to request that a Virginia court of equity prevent a neighbor's cow from trampling his client's vegetable garden.

The content of the Declaration of Independence is also highly legalistic, with a majority of George III's alleged offenses being law-related. The king, it seems, had refused to assent to desirable laws, forbidden his governors to pass laws, and abolished valuable colonial laws and charters. Beyond the laws themselves, the king had assembled legislatures at unusual times, unduly dissolved these bodies, refused to establish courts, used salary and tenure to manipulate judges, and generally harmed the most crucial of legal institutions. The king, really, was the one who had been disrespectful of law and in a profound sense "illegal." The Declaration of Independence hence launched one of the most curious of revolutions: one that professed to be law-abiding!

After the Revolutionary War, confidence in law and legal institutions became an even larger part of American ideology. Doubters of course grumbled, but a legal faith mentally smoothed out some of the social inequities and obscured the dominance of bourgeois and commercial interests. The United States Constitution became an icon through which one could worship in the legal faith. The court emerged as a crucial institution, and the courtroom trial, as observed in person and as re-enacted in newspapers and fiction, served as an important secular ritual. Most importantly, a belief in the rule of law became a central American commitment. This faith was not a conventional religion. It lacked a godhead. A formal priesthood and church did not exist. But during the Early Republic Americans turned frequently to this faith for self-definition and meaning. The nation became a veritable temple of the legal faith.

The bulk of this book concerns individuals and groups which have rejected this faith—"legal heretics" in my terms—but before turning to their stories, it will be useful to sketch the legal faith itself. Heresy, after all, not only communicates an alternative faith but also denies an existing one. Heretics, whether the more familiar religious ones or my less conventional legal variety, share their vision while simultaneously rejecting the controlling one. Dissent requires something dominant. Just what was the American legal faith that some Americans in later years wanted so desperately to disavow?

A faith's doctrines are ultimately its most distinctive features. Believers can discuss, interpret, and revise them. But believers also need something more concrete through which they can worship. Icons, totems, and symbols provoke uncritical religious devotion, and believers can use them to reinforce their faith. An icon, in particular, is like a door that opens onto the faith. Walk through it, and one might explore all the faith entails.

The most important legal icon of the Early Republic was not an image, carving, or statute, as is more common in traditional religion, but rather the United States Constitution. We tend not to think of the Constitution in this way today, preferring instead to consider it our charter or our fundamental law. And indeed, the Constitution's federalism, bicameralism, separation of powers, amendments, and listing of rights are more than enough to keep noisy gaggles of appellate judges and law professors squawking from dawn to dusk. However, the Constitution also exists and works as a symbol for those entering the legal faith. In the Early Republic it became a powerful secular icon.

The good men who assembled for three months in Philadelphia in 1787 to draft the Constitution were deadly serious. They debated, compromised, and agreed to disagree. They then turned things over to the Committee of Style and Arrangement. Counting four lawyers among its five members, the Committee crafted a sturdy, measured, almost businesslike composition. The Constitution has seven articles in the order of declining importance and complexity, and the roughly five thousand words (not including amendments) march along without the flair of metaphors, tropes, or rhetoric.[5] When the novelist E. L. Doctorow listened to the Constitution at the time of the bicentennial in 1987, he found it surprisingly soft-spoken:

> The voice of the Constitution is a quiet voice. It does not rally us; it does not call on self-evident truths; it does not arm itself with philosophy or political principle; it does not argue, explain, condemn, excuse or justify. It is postrevolutionary.[6]

Intriguingly, the framers decided to keep the process that had produced this "postrevolutionary" document to themselves. They voted to keep their arguments and debates secret. They took an oath to lifelong secrecy, and at the end of the deliberations the delegates who took notes were supposed to turn them over to George Washington. "As learned men," the scholar Bertell Ollman has written, "the Framers of the American Constitution were well aware of the advantages to be gained by enveloping their achievement in religious mystery."[7] What's more, they wanted to suggest full agreement. Benjamin Franklin movingly assured the assembled that he had "never whispered a syllable" of his objections to others. "Much of the strength and efficiency of any government in procuring and securing happiness to the people," he asserted, "depends, on opinion, on the general opinion of the goodness of the government. . . ." He then moved that approval of the Constitution be made unanimous, and his motion was approved easily.[8]

These reasoned decisions contributed ultimately to the honoring of the Constitution. Even before the eleventh state, Pennsylvania, ratified the Constitution in June of 1788, it had begun to take on an iconic character. Whenever a new state ratified, rallies and parades marked the event, and the parade in Philadelphia deserves an award for excessiveness. It included city officials, clergy of every denomination, units of light infantry and cavalry, and cadres of the recognized trades, each dressed in distinctive working clothes and carrying a display relating to the trade. In addition, a literal ship of state, named the *Union,* and a float shaped like an eagle, drawn by majestic steeds and featuring a giant representation of the Constitution, paraded by. While the float might have been expected to steal the show, the much discussed "New Roof" was even more symbolically striking. This latter float presented the Constitution as a rooflike structure supported by thirteen pillars and presumably sheltering the Republic. It was drawn by ten white horses, ornamented with bright stars, and crowned at the very top by the figure of Plenty with her sprawling cornucopia.[9]

Newspapers and journals, some of which only months before had discussed the Constitution with critical acumen, contributed to the hoopla. Writers began referring to the Constitution with awe and reverence. Poems and songs sang the Constitution's praises, and one of the popular "federal songs" of the period nicely illustrated the emergent mingling of American exceptionalism and constitutionalism:

> Proud Europe hence may learn and see,
> A Constitution self-controlled;
> By wisdom balanced, firm and free,
> The dread and model of the world.[10]

Lost amidst the gaiety was any sense of how complicated and contested the drafting of the Constitution had been. James Madison, already angling for the title "Father of the Constitution," can be forgiven for calling on the public in 1792 to revere governmental charters such as the Constitution. Public opinion, he thought, "should guarantee with a holy zeal, these political scriptures from every attempt to add to or diminish from them."[11] But Madison was hardly alone. Benjamin Rush, a signer of the Declaration of Independence and leader of the pro-Constitution faction in Pennsylvania, found the Constitution "as much the work of a Divine Providence as any of the miracles recorded in the Old and New Testament. . . ."[12] For Congressman Richard Lee, writing in 1794, the Constitution had enabled the new nation to be "filled with inhabitants and covered with harvests, new habitations reared, contentment in every face, plenty on every board." This, Lee was sure, "was the intention of the Constitution, and it has succeeded."[13]

Enough is enough, Thomas Jefferson concluded, and before his death he warned against treating constitutions "like an ark of the covenant, too sacred to be touched."[14] But the citizens of the ebullient young nation could not be deterred. Schoolbooks of the early nineteenth century spoke of the Constitution as divinely inspired and routinely employed the terms "glorious," "revered," and "sacred."[15] The Washington Benevolent Society, other civic organizations, and many profit-driven entrepreneurs produced not only facsimiles and elegant re-publications of the Constitution but also banners, wall hangings, and even handkerchiefs with all or part of the document. Americans could, and frequently did, carry the Constitution with them. Many could not read the Constitution or anything else for that matter, but that seemed to make little difference. As Max Lerner noted in the 1930s, the people believed in a type of "word-magic." Ignorance of the Constitution's actual content did not bar this magic. "What was wanted was a visible symbol of the things that men hold dear. The American people . . . wanted a visible mark of their accomplishment: *ecce signum.*"[16]

As the example of Daniel Webster suggests, politicians could invoke the Constitution in their campaigns and even erect whole careers on top of the icon. The nation's most prominent orator and statesman between the War of 1812 and his death in 1852, Webster attributed much of his success to the law. "If I am anything," he said late in life, "it is the law . . . that has made me what I am. . . . The law has been my chief stimulus, my controlling and abiding hope, nay, I might say, my presiding genius, and guardian angel."[17] He argued forcefully in Constitutional cases, served under the Constitution as Senator from New Hampshire and Secretary of State, and, most importantly for purposes at hand, fancied himself the "Defender of the Constitution." Like Richard Lee and others before him, Webster credited the Constitution with much of the Republic's greatness. "I believe that no human working on such a subject, no human ability exerted for such an end, has ever produced so much happiness as the Constitution of the United States," Webster said.[18] The Constitution, he was sure, was "complete and perfect, and any change could only result in marring the harmony of its separate parts."[19] The Constitution was "the basis of our identify, the cement of our Union, and the source of our national prosperity and renown."[20]

In the final years of his career, Webster's oratory fell on less and less sympathetic ears. Despite his best efforts, he could not ride the Consti-tution into the White House. Sectional strife made the Constitution in-creasingly contested, and romantics, transcendentalists, abolitionists, and others singled out Webster as rigidly representative of what the law had become.[21] But these disappointments and criticisms notwithstand-ing, Webster's attraction to and invocation of the Constitution during the Early Republic illustrates the iconic nature of the document. One could dispute the meanings of the Constitution and debate the ways to interpret it, but by Webster's time the Constitution had become a symbol and point of entry for the legal faith.[22]

Indeed, Webster even played a role in perhaps the most curious invocation of the Constitutional icon in the early nineteenth century. While William Henry Harrison was hardly the only President to invoke the Constitution with great ardor and devotion, Harrison managed to do it even after his death. After shaking hands for hours in the rain at his 1841 inaugural, the military hero of Tippecanoe retired to what would become his deathbed. His death notice, prepared by Daniel Webster and four others, reported that "the last utterance of his lips expressed the fervent desire for the perpetuity of the Constitution and the preservation of its true principles."[23] Even when invoked by someone in the cold ground, the Constitution could objectify mythic tales of the legal faith, unlock attitudes and assumptions, promise order, and invite patriotism.

If a religious icon allows contemplation of the mysteries and meanings of a faith, religious institutions and rituals provide muscle and participation. The institution supplies personnel and social structure as it also mounts the ritual ceremonies. In most cases a believer has participated in the rituals before, and each new completion of a ritual reinforces the faith. Seeing others perform the established rites provides reassurance that one belongs to a community of believers. Ritual is one of the crucial building blocks of all faiths.

In the American legal faith the court became the most important institution and the courtroom trial the most powerful ritual. Both had taken time to catch hold. In the earliest Puritan colonies of New England, for example, courts not only served a wide range of legislative, executive, and judicial functions but also competed with the equivalent of trials in the churches. A defendant might simultaneously go on trial before religious and civic panels, and distinctions between crime and sin were not necessarily crucial in either setting.[24] To the south in colonial Virginia, even the very idea of a "courthouse" did not exist until well into the eighteenth century. Trials took place in churches, barns, and even taverns, and in the latter in particular something other than decorum reigned. The "gentlemen justices" lacked legal training, and their lives revolved more around the business of tobacco farming than the administration of justice. The judges were frequently late for court, and trials themselves were short on ceremony and formality.[25]

All of this changed as the Revolution approached and as the nineteenth century began to unfold. The court and the courtroom trial began to come into their own, providing an arena in which the most powerful ideas and attitudes were tested and displayed. Complainants, defendants, and litigants sought resolution of specific disputes, and citizens looked to the courtroom proceedings for larger meanings and a better sense of the world around them.

Courtroom proceedings were especially important civic affairs in the more rural areas. Lawyers often rode together on circuit, their arrival at a county seat along with the presiding judge being much heralded. Not only participants but also the curious descended on the courthouse to watch, to argue, and sometimes simply to picnic on the lawn. The courtroom proceedings and especially the trials were *the* most dramatic manifestations of government in rural America.[26]

In the larger cities courts were more regularly in session, and since constables, legislatures, and almshouses were also present, government did not rely as much on courts to establish its identity as it did in the countryside. But this did not make courtroom trials mundane. Courtroom lawyers dominated the profession, and lawyers such as Daniel Webster, Rufus Choate, and William Wirt were celebrities of their era. According the Virginia lawyer and treatise writer St. George Tucker, "The chair maker or cabinet maker is known in his town; a good physician for 100 miles; a lawyer throughout America."[27] Urban judges were hailed or deplored for their rulings, hoisted on the citizens' shoulders or pelted with fruit and vegetables. In the city as well as the country, the trial was an event.

According to the scholar Robert Ferguson, writing in one of the most exquisite works concerning law in early nineteenth-century American culture, courtroom oratory of the period should not be overlooked as an art form. Thoughts of literary "art" might connote images of poems, stories, plays, or novels, but during the Early Republic, Ferguson says, oratory might have ranked even higher. And what better site for the orator than the courtroom. As an early nineteenth-century performance artist, the courtroom lawyer could attempt not only to win his case but also to sway the judge, jury, courtroom audience, and citizenry with his passion, insight, and oratorical skill.[28]

And indeed, one did not even have to attend a courtroom trial to enjoy the oratory and other developments. Early journals such as the *North American Review, Analectic Magazine, Monthly Anthology,* and *Port Folio* covered courtroom trials extensively, and specially published trial reports began appearing in the 1790s in Philadelphia, New York, and New England. Published in pamphlet form and sometimes collected into anthologies, the reports usually followed the order of trial proceedings, beginning with the indictment, turning to opening arguments and testimony, and then offering closing arguments, verdicts, and sentences. The reports ranged from synopses to full transcriptions running hundreds of pages.[29]

In the 1830s and 1840s, trial-related popular culture expanded in form and circulation, and the courtroom trial intruded more and more into the American consciousness. The trial pamphlets gradually died out, but proliferating daily newspapers and cheap fiction kept trials before the American public. Driven by rising literacy rates, availability of surplus income, and modernization in general, these varieties of American popular culture recognized the appeal of the courtroom trial. If what was reported in the daily newspaper or imagined for the inexpensive novel was not always totally faithful to legal norms, that was not a problem. The goal was sales, and sales required not slavish veracity but resonance with the sensitivities and expectations of the readers.

The penny press counted trial reporting as one of its staples. Beginning with Boston's the *Evening Bulletin* and Philadelphia's the *Cent,* both founded in 1830, the new type of newspapers quickly supplanted the commercial and political sheets of the previous decades. Livelier and more reckless, the penny dailies were prepared to entertain as well as inform, and the editors and publishers realized that accounts of trials could do both.

The nation's two largest penny dailies of the early nineteenth century, Benjamin H. Day's the *Sun* and James Gordon Bennett's the *Herald,* were chock-full of trial reporting. Based in New York City, both papers assigned reporters to the lower "police" courts located where the Bowery and Third Avenue intersected, and high-spirited daily columns shared the news.[30] As the *Herald* saw it:

> The mere barren record of person and crime amounts to nothing—to something less than nothing. There is a moral—a principle—a little salt in every event of life—why not extract it and present it to the public in a new and elegant dress? . . . if a Shakespeare could have taken a stroll in the morning or afternoon through the Police, does any one imagine he could not have picked up half a dozen dramas and some original character? The bee extracts from the lowliest flower—so shall we in the Police Office.[31]

In addition to reporting on the lower criminal courts, penny dailies in Baltimore, Boston, New York, and Philadelphia also offered more extended accounts of trials in the higher courts. We today take such reporting in the local sections of our newspapers for granted, but this variety of journalism only found its form and place in the mid-1830s. The great breakthrough came in the spring of 1836, when New York police found the prostitute Helen Jewett dead in her brothel with three-inch-deep hatchet wounds to her head. The subsequent trial of clerk Richard P. Robinson set off a trial-reporting extravaganza unrivaled in prior newspaper journalism. The *Sun* and the *Herald* ran reports on the front page, continuing with column after column of news about who was present in the courtroom, comments from the lawyers, judicial rulings, and lengthy verbatim testimony. According to one journalism historian, the *Herald's* circulation tripled during the two months it gave front-page coverage to the trial.[32]

Dividing lines between fact and fiction in the products of the nascent American culture industry were hazy, and the Robinson murder trial resulted in fictionalized accounts as well as daily journalism.[33] Trials, after all, were as important in the era's fiction as they were in its journalism. Readers of the era's magazines, story-papers, and cheap novels, many of whom were first-generation consumers of fiction, could find in the fictional courtroom trial a forum for dénouement, a locus for resolution of social problems, and an expression of community norms. Stories about trials, in other words, were—as they still are—fun to read.

Antebellum fiction featured lawyer heroes as well as noxious petti-foggers. The lawyer heroes, most commonly hardworking young Protestants with an ancestor who fought in the Revolutionary War, moved to the city to study and practice law. Clients were customarily the poor, the innocent, and the honest. The courtroom trial was an ideal opportunity to put pettifoggers and other rascals in their place. The judge, less a "character" in the fiction than a symbolic embodiment of righteousness, and the jury, the representatives of the people, could be counted on. Happy endings allowed readers to believe all was at least potentially well in their new nation.[34]

The great majority of trials, of course, never were reported in the newspapers or recreated as fiction, but as the nineteenth century reached its mid-point, the courtroom trial established itself as an important aspect of American culture. Through actual trips to the court-house, reading, and conversations with fellow citizens, Americans were exposed to countless courtroom trials. The trial, like the rituals in traditional religions, was inherently dramatic, and Americans could enter into and emerge from the cultural image of the trial time and again.[35] For the average American the ritualized, dramatic courtroom trial did more than establish the guilt or innocence of the defendant. What was right, and what was wrong? Did the laws and legal institutions respect society's norms and aspirations? What are our individual and collective identities under a rule of law? "In almost every trial," Carl Smith has written, "there is a second drama going on in addition to the case at hand: the ceremonial enactment of the law itself and the affirmation of the principles, good or bad, by which society is ordered."[36]

If the Constitution was a sturdy icon for the nineteenth-century legal faith, that was not enough. If the courts emerged as the faith's central institution and the popular culture proffered countless renderings of the courtroom trial, still more was required. The American legal faith, like all faiths, needed its premises, its doctrines, its system of beliefs. These came in the form of legalism, a multifaceted belief in the usefulness, fairness, and legitimacy of laws and legal institutions. Emerging at the time of the American Revolution, legalism and its defining commitment to a rule of law became even more powerful in the early nineteenth century, as social change accelerated and Americans sought images and attitudes to calm their anxiety. Not only lawyers and politicians but also novelists and foreign visitors reflected on law's importance in America.

Legalism—as a variety of belief—related to many of the social and political changes of the Early Republic. The major components of what some have called the "moderate republican" order settled into place—bicameral legislatures, governmental checks and balances, popular sovereignty, federalism, and an independent judiciary.[37] The bar grew still larger and stronger, the judiciary professionalized, and the courts expanded in number and specialized. Control over corporate charters, divorces, and countless other matters moved out of the legislatures' hands and into those of the courts, and litigation became the rambunctious nation's primary method of settling disputes. Confirming all the changes and particularly potent in an increasingly literate society, a published legal literature also became available. In 1760 not a single American lawbook had been printed. But by 1830 almost every state was publishing judicial reports and professional journals, and legal treatises had also appeared.[38] Citizens still groused about their lawyers and about individual decisions in the courts, but law had become the "official discourse," "the principal medium" of the Republic.[39] At the center of American legalism was a powerful commitment to the rule of law. The British jurist Albert Venn Dicey is sometimes credited with first formulating the phrase "the rule of law,"[40] but nineteenth-century Americans subscribed to the rule of law well before Dicey wrote about it.

Using their Constitutional icon and imagining the courtroom trial ritual, Americans believed that the laws were to be made in public, without bias for particular individuals or classes and with an honest commitment to the public good. Lawmakers were to expressly promulgate the laws in clear, general, non-retroactive and non-contradictory form. The laws were to be feasible and predictable, and the people were for the most part to know them or at least be able to find them out. Officials applying the law, especially judges, were to be fair and impartial, treating similar cases in similar ways, extending due process, free from public pressure, to one and all. An alternative popular will theory never seriously contested with this variety of legalism,[41] and Americans largely believed that in their country law ruled man rather than vice versa.

When tooting the nation's horn either in pride or as a warning of danger, lawyers were especially inclined to invoke legalism and the rule of law. David Dudley Field, for example, was hardly able to contain himself. A distinguished lawyer who argued frequently before the United States Supreme Court and made a habit of turning down judicial appointments, Field was wealthy *and* respected. He earned his money representing the likes of New York City's corrupt mayor, "Boss" Tweed, and Jay Gould, a conniving railroad magnate, and gained respect by leading the effort to codify and update American civil procedure. When speaking at the opening of the Law School at the University of Chicago, Field argued that "of all the sciences and arts, not one can be named greater in magnitude or importance than . . . the science of the law." He was sure that Americans had made law their sovereign. "We have enthroned it," he shouted. "In other governments, loyalty to a personal sovereign is a bond for the State. . . . We have substituted loyalty to the State and the law for what with others is loyalty to the person." Indeed, having made a commitment to a legal faith, Americans, in Field's opinion, found law's sacred presence always with them:

> Though [law] may be the most familiar of all things, it is also the most profound and immense. It surrounds us everywhere like the light of this autumnal day, or the breath of this all-comprehending air. It sits with us, sleeps beside us, walks with us abroad, studies with the inventor, writes with the scholar, and marches by the side of every branch of industry and every new mode of travel. The infant of an hour old, the old man of three-score and ten, the feeble woman, the strong and hardy youth, are all under its equal care, and by it alike protected and restrained.[42]

On the opposite extreme from lawyers gushing about the nation's glorious accomplishments were those worrying about the nation having gone astray. Intriguingly, lawyers in the latter camp were as likely to sing the law's praises as those in the former, this time to get the nation back on track. Consider Abraham Lincoln. In 1838, over two decades before assuming the Presidency, the twenty-nine-year-old lawyer rose to address the Young Men's Lyceum in Springfield, Illinois. The nation, as Lincoln surveyed it, was plagued by mobs and gripped by "wild and furious passions." Lurking about were would-be tyrants "of sufficient talent and ambition who will not be wanting to seize the opportunity, strike the blow, and overturn that fair fabric, which for the last half century, has been the fondest hope, of the lovers of freedom, throughout the world." The cure? "A reverence for the Constitution and laws." In fact, Lincoln proposed an oath. Every American, he thought, should "swear by the blood of the Revolution, never to violate in the least particular, the laws of the country; and never to tolerate their violation by others." A man who violated the law, after all, trampled on his father's blood and tore "the character of his own, and his children's liberty."

> Let reverence for the laws, be breathed by every American mother to the lisping babe, that prattles on her lap—let it be taught in schools, in seminaries, and in colleges;—let it be written in Primmers, spelling books, and in Almanacs;—let it be preached from the pulpit, proclaimed in legislative halls, and enforced in courts of justice. And, in short, let it become the *political religion* of the nation; and let the old and the young, the rich and the poor, the grave and the gay, of all sexes and tongues, and colors and conditions, sacrifice unceasingly upon its altars.[43]

Rhetorical law-related excesses might be anticipated from lawyers, codifiers, and future Presidents. Their legal training and practice prompted the law-related hosannas and jeremiads they spilled forth. But thoughtful literary artists as well realized that legalism and faith in the rule of law were becoming central features of the American worldview. James Fenimore Cooper, novelist and son of a land speculator and judge, had his moments of disenchantment with America. He was kicked out of Yale, spent his obligatory time at sea searching for himself, and even for awhile expatriated himself to Europe. Later, his over thirty novels as well as his additional works of autobiography and social criticism made him the nation's best-known literary figure. According to critics, "the flood of fiction from his imitators largely began the commercial life of American fiction."[44]

Especially interesting in a consideration of the legal faith are Cooper's five Leatherstocking novels. Virtually the only works by Cooper that are still read in contemporary America, the works appeared between 1823 and 1841 and explore the quests of Natty Bumppo, "Leatherstocking" himself—a "Pathfinder," a "Deerslayer," a mythic embodiment of the independent American moving west. Lumbering by modern standards, the novels provide a type of national narrative. They also wrestle with the pitfalls and possibilities of a legal faith. *The Pioneers* seems in particular a debate on what law should or should not be.

The Pioneers begins in 1793, but Cooper makes a point of announcing that he is writing in 1823. Things may be unsettled and contested in the novel, but thirty years later in real time the problems of fictional time have resolved themselves. In the center of the State of New York roads now run in all directions, churches and schools are abundant, and hearty yeomen are planting both their crops and family roots. In short, Cooper intones, "the whole district is hourly exhibiting how much can be done, in even a rugged country, and with a severe climate, under the dominion of mild laws, and where every man feels a direct interest in the prosperity of a commonwealth of which he knows himself to form a part."[45]

Natty Bumppo—the legendary hunter, first white settler in the area, and an "unlarned man" who "never so much as looked into a book or larnt a letter of scholarship"—would be surprised. From the beginning of the novel he is disgruntled with the people, the settlements, *and* the laws. When the leader of the settlement, Judge Marmaduke Temple, boasts of the good laws being passed by the legislature to stop fishing with nets or the killing of deer in teeming season, Bumppo is dubious: "You may make your laws, Judge, but who will you find to watch the mountains through the long summer days, or the lakes at night? Game is game, and he who finds may kill, that has been the law in these mountains for forty years, to my sartain knowledge; and I think one old law is worth two new ones." Bumppo is not about to change his opinion, but for the benefit of others as well as for himself, the Judge continues the argument: "Armed with the dignity of the law, Mr. Bumppo, a vigilant magistrate can prevent much of the evil that has hitherto prevailed and which is already rendering the game scarce."[46]

As the novel unfolds, a mystery regarding disputed land claims and also a romance tediously run their courses, but the debate regarding law remains engaging. Rambunctious settlers without Bumppo's commitment to nature's ways or Temple's civic spirit ax the maples, wastefully catch too many fish, and use a cannon to blast flocks of pigeons to the edge of extinction. Bumppo is right about the costs of settlement, but Temple is also right in calling for legal restraints. In the end, Bumppo himself goes on trial, and both Cooper and the community delight in the trial-day processional featuring a sword supposedly used in one of Cromwell's victories, constables carrying staves, a judge wearing an old-fashioned military coat with silver epaulets, and circuit-riding lawyers, one or two of whom "had contrived to obtain an air of scholastic gravity by wearing spectacles."[47] At trial, with Temple directing the scene, the jury finds Bumppo innocent of assaulting a local official who tried to bluster his way into Bumppo's hut but guilty of resisting the execution of a search warrant.

In the aftermath, Judge Temple has more than his share of explaining to do, especially to his only child Elizabeth, whom Bumppo had saved from a vicious panther. "Surely, sir," pouts Elizabeth, "those laws that condemn a man like Leatherstocking to so severe a punishment, for an offense that even I must think very venial, cannot be perfect in themselves." Granted, Temple says, but "Society cannot exist without wholesome restraints and respect for the persons of those who administer them." "Try to remember, Elizabeth," Temple pontificates, "that the laws alone remove us from the condition of the savages. . . ."[48] He then gives Elizabeth money for Bumppo's fines, and when Bumppo escapes before Elizabeth can deposit the cash, Temple arranges a pardon in Albany. Closing the book and putting out their candles, readers in Cooper's time no doubt gave their hearts to Bumppo, especially after he symbolically burned down his hut and moved west. But despite this, most of Cooper's readers also recognized Judge Temple's attitude about law as the dominant and desirable one.

So, too, did the many European visitors who traveled to the United States in the early nineteenth century. Well-heeled and curious, these visitors wanted to observe how a country might function without an aristocracy, castes, and an official church. As a result of his subsequent writings more so than of his actual stature at the time of his visit, Alexis de Tocqueville was the most famous of the visitors. The French aristocrat and government official toured the United States in late 1831 and early 1832 at the request of his government. His official charge was to investigate and report on the new penitentiaries being developed in

America, but his two-volume *Democracy in America* (1835) went further than anticipated, commenting on the full sweep of institutions, politics, and manners.

The American legal faith, it is fair to say, made a tremendous impression on de Tocqueville. American lawyers seemed to him a viable substitute for the nobles, wealthy, and literati of European nations. Lawyers were "the highest political class," the "most cultivated circle of society." "If I were asked where I place the American aristocracy," de Tocqueville said, "I should reply without hesitation that it is not composed of the rich, who are united together by no common tie, but that it occupies the judicial bench and the bar."[49] The American courts, meanwhile, seemed "the most visible organs by which the legal profession is enabled to control the democracy."[50] The people respected judges, completed their civic educations by serving on juries, and accepted courtroom decisions. In addition, the American people also respected law itself. How curious this was, especially since in Europe the masses looked at the laws with suspicion. "However irksome an enactment may be, the citizen of the United States complies with it," he wrote, "not only because it is the work of the majority, but because it originates in his own authority, and he regards it as a contract to which he is himself a party." Turning on its head the European norm, opulent Americans might view the laws with suspicion, but the mass of Americans looked upon the laws with "a kind of parental affection."[51]

De Tocqueville did not get everything right. He may not always have understood America better than the Americans. But he did accurately sense the power of the legal faith, the same faith that inspired lawyers and politicians and led to literary contemplation. De Tocqueville's most famous comment on the legalistic character of early nineteenth-century American culture merits quoting at length:

> Scarcely any question arises in the United States which does not become, sooner or later, a subject of judicial debate; hence all parties are obliged to borrow the ideas, and even the language, usual in judicial proceedings in their daily controversies. As most public men are, or have been, legal practitioners, they introduce the customs and technicalities of their profession into the affairs of the country. The jury extends this habitude to all classes. The language of the law thus becomes, in some measure, a vul-

gar tongue; the spirit of the law, which is produced in the schools and courts of justice, gradually penetrates beyond their walls into the bosom of society, where it descends to the lowest classes, so that the whole people contracts the habits and the tastes of the magistrate.[52]

More so than even Thomas Paine had imagined, the law had become king in America.

In the years since Daniel Webster puffed out his orator's chest, Cooper crafted his curiously argumentative novels, and de Tocqueville gave the French government much more of a report than it anticipated, the American legal faith has both changed and held firm. All faiths, of course, must have some degree of flexibility and fluidity to survive. Otherwise, they become brittle, shatter, and disappear. All faiths must also have commitments to which they remain true, features that may be thought of as their defining ones. Hence, the icons, institutions, rituals, and premises of the American legal faith have readjusted themselves, while the core belief that in the United States the law is king continues to hold.

As for the Constitution as icon, actual physical reproductions have continued to appear. Icon avalanches, in fact, occurred at the time of the centennial in 1887, sesquicentennial in 1937 and bicentennial in 1987. Also available in great numbers are couplings of the Constitution with a constitution of a given state or with other honored pronouncements from America history such as Lincoln's "Gettysburg Address." Then, too, there are countless little books praising the Constitution as the "soul," "voice," "citadel," or "sentinel" of the nation. All of these impressive facsimiles and reproductions, like the carvings and paintings of saints in early Christianity, are icons of a faith, albeit a legal one.[53]

More profoundly, though, worshiping through the icon has shifted over the years. During the late nineteenth and early twentieth centuries—the era legal historians call the "age of legal formalism"—business leaders and members of the United States Supreme Court fetishized the Constitution, converting it into an object with incredible power to protect and aid the society. The obsessive reverence for the Constitution was perhaps most evident in *Lochner v. New York* (1905), a

Supreme Court opinion invalidating a New York statute limiting the number of hours one could work daily and weekly in a bakery, but many other comparable opinions displayed the same extravagant devotion to the Constitution well into the 1930s. Max Lerner, editor of the *Nation*, even warned in the 1930s that the fetishizing of the Constitution was one step toward fascism.[54]

The extreme veneration of the Constitution during this period may help explain the tremendous hue and cry following the publication of Charles A. Beard's *An Economic Interpretation of the Constitution* (1913). A widely read progressive historian, Beard argued that commercial and property interests had directed the drafting and ratifying of the Constitution. No matter how measured Beard's tone, this argument hardly sat well with the fetishizers. President Taft denounced the book as unseemly muckraking besmirching the reputations of the Founders, and Warren Harding, himself destined for the White House, attacked Beard's "filthy and rotten perversions" in an article entitled "Scavengers, Hyena-Like Desecrate the Graves of the Dead Patriots We Revere."[55] Constitution worship made Beard's *An Economic Interpretation of the Constitution* the most controversial book ever written by an American historian.

Subsequent to the excoriation of Beard's work, the United States Supreme Court changed both its membership and its stance toward the Constitution, and the Constitution regained a more flexible—but still iconic—character. Americans, despite greater literacy than their ancestors two centuries ago, remained obtuse regarding the actual content of the Constitution, and the famous anecdote involving novelist Upton Sinclair cannot be retold too often. Sinclair, it seems, once began a California rally by reading aloud the Bill of Rights in the Constitution, only to be arrested for such disorderly subversion.[56] But if the content of the Constitution is unknown, by police chiefs and prosecutors among others, Americans can still worship through the Constitution as icon. Writing in the 1930s, the distinguished legal scholar Karl Llewellyn described the American public's command of the Constitution as "pervasive ignorance and indifference to almost all detail." Loyalty, he thought, ran "in the first instance to a phrase, without more: 'The Constitution.'"[57] The phrase, this icon, was and remains a way for Americans to pass into the legal faith and all the larger beliefs and possibilities that faith entails.

Fig. 1. Abolitionist William Lloyd Garrison at 74. Photo courtesy of The Boston Athenaeum.

Fig. 2. Women's rights activist Elizabeth Cady Stanton in her senior years. Photo courtesy of The Boston Athenaeum.

Fig. 3. Eugene Debs at the time of the 1894 Pullman strike. Photo courtesy of The Boston Athenaeum.

Fig. 4. Socialist leader Eugene Debs delivering his Canton, Ohio, speech in 1918. Photo courtesy of the Eugene V. Debs Foundation.

Fig. 5. Eugene Debs upon his release from the Atlanta Federal Prison in 1921. Photo courtesy of the Eugene V. Debs Foundation.

Fig. 6. Bobby Seale and Huey Newton standing armed before the Black Panther Headquarters. Photo courtesy of AP/World Wide Photos.

Fig. 7. Huey Newton taking questions at a 1967 San Francisco news conference. Photo courtesy of AP/Wide World Photos.

Fig. 8. A pensive Eldridge Cleaver in 1971. Photo courtesy of AP/Wide World Photos.

Fig. 9. Joseph M. Scheidler, founder and leader of the Pro-Life Action League. Photo courtesy of the Pro-Life Action League.

Fig. 10. Randall Terry, founder of Operation Rescue and political candidate. Photo courtesy of Randall Terry for Congress, 1988.

American courts and courtroom trials have also over the decades shifted and reshaped themselves, but the courtroom trial retains its power as a ritual of the legal faith. The chief institution mounting the ritual is no longer the court itself. America's courts are of course still there, and the full-time professional staffs of judges, prosecutors, and public defenders for indigent defendants keep the tawdry assembly line of American criminal justice moving.[58] But most Americans have never participated in or even witnessed a courtroom trial. They get their image of the courtroom trial from the countless trials in American popular culture.

Much more so than in the early nineteenth century, trials are a staple for the popular culture industry. Print and broadcast journalism routinely reports on trials, a cable channel features trials, and the tabloids feast on the courtroom activities of the rich and reckless. In addition, fictional trials are around every corner in American novels, movies, and prime-time television. Other nations' popular cultures rarely if ever accord trials the importance they receive in American popular culture. The courtroom trial is in fact so common in American popular culture that it is "naturalized," that is, taken for granted. It does not even register as a convention used by writers and filmmakers.[59]

As is the case in all rituals, the modern popular cultural courtroom trial is highly standardized. The setting itself is usually a wood-paneled and well-upholstered courtroom, one that might still be found in an older federal courthouse but a far cry from the peeling paint and hard plastic chairs of the typical urban courtroom. The judge's bench stands like an altar at the exact center-front and rises above, suggesting something higher and truer. Almost all proceedings are criminal rather than civil, and even when we encounter a fictional civil trial—as, for example, in *The Verdict* (1982) starring Paul Newman or in many *L.A. Law* episodes—the proceedings resemble a criminal prosecution with one party allegedly an elusive and venomous wrongdoer. The action occurs primarily on the bench, on the witness stand, and in the "well"—the flat, unadorned space at the foot of the bench and adjacent to the jury-box. The overall tone is feisty and confrontational, with each side perceived by the other to be playing unfairly. A jury is virtually mandatory, and readers and viewers often vicariously join the jury in the attempt to make sense of things. Overall, the cultural convention is an opportunity to find meaning in the legal faith, and this opportunity sometimes gets the better of a writer. According to David Kelley, a lawyer and one-time executive producer of *L.A. Law,* many television writers "fall into the trap of writing courtroom stuff very ponderously. It's overwritten. It's like bad French cooking, where everything is bathed in too much cream sauce."[60]

Little of this has much to do with what actually takes place in the courthouse. Most real-life criminal charges are dropped or plea-bargained, and less than 10 percent lead to a trial. In those cases that do go to trial, the defendant commonly avoids taking the stand in order to conceal past convictions. Witnesses do not break down on the stand, defendants are usually convicted, and judges tightly control the proceedings. But the point is not accuracy. Trials in the popular culture give readers and viewers access to the legal faith. They do not physically participate in real trials but rather allow their minds to pass through the ubiquitous culturally constructed ritual.

The Constitutional icon and trial ritual lead ultimately to legalism and the rule of law, the belief in impartial judgment according to neutral rules. However, during selected periods in the course of the twentieth century the legal faith seemed to wobble. Immediately following World War I, for example, the President, the Congress, the judiciary, and a majority of the population seemed inclined to cut legalism's corners in order to suppress a perceived subversive menace.[61] In the early 1970s, the Watergate scandal revealed not only election shenanigans but also pervasive disrespect for legal institutions and rules on the highest rungs of government. After both extended episodes the nation seemed to right itself, employing the rule of law as a political rudder much as Abraham Lincoln suggested in the 1830s. Legalists and civil libertarians pointed out in the 1920s how the rule of law had been savaged during the Red Scare, and eventually the appellate courts articulated new rules to guard against future breakdowns. In the 1970s, Richard Nixon was forced from the White House, and his sweaty helicopter departure signaled the way Americans were more enamored with the rule of law than with the aura of the Presidency.

In the present, academics continue to wrestle with the rule of law, trying to define it, expose it, and even transcend it.[62] Prominent members of the judiciary, including Justices of the United States Supreme Court, refine and defend it.[63] But despite all this intellectual and political hubbub, the great majority of citizens continue to hold the rule of law dear. The Danish scholar Helle Porsdam, a modern-day de Tocqueville, has asserted that "Americans practically think and breathe in legal terms." Law is so central in American life "that it is no longer possible to reflect seriously about American culture without accounting for the role of the law."[64]

None of this is to argue that the rule of law really is the ultimate foundation of American life or in some grandly cross-cultural way the badge of civilization. The issue is instead legal faith, the way that by using appropriate icons and rituals Americans have since the Early Republic believed and worshiped in law. The legal faith is one feature of Americanism that distinguishes it on the world stage.

And what of dissenters? Native peoples, defeated and moved west to arid lands whites did not want, could understandably wonder what relevance the legal faith had to them. Through most of the nation's history, people of color and women as well found a legal faith that had different promise for white men than it did for them. Southerners, the poor, recent immigrants, and others also had reason to engage in quiet acts of private resistance against a government and society hiding behind what must have seemed the facade of legalism. In addition, American history has featured citizens who rejected the legal faith in a more public, coherent, and aggressive way. These groups and individuals are, in my terms, America's "legal heretics." Their words and actions are all the more striking because they are offered within America, within the "temple" of legal faith. Contemplation of the legal heretics will underscore the faith itself and, perhaps, suggest alternatives.

William Lloyd Garrison
From Abolition to Anarchism

As the citizens of the United States began to worship in the legal faith, they also developed the sacred personages, sites, and dates of Americanism as it is more generally understood. Hence, the nation in the early 1800s came to recognize its "Founding Fathers"—a whole passel of them in fact. The nation cast Lexington and Concord, Bunker Hill, and Independence Hall in Philadelphia as places where the United States had been "born." And the nation adopted the Fourth of July, the day in 1776 on which the delegates to the Second Continental Congress signed the Declaration of Independence, as a national "birthday." On the "Glorious Fourth," as it was frequently dubbed, Americans assembled, paraded, held special church services, and—surprising as it might seem today—married in especially large numbers. How proud the young nation was of its coming into being. How much it wanted to sing to itself and the whole world of its origins.[1]

But as invigorating as the mythology of a young nation might be, it also provided a context for grousing and complaining. In the 1830s, the Fourth of July in particular became a date for criticism as well as praise. Dissidents and malcontents were sometimes at their best on the Fourth. The nation had betrayed its promise. America was dishonest, immoral, or wrong-headed. On the Fourth of July critics could vent their spleens on what they took to ail the nation.[2]

The abolitionist William Lloyd Garrison was in a sacrilegious mood of this sort when on an extremely hot Fourth of July in 1854 he traveled from Boston to Framingham for an outdoor gathering of the Massachusetts Anti-Slavery Society. Upon reaching the meeting site, he strode forward with the erect posture and brisk gait many took to be so perfectly representative of his character. His platform was draped in black to symbolize the ongoing sin of slavery and festooned with an American flag hung upside down to suggest a nation gone astray. High above, two white flags with the words "Kansas" and "Nebraska" flapped in the wind. Henry David Thoreau and three thousand others waited on Garrison's words.

His speech itself was short, stressing the superiority of "the higher law of God" to man's law, but as he appeared to conclude, Garrison promised the assembled something which "would be the testimony of his soul."[3] He lit a candle, ignited a copy of the Fugitive Slave Act, and shouted the well-known call from Deuteronomy, "And let the people say Amen." Encouraged by the crowd's response, Garrison next ignited copies of two legal pronouncements: Judge Edward Loring's decision returning escaped slave Anthony Burns to Virginia and Judge Benjamin Curtis's directions to a grand jury investigating attempts to rescue Burns. Again he called on the crowd, and again some portion of it shouted "Amen." Finally, Garrison raised a copy of the United States Constitution, called it "an agreement with hell," and set it aflame with his candle. As the Constitution burned brightly, he declared, "So perish all compromises with tyranny." In response to his call, the crowd for a third time cried "Amen!"[4]

Garrison's words and conduct could be seen as only calculated theatrics designed to attract attention and refortify his flagging reputation.[5] But from a legal perspective his gestures are more significant. Garrison's choices of items to incinerate—a statute, judicial orders, and especially the Constitution—were not random. His outraged critique of slavery had come by the 1850s to incorporate a comparably outraged critique of the law-related ideology which had assumed a preeminent place in the youthful republic.

Garrison's intellectual and political journey from abolitionism to anarchism and legal heresy merits retracing. He adopted his "immediatist" variety of abolitionism as a young man and held firm in his abolitionist views until the slaves were finally freed. But working as a journalist, the young Garrison did not initially progress from his law-related experiences and observations to a full rejection of the legal faith. His antilegalism developed more slowly and unevenly, and only after adopting a belief in man's ability to synchronize perfectly with God's preferences did Garrison become a legal heretic. In the 1830s and 1840s he rejected once and for all the Constitution, the most powerful icon of the legal faith, and fully abandoned a belief in man-made law. In the opinion of some, both in Garrison's own era and today, his position was flawed, shortsighted, even silly, but against the backdrop of the American legal faith, the position is intriguing. William Lloyd Garrison is our first American legal heretic.

The variety of abolitionism which Garrison adopted as a young man may have been so staunch and unwavering because it was linked so intimately to his own personal struggle for achievement and self-definition. Born in a less than modest frame house in Newburyport, Massachusetts, in 1805, Garrison, his siblings, and his mother were abandoned in 1808 by Abijah Garrison, an alcoholic seaman and dismal failure as a father. As a boy, Garrison heard the taunts of other children as he sold homemade candies on the streets and carried his tin pail to the homes of the wealthy to beg for food scraps. Fanny Garrison, his mother, worked in various menial positions and eventually moved all or part of her family from Newburyport to Lynn to Baltimore and then back to Haverhill in search not so much of prosperity as of basic survival.

Only in 1818, when as a thirteen-year-old he garnered an apprenticeship with Ephraim Allen, owner and publisher of the Federalist *Newburyport Herald*, could Garrison begin imagining his way out of poverty. He loved his work and poured himself into it. The increasingly precocious teenager even submitted anonymous letters to the *Herald* signed, improbably, "An Old Bachelor." One, dated May 21, 1822, showed more than a trace of misogyny in its suggestion that American women were too idolized, flattered, and "puffed up and inflated with pride and self-conceit."[6] What's more, the youth as old grump argued, too many women too easily won breach of promise to marry suits in the courts. When his commitment to Allen ended in his twentieth year, Garrison began shaping his career as a printer, writer, and editor for various Federalist, temperance, and abolitionist journals. Six years later in 1831, at the age of 26, he founded the *Liberator*, the Boston abolitionist journal he would publish for the next thirty-five years.[7]

The *Liberator* reflected the "immediatist" version of abolitionism which Garrison had adopted in the late summer and early fall of 1829. The position that slavery was fundamentally wrong and should be ended immediately and completely had been articulated as early as 1815 by the Tennessee Manumission Society. Leading American texts championing the position included George Bourne's *The Book and Slavery Irreconcilable* (1816) and James Duncan's *Treatise on Slavery* (1824). In England, where the development of an immediatist position paralleled developments in the United States, the Quaker Elizabeth Heyrick anticipated strategies of a later era by organizing a successful consumer boycott of West Indian produce. Her immediatist text, *Immediate, Not Gradual Emancipation* (1824), was an especially eloquent plea for immediate emancipation.[8]

If Garrison achieved some prominence as an immediatist, it was not because of the innovativeness of his position but rather because of the fierceness with which he maintained it. Having accepted a position as co-editor of the *Genius of Universal Emancipation*, a Baltimore antislavery weekly, he stated in a September 2, 1829 editorial that, questions of expediency notwithstanding, slaves were entitled to immediate emancipation.[9] Fifteen months later when he launched the *Liberator*, Garrison was even more certain. In the very first issue Garrison announced, "I shall strenuously contend for the immediate enfranchisement of our slave population." Indeed, his often quoted expression of determination from the same issue—"I will not equivocate—I will not excuse—I will not retreat a single inch—and I WILL BE HEARD"—goes to the very same issue.[10]

Not surprisingly in the context of his era, Garrison's call for immediate emancipation dripped with religious rhetoric. "Religious professors of all denominations," he said, "must bear unqualified testimony against slavery. No slaveholder ought to be embraced within the pale of a christian church; consequently, the churches must be purified as 'by fire.'"[11] The slaves were like "the Israelites in Egypt," while slaveholders adopted "the language and policy of Pharaoh."[12] Owning a slave was literally sinful. The slaveowner placed himself between his slaves and God, thereby denying the former the opportunity to be accountable moral actors. Slaveowners in fact competed with God for the loyalty and the direction of human beings. This conduct, Garrison insisted, led to still more sins: sexual laxity, violence, ignorance of the Bible, and profanity.[13] In the face of this sinful horror, this rebellion against God, Garrison and his immediatist colleagues were certain the only appropriate step was instant cessation. Give the slaves their freedom; allow them to relate directly to their God.

This immediate freedom, meanwhile, did not mean former slaves would instantly be on equal footing with white Americans. As Garrison conceived of it, immediate emancipation did not automatically include suffrage, the right to hold office, or freedom from "the benevolent restraints of guardianship." Garrison instead argued "for immediate personal freedom of the slaves, for their exemptions from punishment except where law has been violated, for their exclusive right to their own bodies and those of their own children, for their employment and reward as free laborers, for their instruction and *subsequent* [italics added] admission to all the trusts, offices, honors and emoluments of intelligent freemen."[14]

After false rumors spread that Garrison and the *Liberator* had contributed to Nat Turner's Rebellion in 1831, many southerners took Garrison to be the most noxious enemy the North could muster. Southern editors condemned him, and Georgia's legislature even offered a five thousand-dollar reward for his arrest and prosecution.[15] However, a closer study of Garrison's abolitionist thought would have allayed some of the fears. He did not endorse slave rebellions or other violent acts to break the chains of slavery. Immediate abolition, he said, "calls for no bloodshed, or physical interference; it jealously regards the welfare of the planters. . . ."[16]

If Garrison had reassuring, albeit largely unheard, words for the slaveowners, his position with regard to those who would send freed slaves to colonies in Africa was more aggressively hostile. Founded in 1817, the American Colonization Society had proposed the resettlement of the former slaves in Africa. The proposal attracted support from several prominent slaveowners, Henry Clay included, and some resettlement did take place on the west coast of Africa in what became the nation of Liberia. Garrison admitted in the first issue of the *Liberator* that in an address delivered in 1829 in Boston's Park Street Church he had "unreflectingly assented to the popular but pernicious doctrine of *gradual* abolition," but he now recanted and asked "pardon of my God, of my country, and of my Brethren the poor slaves, for having uttered a sentiment so full of timidity, injustice and absurdity."[17] Subsequent issues of the *Liberator* went on to excoriate the American Colonization Society, and if the slaveowners were like Pharaoh holding the slaves captive in the South as Egypt, the society, in Garrison's opinion, stood in the shoes of none other than evil Lucifer.[18]

Garrison's most extended treatment of the colonization alternative to immediatism came in *Thoughts on African Colonization*, a 236-page pamphlet he published in 1832.[19] Declaring himself ideologically at war with colonization, Garrison in the pamphlet asks why colonization was appealing not only to slaveholders and racists but also to good Christians. By way of an answer, he offers an intriguing narrative about an African Colonization Society agent who obtains permission to address a northern congregation and wins it over with promises to end the slave trade, slavery, and racial intolerance and also to civilize and evangelize Africa. "Exquisite! The picture is crowded with attractions, delightful to the eye. The story is skillfully told, and implicitly believed; but like every story, it has two sides to it." Garrison then goes on to give the other side, arguing that colonization was unfeasible because many more slaves were being born in America than could ever be returned to Africa and that colonization actually perpetuated slavery and racial intolerance.[20]

Garrison's hostility toward the American Colonization Society was justified. Racist in its presumptions, the society was stronger in the South than in the North, and it never really accomplished much. In the period from 1820 to 1832, when the United States had roughly 2.5 million slaves and free blacks, the society managed to ship only 2,885 emigrants to Africa.[21] Rather than attempting to end slavery, Garrison argued, the society really wanted to rid America of freed slaves. Freed people of color haunted members of the society, Garrison said, because they were "mirrors which reflect the light of liberty into the dark bosoms of the slaves."[22]

In his attacks on the "colonizationists" and in general, Garrison through immediatism effectively staked out the highest moral ground, and this may have been as important to him as the hope that slaves would be immediately freed.

> I utterly reject, as delusive and dangerous in the extreme every plea which justifies a procrastinal and an indefinite emancipation, or which concedes a slave owner the right to hold his slaves as *property* for any limited period, or which contends for the gradual preparation of the slaves for freedom; believing all such pretexts to be a fatal departure from the high road of justice into the bogs of expediency, a surrender of the great principles of equity, an indefensive prolongation of the curse of slavery, a concession which places the guilt upon any but those who incur it, and directly calculated to perpetuate the thraldom of our species.[23]

Garrison, after all, was battling for both the slaves' freedom *and* the hearts and minds of whites, and by disdaining compromises, he strategically claimed the noblest truths for his side.[24]

Garrison's immediatism also hints of the legal heresy which he would come to articulate and represent later in his life. Immediate emancipation and its concomitant commitment to the highest justice, he asserted, "simply demands an entire revolution in public sentiment, which will lead to better conduct, to contrition for past crimes, to a love instead of a fear of justice, to reparation of wrongs, to a healing of breaches, to a suppression of revengeful feelings, to a quiet, improving, prosperous state of society."[25] As noted by the historian David Brion Davis, immediatism "marked a liberation for the reformer from the ideology of gradualism, from a toleration of evil within the social order, and from a deference to institutions that blocked the way to personal salvation."[26] Man-made law would prove to be one such institution.

What was the nature of Garrison's legal thinking during his early career? What roles did law and legal institutions play in his understanding of slavery and call for immediate abolition? He had ample opportunity to perceive and reflect upon law and legal institutions, but even though his immediatist abolitionism took firm and lasting shape during the 1820s and early 1830s, he was not as yet fully heretical in his legal views. Garrison's calcified attitudes and bearing disguised the fact that he was still a young man.

If law came to life for Garrison at this stage of his personal and professional development, it was largely through his journalistic endeavors. Like Ben Franklin and other poor and largely self-educated men before him, Garrison used journalism and publishing not only to inform his readers but also to express and shape himself. His newspapers, biographer James Brewer Stewart has written, "could become an extended representative of his own personality, knowledge, convictions, self-image, and power of expression. Influence and respect could come to him as it did to all successful editors by succeeding in 'selling himself.'"[27] But the consuming project of selling oneself can also impede further intellectual and political growth, and such was the case with Garrison's legal thought.

Two particular law-related episodes—controversies involving Francis Todd in 1829–30 and Prudence Crandall in 1833–34—are illustrative. The Todd controversy grew out of Garrison's work as editor of the *Genius of Universal Emancipation*, the previously mentioned antislavery weekly published in Baltimore. Already dubbed "Lloyd Garrulous" by some detractors because of his lengthy and pungent commentary,[28] Garrison published in each issue of the *Genius* the figure of a chained and kneeling African American asking, "Am I not a man and brother?" Directly beneath this eye-catching graphic appeared a so-called "Black List," recording horrors related to slavery—auctions, whippings, kidnappings, murders, and other atrocities.[29]

In the issue of November 13, 1829, Garrison noted that the *Francis*, a ship which had recently departed for New Orleans carrying a cargo of slaves for sugar plantations, was owned by Francis Todd, a Newburyport merchant. Garrison recalled Todd from Newburyport and on a deeper level also no doubt remembered begging for scraps, tin pail in hand, among the Newburyport merchant class. Piqued that a wealthy and respected northerner would stoop to participating in the domestic slave transport, Garrison huffed and puffed in the next issue of the *Genius*. "So much for New England principle," he said. Todd and Captain Nicholas Brown, another respected Yankee, were "enemies of their own species" for transporting seventy-five slaves in the narrow space between decks.[30] Proud of his efforts and spoiling for even more of a fight, Garrison then dispatched copies of his work to Todd himself.

Todd was, to say the least, displeased. He filed suit for libel against both Garrison and Benjamin Lundy, the newspaper's owner and co-editor. A month later, after a presentment from a Baltimore grand jury, Thomas Jennings and Richard W. Gill, deputies of the Maryland attorney general for Baltimore City, brought forward a formal criminal indictment for malicious libel.[31] In the early antebellum period private libel actions were only beginning to supplant criminal libel actions pursued by public prosecutors.[32] Both actions were viable in Maryland, but in keeping with the jurisdiction's procedural standards, the private action brought by Todd was suspended while the prosecutors attempted to make their criminal case.

At issue in the prosecution was the truthfulness of the statements Garrison published regarding Todd's conduct; publication of falsehoods could demonstrate the malicious intent needed for conviction. The prosecutors, in this regard, showed through testimony and evidence that there were eighty-eight rather than seventy-five slaves aboard the *Francis*, that they were unchained, and that they moved freely below decks. In response, Charles Mitchell, Garrison's defense counsel, offered no testimony or evidence but instead spoke for almost two hours on the outrageous nature of both slavery and the libel laws. Weighing, on the one side, testimony and evidence which showed Garrison's factually erroneous efforts to impugn Todd and Brown, against, on the other side, expressions of moral outrage, the jury required only fifteen minutes to return a guilty verdict. Garrison, now identified as solely responsible for the criminal articles because Lundy had been out of town at the time of the libelous publication, was fined fifty dollars plus costs. Lacking the funds to pay the fine, he was sentenced to six months in the Baltimore Jail.[33]

Fortunately for Garrison, Arthur Tappan came to his rescue. A silk and feather merchant with an early department store in Manhattan, Tappan made his clerks live in supervised boarding houses, be under lock and key by 10:00 P.M., and attend church faithfully. He also grossed over a million dollars annually. Driven by a compulsive piety and totally humorless, Tappan seemed to find some release in giving away his money, and in the 1820s he emerged as New York's most generous phil-anthropist. Garrison and his intolerance of merchants who did not walk the straight and narrow, who engaged in the slave trade no less, appealed to Tappan, and Tappan paid Garrison's original fine, enabling him to leave jail after forty-nine days.[34]

Striding from the Baltimore Jail, Garrison was not only unrepentant but also fortified. He had used his imprisonment to think and write. His scrawled sonnets—prison graffiti are hardly new—decorated the walls of his cell. The nastiest of his letters flew off to Francis Todd; to Henry Thompson, Todd's Baltimore agent who had testified against Garrison at trial; to Judge Nicholas Brice, who had presided at the trial; and to Richard W. Gill, one of the prosecutors. His letter to Brice promised an exposé which would "secure to you a deathless notoriety," and he warned Gill, "Beware of my pen!"[35] Last but not least, Garrison wrote and distributed a pamphlet, *A Brief Sketch of the Trial of William Lloyd Garrison, for an Alleged Libel on Francis Todd of Newburyport, Mass.*[36]

The latter is an early, charged, and ultimately uneven commentary by Garrison on the law and legal institutions. Garrison cast his case snidely as "highly illustrative of Maryland justice" and hoped his pam-phlet would expose "the defectiveness of the indictment, and the arbi-trariness of the court." Irritated and outraged, Garrison nevertheless seemed to maintain some higher faith in constitutional protections and legal rights, a faith which had been betrayed in his own case:

> As for the law (if it be law) which has convicted me, I regard it as a bur-lesque upon the constitution—as pitiful as it is abhorrent and atrocious. It affords a fresh illustration of the sentiment of an able writer, that "*of all injustice, that is greatest which goes under the name of Law; and of all sorts of tyranny, the forcing of the letter of the Law against the equity, is the most insupportable.*"[37]

Still shaping his thoughts on law, Garrison was in the same pamphlet less ambiguous with regard to the press and the types of freedoms which the press needed. For the Baltimore newspapers, he mustered a string of insults: "The Baltimore presses are celebrated for their craven spirit, their abject servility, their cormorant selfishness, their stagnant quies-cence. The loss of an advertisement, or the withdrawal of a subscriber, is of far greater consequence than the exposure of corruption, or the reform of abuse." His own case, meanwhile, concerned nothing less than freedom of the press. He discussed in the pamphlet the recent history of censorship in England and France. He asserted that "whatever relates to the freedom of the press, is ultimately connected with the rights of the people. Every new prosecution for libel, therefore, (however insignificant in itself,) may be viewed as a test of how far that freedom has been restricted by power on the one hand, or perverted by licentiousness on the other."[38] Few if any judges in the early 1830s would have taken seriously Garrison's First Amendment argument against criminal libel proceedings,[39] but it might have found a more sympathetic judicial ear a century later.

Garrison concluded the pamphlet with an appeal to the people for a change of the verdict. When such a change, not surprisingly, failed to materialize, Garrison declined the opportunity to fight another round and ducked out on the civil libel action which had been suspended while the State of Maryland pursued its criminal libel. In the civil action the Maryland jury found for Todd and ordered Garrison to pay one thousand dollars—a large judgment in the era. Beating a hasty path north and thereby able to avoid enforcement of the civil judgment, the young journalist rationalized his flight by saying justice was impossible with a Maryland jury.[40] Further thoughts on the law and its role in social life and relationship to a man's conscience would have to come on a later day.

Three years after his flight, Garrison was more established and working in Boston as the editor of the *Liberator*. Abolition remained the driving cause of his life, but unlike some abolitionists, he also spoke out against the pervasive white racism of the North. His stance was well known and appreciated among free blacks. Indeed, the *Liberator's* greatest appeal was not as contraband for illiterate southern slaves but rather as political commentary for free northern blacks, who actually constituted the majority of the journal's subscribers.[41] Through his championing of some modicum of equality for free blacks in the North, Garrison came in touch with Prudence Crandall and law, legal process, and legal institutions.

Crandall, a thirty-year-old Quaker abolitionist, worked as a schoolmistress in Canterbury, a small town in northeastern Connecticut. In 1833 she admitted a black pupil to the girls' boarding school she operated in a house near the town green. Some townspeople were offended, organized a boycott of the school, and succeeded, at least temporarily, in closing the school. Crandall might have abandoned her efforts, but since Garrison had supported the development of educational opportunities for blacks and published editorials in the *Liberator* about the need for manual labor colleges for blacks, Crandall wrote him with the daring idea of reopening her school exclusively for black girls. Garrison in turn urged her on. She advertised in the *Liberator* her new school for "young Ladies and little Misses of color,"[42] and Garrison warmly endorsed both "Miss P. Crandall, (a white lady)" and the school. "An interview with Miss C.," he said in an editorial, "has satisfied us that she richly deserves the patronage and confidence of the people of color."[43]

Once again Arthur Tappan dug deliberately into his deep pockets, and in a few weeks fifteen girls had been recruited in Boston, Providence, and New Haven. But if Crandall's willingness to admit a single black girl had troubled the Nutmeg bigots, her plan to open an all-black school provoked panic. Town meetings grew rabid. Grocers refused to sell supplies to the school. Physicians withheld services for the school's staff and students, and townsfolk filled the school's well with manure. One of Crandall's pupils reported in an anonymous letter published in the 22 June 1833 issue of the *Liberator* that:

> [The] Canterburians are *savage*. . . . The place is delightful; all that is wanting to complete the scene is *civilized men*. . . . When we walk out, horns are blown and pistols fired.[44]

When harassment won't work, legislation might. The Canterbury town fathers turned to the Connecticut legislature in Hartford, and the lawmakers quickly passed a statute prohibiting the establishment of schools for students from outside Connecticut without the formal approval of the local town government, something Crandall had no hopes of obtaining. Church bells rang and canons boomed in Canterbury as the locals celebrated the lawmakers' speedy action. Canterbury officials then quickly used the new law to close the school and arrest Crandall.[45]

Having made Crandall's struggle to operate her school a journalistic cause célèbre, Garrison resolved to do the same with her prosecution. In a letter to a lifelong friend, the printer Isaac Knapp, he deemed Crandall, "a wonderful woman, as undaunted as if she had the whole world on her side,"[46] and he cast the Canterbury litigation as a test case:

> If we suffer the school to be put down in Canterbury, other places will partake of the panic, and also prevent its introduction in their vicinity. We may as well, "first as last," meet this prescriptive spirit *and conquer* it.[47]

Unfortunately, the ambitious Garrison was also committed to a lecture tour in England, and he had to ask colleagues at the *Liberator* to keep the case on the front page and also to give Crandall full support and counsel while he was out of the country.[48]

Lengthy litigation and an appeal followed. At a first trial the jury was unable to reach a verdict, but at a second Crandall was convicted of violating the newly minted Connecticut statute and fined on hundred dollars. She then appealed to the Connecticut Supreme Court, and a year later that Court entertained elaborate and stirring appellate arguments regarding the citizenship of blacks and the protection of their privileges and immunities under Article IV of the United States Constitution. Speaking for the majority of the Court, Justice Wilson acknowledged that the questions involving "the rights of a large and increasing population, and the correct construction of a clause in the constitution" were "of the deepest interest to this community." He then went on, in a sudden shift that sets something of a standard for legalistic anticlimax, to reverse the trial court conviction on narrow procedural grounds. The trial court charges, it seems, failed to state that Crandall's school was unlicensed, and this statement was necessary to bring Crandall's activities under the precise wording of the Connecticut statute.[49]

Crandall had her legal victory in hand, but like many before and after her, she realized how empty such a victory might be. While the lengthy legal battle was being fought in the courts, her school had ceased to operate. Her Canterbury opponents continued to harass her and vandalized her premises, maliciously stringing dead cats on the school fence.[50] Crandall found comfort in the companionship of the Reverend Mr. Philleo, a Baptist minister, and she decided to marry him and relocate to Illinois.

For his own part, Garrison had returned well before the decision of the Connecticut Supreme Court, but his letters reveal declining sympathy for both Crandall and her cause. Had he perhaps been improperly enamored with Crandall? No pathway leads to his heart of hearts. But Garrison scrambled in an 1834 epistle to Helen Benson, his fiancée and the daughter of a Providence merchant and abolitionist, to deflect suspicion that he had "galanted" Crandall through the streets of Boston.[51] In another letter to Benson, he complained of Crandall's growing vanity and even admitted, in a rare burst of self-criticism, that he himself might have the same trait:

> One thing she [Crandall] must guard against—namely, being exalted in her mind by the abundant panegyric of her friends. Certainly, she deserves the sympathy, the affection, and the praise of all those who feel for the suffering and the dumb—for what disagreement and opposition she has voluntarily encountered! . . . Still (and I am aware that these remarks are strictly applicable to me as to her,) she must be careful lest she be 'exalted above measure'. . . . How contemptible, how foolish, how disgusting is personal egotism![52]

When told of the dead cats dangling on Crandall's fence, Garrison proffered to the Canterburians not outrage but puns. "You have added another black act to the long *cat*-alogue of your offenses. The *cat*-astrophe will be duly chronicled, not *dog*-matically but *cat*-egorically."[53] Garrison did not approve of the Reverend Mr. Philleo, and wondered if "the thought of being indissolubly allied to a worthless person" was supportable.[54] However, when all was said and done, Garrison said in a letter to his friend and future brother-in-law George Benson, it was probably best for Crandall to marry and "move off with flying colors."[55]

A defendant in the Todd litigation in Baltimore or a champion of Crandall's cause in the Connecticut courts and legislature might have sprung from either or both episodes to a variety of legal heresy. The law's biased workings and alignment were evident. But although genuinely outraged in both instances by the workings of the law, Garrison was maturing, still shaping and promoting himself as a political journalist, and, with good reason, fixated on the ongoing reality of American slavery. His rejection of the legal faith was soon to come but still deferred.

Like other American legal heretics who would follow him, Garrison was able to move to a sharper, more radical critique of the American legal faith because he developed both a more cohesive personal community *and* a more coherent worldview. Beginning in the mid-1830s, as he entered his fourth decade, Garrison could draw support and insight from his solidarity with others and his developing philosophy. In particular, his sense of "perfection," that is, the possibility of walking hand in hand with God, enabled Garrison to extend his antislavery journalism and activism into new areas.

Garrison's emergent personal community included both his family and his circle of abolitionist colleagues, and lines between the two groups blurred. In September 1834, he and Helen Benson married, and rather than aspiring to a public role, Helen served the abolitionist movement by being her husband's devoted private helpmate. They had six children, and one daughter remembered in a loving memoir the way she as a young girl warmed her hands on her father's bald head.[56] Through Helen, Garrison also acquired the extended family of loyal in-laws which had been notable for its absence during his youth and early adulthood, and many of Garrison's in-laws were, like his father-in-law, active abolitionists.

In Boston, abolitionist family members blended with abolitionist friends, and Garrison's circle became known nonpejoratively as the "Boston Clique." Members of the Clique were fond of and, for the most part, loyal to Garrison, and he in turn relished his special role within the Clique. Reflecting on this role, the historian Lawrence J. Friedman compares it to that of a messiah, a father figure, or a minister before settling instead on Max Weber's notion of an effective group leader, albeit one who behaved like "a brilliant mad scientist"![57] Garrison and Helen named four of their children after abolitionist contemporaries, and Garrison "constantly attempted to make each member of the Clique feel loved, respected, and even indispensable—so much so that Clique abolitionists often turned to him in moments of confusion and diffi-culty."[58] Garrison remained active on the national stage and also trav-eled several times to England for conventions and lecture tours, but sup-ported now by his family and the Boston Clique, Garrison matured into a less reckless rooster.

The settling into place of Garrison's worldview and religious faith in the mid-1830s also facilitated bolder, more systematic thinking about law and legal institutions. He had always been deeply religious. His mother had been a devout, bordering on fanatical Baptist, and even after he launched his career, Garrison remained respectful of her teach-ings and advice.[59] As previously noted, the religious rhythms and im-ages of his youth and early adulthood infused his abolitionist work, and throughout his long career as a journalist and agitator he referred con-stantly to the Bible for support.[60] But this is not to argue that Garrison's religious beliefs and modes of worship were fixed. In the mid- and late 1830s he increasingly accepted a more personal faith of individualistic perfectionism.

Essentially, perfectionism held that by fully accepting God, men and women could be "perfect." That is, they could in their daily lives shed their sinfulness and live fully in keeping with God's will. This, in turn, would enable them to both achieve salvation and, in the meantime, re-generate the earthly society in which they lived.

Many in Garrison's era had perfectionist beliefs. Quakers believed that an "inner light" of God dwelled within every man, and this inter-nal beacon could not only illuminate moral choices but also shine brighter and brighter if carefully attended.[61] The Great Revival of the early nineteenth century rejected predestination in favor of conversion, and when literally thousands of revivalists gathered at places like Cane Ridge, Kentucky, no shortage of them subscribed to a countrified per-fectionism.[62] Then, too, among the New England gentry liberal theol-ogy beginning with Unitarianism and leading to transcendentalism em-bodied perfectionism. Ralph Waldo Emerson's sense of self-reliance as well as Henry David Thoreau's variety of civil disobedience were, in spe-cialized ways, perfectionist.[63] Emerson once confided to educator and fellow transcendentalist Bronson Alcott that he could "never speak handsomely in the presence of persons of Garrison's class,"[64] but men as different as Emerson and Garrison were both enamored with the perfectionism of their time and culture.

Garrison did not refine his perfectionist belief within the Methodist, Presbyterian, and Baptist churches. These types of Christians, it seemed to him, were more interested in playing with doctrinal niceties and conducting in-house purges than in proclaiming the message of Christ. In an 1836 letter to Samuel J. May, a Unitarian clergyman, Garrison employed references to religions he found even tawdrier than the Protestant churches to express his outrage:

> Judaism and Romanism are the leading features of Protestantism. I am forced to believe that, as it respects the greater portion of professing Christians in this country, Christ has died in vain. In their traditions, their forms, their vain janglings, their self-righteousness, their will-worship, their sectarian zeal and devotion, their infallibility and exclusiveness, they are Pharisees and Sadduccees, they are Papists and Jews.[65]

For an alternative source of perfectionist dialogue Garrison turned to John Humphrey Noyes, surely a man with whom mainstream Protestants wanted no truck. A Vermonter six years Garrison's junior, Noyes met and corresponded with Garrison in 1837. Unlike the revivalist Charles Grandison Finney, who interpreted perfectionism more as an aspiration, Noyes understood it to be actually obtainable. Men and women had free will, he argued, and they could as a result truly become Christlike. Noyes in fact considered himself to have become perfect, via a spiritual crucifixion experienced in, of all places, a New York rooming house, and went on from there to articulate models of marriage and communal living appropriate for a sanctified terrestrial utopia.[66]

Garrison stopped far short of purchasing Noyes's whole package, but the notion of a pure, personal holiness appealed to him. Shortly after his exchange with Noyes, Garrison stated in an 1837 letter to fellow abolitionist Henry C. Wright that his perfectionist views were "simple" but destined to "make havoc of all sects, and rites, and ordinances of the priesthood of every name and order."[67] Garrison's review of his biblical sources, in particular the gospels of Paul and John, seemed to confirm perfectionism. He began to advocate perfectionism to the members of the Boston Clique, and he was even moved to publish the poem titled "True Rest":

> . . . It is to be Perfect in love and holiness;
> From sin eternally made free;
> Not under law, but under grace;
> Once cleansed from guilt, forever pure;
> Once pardoned, ever reconciled;
> Once healed, to find a perfect cure;
> As Jesus blameless, undefiled;
> Once saved, no more to go astray;
> Once crucified, then always dead;
> Once in the new and living way,
> True ever to our living Head;
> Dwelling in God, and God in us . . .[68]

Such inspired poesy may have appealed to radical Hicksite Quakers such as Arnold Buffum, Lucretia Mott, and the Grimké sisters, but others, including the wealthy and beneficent Arthur Tappan and virtually all religiously orthodox abolitionists, were less receptive.[69]

What impact did perfectionism have on Garrison's thoughts regarding law? The heart of the matter involves allegiance. Many in Garrison's era distinguished between the teachings of a moral code or religious faith on the one hand and the prescriptions of the society's written laws on the other. But Garrison took it further and, due to his perfectionist beliefs, actually expressed literal allegiance to the true government of God. He believed that this government could and did exist, and that he and others could and should live through such a government. Man's laws, courts, and constitutions obviously plummeted in significance once one became "perfect." Man's government could still be adjusted and improved, but, more importantly, it could be put aside. Seeing with the assistance of an inner beacon, living in a personal relationship with God, and expressing allegiance to God's government led directly to legal heresy.

Expressions of this heresy began to blossom amongst the numerous and unwieldy antislavery notices, articles, and editorials in the *Liberator*. In a lead editorial which appeared on June 23, 1837, Garrison chal-

lenged the notion that anyone owed allegiance to "human governments." Such governments, he said, were based on distrust of God's
promises, a longing for power over others, a rejection of the equality and
brotherhood of man, and a need to retaliate. Human government, he
said, is better than anarchy only "as a hail storm is preferable to an earth-
quake, or the smallpox to the Asiatic cholera." Sensing perhaps, the variety of anarchism with which he was flirting, Garrison stopped short,
saying, "But we are going more deeply into the subject than we intended
at the outset."[70]

However, Garrison could not stop. On December 15, 1837, as the *Liberator's* seventh year of publication drew to an close, Garrison published
a new prospectus for the 1838 volume. Henceforth, he announced, the
journal would not only vigorously oppose slavery but also turn to "other
topics which, in our opinion, are ultimately connected with the great
doctrine of inalienable rights. . . ." The time was right, Garrison said, for
"the emancipation of our whole race from the dominion of man, from
the thraldom of self, from the government of brute force, from the
bondage of sin—and bringing them under the dominion of God, the
control of an inward spirit, the government of the law of love, and into
the obedience and liberty of Christ, who is the same yesterday, today
and forever." In the earthly kingdom of God, Garrison insisted, the
"government is one of love, not of military coercion or physical re-
straint; its laws are not written on parchment, but upon the hearts of its
subjects . . ."[71]

In September 1838, Garrison founded the New England Non-Resistance Society and boldly suggested that the founding date of the Twentieth of September would ultimately have greater importance than the
Fourth of July.[72] On February 1, 1839, he also founded a new publication, the *Non-Resistant.* Beyond a rejection of bearing arms, military
service, and all physical aggression, the Society and new journal es-
chewed the legal faith and respectful conduct within its prescriptive and
proscriptive bounds. It was unacceptable to hold elected office, serve on
the bench, vote for others, and even to file a lawsuit. Stunned by the
emerging expansiveness of Garrison's anti-legalism, the abolitionist organizer Henry Brewster Stanton demanded to know in a famous 1839
public confrontation whether voting was a sin. "A sin for me," Garrison

answered bluntly.[73] According to the Society's "Declaration of Sentiments" Garrison and his colleagues were stepping beyond civil government:

> We recognize but one KING and LAWGIVER, one JUDGE and RULER of mankind. We are bound by the laws of a kingdom which is not of this world; the subjects of which are forbidden to fight; in which MERCY and TRUTH are met together, and RIGHTEOUSNESS and PEACE have kissed each other; which has no state lines, no national partitions, no geographical boundaries; in which there is no distinction of rank, or division of caste, or inequality of sex; the officers of which are PEACE, its extractors RIGHTEOUSNESS, its walls SALVATION, and its gates PRAISE; and which is destined to break in pieces and consume all other kingdoms.[74]

Just why those who wanted nothing to stand between themselves and their God needed new organizations and publications remained unclear, as did a whole raft of secondary questions: Was it right to pay taxes? Could one use government currency or rely on insurance companies chartered by the government? Might one, short of bringing a lawsuit, testify in court in conjunction with somebody else's lawsuit?[75] But nevertheless, selected readers of Garrison's publications and certainly members of the new Non-Resistance Society traveled down the road with Garrison from abolitionism to legal heresy. A follower from Indiana reported he was more easily able to collect debts when debtors knew he would not resort to legal proceedings.[76] Another follower announced that he ran a worldwide business while spending less than eight dollars annually on legal costs.[77] These mergers of sharp business practices with Garrisonian legal heresy were perhaps not quite what Garrison anticipated, but a stable social situation and perfectionist Christian anarchism enabled Garrison in his fourth decade to articulate a wide-ranging rejection of the nation's legal faith.

All that remained for Garrison's legal heresy to be complete was a rejection of the United States Constitution, but this step was the most ominous of all. Law and courts and legislatures could easily be seen, from the perspective of Garrison's increasingly controlling Christian

anarchism, as flawed, as merely man-made, and as entities not demanding allegiance. But as indicated in the previous chapter, the United
States Constitution of the early nineteenth century had taken on an
iconic character. To be sure, it remained a text that could be read and a
law of a special sort. But the Constitution had also become a symbol
and a sacred icon in the legal faith. It was carefully preserved on its original parchment. New citizens swore to respect and abide by it. Politicians like Daniel Webster constructed their careers on the ostentatious
veneration of it. In order to become a complete legal heretic, Garrison
would have to be an iconoclast. He would have to smash the Constitution as icon of the legal faith.

The tortured twists and turns of Garrison's thoughts during the 1830s
indicate how difficult a rejection of the Constitution would be. In his
1832 *Thoughts on African Colonization*, the lengthy pamphlet in which
he excoriated the American Colonization Society, he singled out a particular clause in the compact—Article I, Section 2, which counted the
slaves in apportioning Congressional representation—and urged that it
"be erased."[78] In an August 6, 1833, letter he wrote to the *London Patriot*,
he acknowledged that many considered the Constitution a "sacred compact" and formally recognized it as binding, but he also called it "the
most bloody and heaven-daring arrangement ever made by men for the
continuance and protection of a system of the most atrocious villainy
ever exhibited on earth." Then, apparently forgetting that he had just
recognized the compact as binding, he went on in the same letter to declare: "Such a compact was, in the nature of things, and according to the
law of God, null and void from the beginning. No body of men ever had
the right to guarantee the holding of human beings in bondage."[79] In a
more positive vein, Garrison in the same year at the founding meeting
of the American Anti-Slavery Society praised the Constitution for insu-
lating the District of Columbia from southern control and leaving up
to the individual states the decision about whether or not to tolerate
slavery. The Society adopted a constitution largely as drafted by Garrison, and the document stated that each state, according to the United
States Constitution, has the right to abolish slavery. The Society, in the
same document, also pledged "in a constitutional way" to influence

Congress to end the domestic slave trade and prevent the extension of slavery to new states.[80]

By the mid-1830s, with the abolition of slavery on a state-by-state basis having ground to halt, Garrison seemed to realize that abolition would be greatly aided if it could be demonstrated that the Constitution in reality outlawed slavery.[81] Abolitionists could then invoke the Constitution as a controlling reference in their demands that slavery be terminated. In order to achieve this goal, Garrison engaged in constitutional reasoning which was as much bizarre as it was resourceful. Beginning with the Preamble, he declared that it "presupposes oppression and slavery, in any and every form, wholly unwarrantable, and consequently is a warrant for a general emancipation of slaves." Turning to Article IV, Section 2, which explicitly stipulated the return of persons held to service or labor who had escaped, Garrison argued it was irrelevant because according to law slaves were "things" rather than "persons." The correct understanding of the Constitution, he then concluded, was one which cut fully against slavery. Northern courts upholding slavery and returning runaway slaves were themselves acting unconstitutionally.[82]

If Garrison's constitutional reasoning at this stage seems truncated, there were at least others in the same period who more successfully developed an antislavery interpretation of the Constitution. Perhaps the most prominent was Lysander Spooner, an abolitionist and Massachusetts lawyer. He began his argument with an Enlightenment-era version of natural law, arguing that any written law, constitutions included, must be consistent with natural law and man's inherent natural rights in order to be binding; any law or constitution sanctioning slavery must, as a result, be invalid. Spooner then went on to review colonial charters, the Declaration of Independence, state constitutions of 1789, the intentions of the Constitution's framers, and the Constitution itself and to conclude that nowhere had there been unambiguous positive legislation which legalized slavery. This lacuna, Spooner thought, was crucial because, given the language of the Declaration of Independence declaring life, liberty, and the pursuit of happiness to be natural rights, slaveowners had the burden of showing that slavery had been constitutionally established. As for the words of the Constitution itself, Spooner noted that what is normally called the "fugitive slave clause" does not even contain the words "slave" or "slavery." The exact words were instead "persons held to service or labor," and this referred to apprentices or indentured services. Very young and very old slaves, after all, were not expected to provide "service" or "labor"; they were instead taken to be property. What about the extensive case law that constitutionally recognized slavery? Spooner returned to the beginning of his argument, saying the courts had failed to recognize that slavery had not been established.[83]

Garrison characterized Spooner's thought as "ingenious—perhaps, as an effort of logic, unanswerable,"[84] but by the time of this comment Garrison had himself drawn different conclusions. Starting in the late 1830s, he began to abandon his prior argument that the Constitution was antislavery, and by the early 1840s, he began to reject the Constitution because it was a proslavery document. One might maneuver through the actual words of the Constitution as Spooner had done, but as Garrison came to look at things, the bargain through which the Constitution was formed recognized slavery. "In the adoption of the American Constitution, and in the formation of the Federal Government," he argued, "a guilty and fatal compromise was made by the people of the North with southern oppressors, by which slavery had been nourished, protected and enlarged up to the present hour, to the impoverishment and disgrace of the nation, the sacrifice of civil and religious freedom, and the crucifixion of humanity."[85] Buoying Garrison in his proslavery interpretation of the Constitution were the newly published papers of James Madison. Garrison published lengthy excerpts from the papers in the *Liberator* and argued that they once and for all established the proslavery nature of the Constitution. The Madison papers "demonstrate that the slave population were sacrificed on the altar of political expediency—with some tinges of conscience, it is true, but nevertheless sacrificed. . . ."[86]

In the same way that Lysander Spooner developed an antislavery interpretation of the Constitution more elaborate than anything penned by Garrison, others outdid Garrison in terms of a proslavery interpretation as well. William Ingersoll Bowditch pointed out that, thoughts of natural rights notwithstanding, constitution framers and legislators have yet to make laws congruent with these lofty aspirations. Colonial legislators were competent to legislate on slavery and did so, and using the already recognized "common meaning" rule, it seems clear that the framers intended to accept slavery. Writing in a pamphlet titled *The Constitution, a Pro-Slavery Compact*, Wendell Phillips, Garrison's friend and a member of the Boston Clique, argued that debates in the Articles of Confederation Congress and at state conventions to ratify the Constitution as well as the *Federalist Papers* made clear that slavery was part of the American constitutional regime. The Constitution was written, Phillips said, by "forty of the shrewdest men and lawyers in the land," and only "a desperate man" would set out to prove "that slavery is not referred to at all."[87]

Debates among abolitionists about the character of the Constitution were hardly inconsequential, and some of the most unfortunate splits in the abolitionist ranks occurred because of this very issue. Perhaps the most poignant involved Garrison and the heroic and legendary Frederick Douglass. After his escape from slavery in Maryland in September 1838, Douglass read the *Liberator* devotedly, and when in the early 1840s he became a speaker on the antislavery circuit, Douglass found Garrison especially admirable and appealing. While some of the other antislavery speakers strove for the common touch by telling supposedly cheerful jokes about African Americans, Garrison stood above such racism.[88] For his own part, Garrison was initially paternalistic toward Douglass, saying that Douglass needed "nothing but a comparatively small amount of cultivation to make him an ornament to society and a blessing to his race."[89] But as the years went by, Garrison came to hold Douglass in the highest esteem. Garrison seemed to cope relatively well when the audience at an 1847 meeting of the American Anti-Slavery Society in New York City interrupted him with chants of "Douglass, Douglass."[90] Even when Douglass insisted on founding the *North Star*, an abolitionist journal which would compete with the *Liberator*, Garrison was able grudgingly to come to terms with the development.[91] A teacher might pause when his student's accomplishments equal or surpass his own, but shared commitments may also enable the teacher-student relationship to evolve into something more balanced and mutually enriching.

Yet when Douglass broke publicly with Garrison with regard to the Constitution, the break was more than Garrison could handle. As late as the spring and summer of 1848 Douglass continued to cast, deplore, and reject the Constitution as a proslavery document, and only in 1849 did he begin to waver. The *North Star*, published in Douglass's new home of Rochester, articulated the position that the Constitution empowered, indeed demanded, that Congress abolish slavery. Echoing Spooner and others, Douglass pointed to the Preamble, the constitutional guarantee of a "republican form of government, and the Fifth Amendment's protection of life, liberty and property" as indicators that Congress could and should act to end slavery. History had made the Constitution proslavery, Douglass concluded by 1850, but its actual provisions, when coupled with moral and natural law principles, made the Constitution in a more fundamental sense an antislavery instrument.[92] Garrison at this point boiled over and let fly with an editorial that was mean and bitter even by his own standards. "Mr. Douglass now stands self-unmasked," Garrison said, "his features flushed with passion, his air scornful and defiant, his language bitter as wormwood, his pen dipped in poison; as thoroughly changed in his spirit as was ever 'arch-angel ruined,' and as artful and unscrupulous a schismatic as has yet appeared in the abolition ranks."[93]

Well before his painful split with Douglass, Garrison had sprung from his proslavery interpretation of the Constitution to a call for "disunion." Beginning in 1842, Garrison began urging antislavery societies to declare themselves in favor of dissolving the Union. Some thought Garrison a traitor, but he reminded readers of the *Liberator* that Thomas Jefferson and the Declaration of Independence had also recognized the right to terminate an unjust government. The tyranny of the South over the North, Garrison thought, was "a million times more frightful than was the oppression of the mother country." He proposed ending the Union "not as a THREAT, but as a MORAL OBLIGATION."[94] At the annual meeting of the American Anti-Slavery Society in May 1844, Garrison urged the Society to disavow allegiance to one nation under the Constitution. After spirited debate, disunionism became the official stance of the Society by a 59–21 vote.[95]

For some, the disunionist ramifications of Garrison's ultimate interpretation of the Constitution were merely extensions of the "immediatist" variety of abolitionism with which Garrison had begun. "It was the statement of a moral imperative, a reveille to the conscience; and it was made by an agitator who knew that those who heard the call were in no condition immediately to translate it into practice."[96] But as the historian William M. Wiecek has reminded us, Garrison's advocacy of disunion was not only a strategic stance related to the abolition of slavery; it was also a deeply personal repudiation of one's allegiance to the United States.[97] The rejection of the Constitution, the great icon of the legal faith, was crucial in the act of personal disallegiance.

In the multi-volume account of their father's life which they began publishing shortly after their father's death, two of Garrison's sons testify to this personal dimension. Those hostile to their father's call for disunion continued to subscribe to the "sub-sacredness" of the Constitution and offered "half-way measures" destined to come to naught. Only their father and other Garrisonian abolitionists "yielded to this religious purification of themselves before their Creator."[98] From perfectionist and Christian anarchist perspectives, the laws and the courts of man possessed no binding power. Voting, office holding, and lawsuits were inappropriate. And now, by championing disunion, the most significant symbol of the legal faith had also been transcended.

When Garrison denounced the Constitution in his speech at Framingham on the Fourth of July, 1854, his words were significant. The speech, described by one of Garrison's biographers as "the most calculated and most dramatic of his life,"[99] was a type of confirmation ceremony for his alternative faith. Garrison, after all, did more than condemn the Constitution. He burned it, and then, with the remains at his feet, he stomped on them. He crushed them. He ground the very ashes of the icon of the legal faith under his heel. Garrison had truly become a legal heretic.

A decade later, in the midst of the Civil War, Garrison recalled his words and conduct in Framingham on the Fourth of July, and he was hardly about to recant. He had "committed to the flames the Constitution of the United States," and he would proudly do it all over again. "No act of ours do we regard with more conscientious approval or higher satisfaction," he wrote. "None do we submit more confidently to the tribunal of Heaven and the moral verdict of mankind."[100]

In retrospect, Garrison may have taken the Constitution to be more fixed than necessary. Yes, the original Constitution does appear to have accepted slavery and incorporated it into the Republic. Yes, the Constitution stood in the way of abolition and the freedom of millions of people. But the Constitution was neither as fully posited nor totally predictable as Garrison came to think.[101]

This problem acknowledged, it is Garrison's whole legal heresy and not just his anticonstitutionalism that demands attention. In the midst of the very era in which laws and legal institutions were proliferating and the legal faith was taking hold, Garrison was skeptical. Starting from a staunch immediatist abolitionism he came to believe in God's government on earth and in man's ability to grasp and live by and through this government. His perfectionist Christian anarchism led him to see man's laws, legal institutions, and constitutions as inherently corrupt. Others in the mid-nineteenth century engaged the law critically and tried to move it in preferred directions, but Garrison went further. As legal heretic, he demonstrated the possibility of completely rejecting the legal faith.

3

Elizabeth Cady Stanton
Women's Natural Rights and the Revolt against Gendered Legalism

During the nineteenth century, recitation of the Declaration of Independence was a virtually obligatory part of the Fourth of July celebrations. Distinguished orators as well as aspiring amateurs vied with one another to capture the document's tones and thunder.[1] But just as the holiday as a whole could be turned on its head, so, too, could the document. Throughout the antebellum period and later, malcontents, rebels, and legal heretics invoked and manipulated the Declaration of Independence to vent their discontent.

Elizabeth Cady Stanton engineered perhaps *the* most striking reconstruction of the Declaration of Independence in all of American history. A thirty-three-year-old resident of Seneca Falls, New York, Cady Stanton suggested in 1848 that the demands and concerns of progressive women be expressed with reference to the Declaration. To be sure, the document would have to be revised to include women, but that was exactly the point. In Cady Stanton's opinion, the laws, legal system, and legal faith failed to recognize women as human beings with the full panoply of natural rights. The so-called "Declaration of Sentiments" that she and her colleagues wrote drew much of its power by playing off the Declaration of Independence. It rightfully became the most symbolically famous document in American women's history.

A century and a half later, Cady Stanton's philosophy and accomplishments might be taken for granted, but in her era she proffered a profound legal heresy. Her sensitivity to women's rights began with a privileged but restricted childhood, one in which she was reminded powerfully that her gender limited who she might be. After marriage and as a young adult, she vibrantly articulated a philosophy of women's natural rights, and after the Civil War she saw many of her demands accepted, even though she herself continued to encounter personal difficulties. Elizabeth Cady Stanton's legal heresy was not the same as William Lloyd Garrison's Christian anarchism, but in its pointed attack on gendered legalism it was every bit as radical.

Countless nineteenth-century women painfully experienced the ways law limited and restricted their lives, but in Elizabeth Cady Stanton's case gender inequality under the law literally began at home. She grew up in a family that not only treated girls as inferior but also was headed by a patriarchal figure who himself personified the law. Psychobiography is always a bit of a crapshoot. Practitioners are often inclined to exaggerate unconscious and irrational drives and also childhood experiences, choosing those aspects of a subject's makeup and personal history that fit a given thesis. Then, too, the psychobiographer is often captured by his or her present, projecting contemporary notions and maladies into eras when they may not be relevant.[2] But these qualms and others having been acknowledged, Cady Stanton's girlhood experiences constitute the basis for her later rebellion against the patriarchal legal norms. Her legal heresy is grounded in her youth.

Cady Stanton was born in 1815 in Johnstown, New York. Her mother, Margaret Livingston Cady, hailed from one of the state's oldest and most established families—the Livingstons of Albany. Her father, Daniel Cady, was a land speculator and prominent lawyer, with a reputation for courtroom oratory perhaps not equal to that of a Daniel Webster, but lofty nevertheless. His wealth and his fame as a lawyer carried him into both the New York Assembly and the United States House of Representatives and the elite social circles enjoyed by the Livingstons. He married Margaret Livingston in 1801 and, already a Federalist, grew even more conservative as he soaked up the patrician values of his wife and in-laws.

The Cadys lived well. Their Johnstown mansion, on the prestigious corner of Market and Main Streets, was the grandest in town. At one point they employed a dozen servants, including maids, nannies, a cook, a laundress, and assorted handymen. What's more, things were in their place and spit-and-polish clean. The Cadys were strict Calvinist Presbyterians, and disorder on the home front would not have boded well for salvation.

Margaret Livingston Cady gave birth to eleven children, but only six lived past their early youth: Elizabeth, her brother Eleazer, and her sisters Tryphena, Harriet, Margaret, and Catherine. It was no secret that the Cadys preferred male children. They assumed that sons would maintain and enhance their financial status while daughters would be married off, perhaps at a financial loss. The Cadys grieved when two sons, including Daniel Cady's namesake, died young, and Elizabeth and her sisters grew up feeling they were disappointments simply because they were female. Cady Stanton's first clear childhood memory in fact involved friends, neighbors, and relatives commiserating with her parents when Margaret, yet another girl, was born in 1820.[3]

In subsequent years sexism and sadness continued to meld in the Cady family. In 1826, when Elizabeth was eleven, Eleazer Cady, her last surviving brother, died just two months after graduating from Union College. The Cadys were devastated, and Elizabeth remembered painfully in her autobiography the darkened parlor with her brother's casket. Sitting among the draped pictures and mirrors, Daniel Cady took his daughter on his knee and said, "Oh, my daughter, I wish you were a boy."[4] After the burial, the Cadys visited the cemetery every evening for months, and a sobbing Daniel Cady frequently threw himself on the grave of his dead son. Elizabeth tried her best to comfort him but realized that in his eyes "a girl weighed less in the scale of being than a boy."[5] She could not be what her deceased brother had been and promised to become.

In 1827 Margaret Livingston Cady, eight years after her last birthing experience and over twenty-five years after her marriage, bore another son in one last desperate effort to produce a male heir. Named Eleazer after his deceased brother, the child lived only until 1828. Now in her mid-forties, Margaret Livingston Cady suffered some sort of breakdown when the child died and turned the family's daily affairs over to her grown daughter Tryphena and the latter's husband. Daniel Cady merely dug deeper and deeper into his work, eventually obtaining an appointment to the New York Supreme Court.

When Daniel Cady managed to look up from the papers in his law office, he often found his daughter Elizabeth there. She idolized him, wanted desperately to ease his sense of loss, and hoped somehow to be the son he did not have. He could never see her as a person rather than as a girl, but he was capable of tenderness. He was proud of her horsemanship and her interest in Greek, and he let her read his lawbooks and occasionally see his clients. She was also allowed to troop with him to the courthouse, the jail, and to other lawyers' offices.

One of her father's cases in particular made a powerful impression on the young Elizabeth. Flora Campbell, a family servant, sought Daniel Cady's help in recovering a farm that her husband had purchased with her money and then willed to a wayward son. Daniel Cady wrung his hands, showing Flora Campbell the New York statutes that gave title in a woman's assets to her husband upon marriage. Elizabeth angrily proposed to cut the discriminatory language from her father's lawbooks with a knife, but when he learned of the plan literally to excise the unwanted law, Daniel Cady explained that law was found not just in the lawbooks but in the society all around them. Perhaps, he suggested, his daughter could work to change the laws when she became an adult.[6]

Eventually, she would do just that, but her project would be an immense undertaking. Flora Campbell's inability to hold property independent of her husband represented only one small aspect of women's subordinated position under nineteenth-century American law. So-called "coverture" was intact, and it systematically entailed the elimination of virtually all rights under the law for married women. They had no legal control over the wages they might earn, contracts they might enter, or the discipline of their children. Divorce was rare by modern standards, but when it occurred, women almost always lost the custody of their children. For the most part, the law did not even punish husbands for beating or raping their wives, rape being thought of as impossible within marriage. Wives, after all, assumed a dependent, inferior position to their husbands and, presumably, granted standing consent for sex, even if it had to be forced.[7]

Most importantly in a political sense, women were denied the right to vote. In the words of the historian Ellen DuBois, "Women were so far outside the boundaries of the antebellum political community that the fact of their disenfranchisement, unlike that of black men, was barely noticed."[8] Most revolutionary leaders had not even contemplated women's suffrage, and John Adams, one of the few who did, argued that granting women voting rights would open up the possibility of propertyless adult men and younger men demanding the same rights.[9] In the 1820s and 1830s those who addressed women's suffrage were less likely to be outraged by its absence than to cite the absence as evidence that full-bodied democracy was not necessarily inevitable.[10]

Cady Stanton's father and her times invited her to assume the law, the legal profession, and a fully enfranchised life were beyond her. Although she was an excellent student at a local academy, Cady Stanton could not attend the all-male colleges of her era. Her best option was a boarding school, the Troy Female Seminary in Troy, New York. Founded by Emma Willard and later renamed after her, the school at least respected young women's capabilities and tried to provide something comparable to a college education. Cady Stanton admired Emma Willard herself and developed a fondness for dancing that would stay with her throughout her life, but in general the school disappointed her. In addition, she ran head on into the Second Great Awakening when Charles Grandison Finney himself conducted revivals at the school. "Owing to my gloomy Calvinistic training in the old Scotch Presbyterian Church, and my vivid imagination," she said later, "I was one of the first victims."[11] In an early version of religious deprogramming, her parents shipped her off to Niagara for six weeks to flush the excessive religiosity from her system.

After graduating from the Troy Female Seminary in 1833, Cady Stanton settled into the inactive tedium of a young bourgeois woman, although she did claim in a Troy Female Seminary alumnae survey that she was "reading law" in her father's office.[12] Lively, smart, and attractive in the heavyset way that appealed to men of her era, she might have married one of the young men who boarded with her family while studying law with her father. Her sisters Tryphena, Margaret, and Catherine had, after all, married lawyers, and a vicarious career in the law might have been better than no career. But instead—and much to her parents' dismay—she chose as a husband Henry Brewster Stanton, the abolitionist lecturer and organizer who had confronted William Lloyd Garrison on the question of voting's sinfulness. Cady Stanton met her future husband at her cousin Gerrit Smith's home in Peterboro. When the couple married hurriedly in 1840, Cady Stanton's parents did not attend.

The marriage to Stanton, obviously, was an act of rebellion on Cady Stanton's part. The Cadys most decidedly deemed abolitionists to be undesirable mates. Such rebellion might have been unnecessary if Cady Stanton had been able to pursue the life in the law so powerfully personified by her father, if somehow the opportunities available to her under the law had matched her abilities. Years later, in an 1855 letter to Susan B. Anthony, Cady Stanton recounted the "terrible scourging" she had received at her father's house for being outspoken on emerging women's issues. "I have never felt more keenly the degradation of my sex," said Cady Stanton. "To think that all in me of which my father would have felt a proper pride had I been a man, is deeply mortifying to him because I am a woman."[13]

Elizabeth Cady Stanton's marriage in and of itself did not lead to her radicalization and articulation of a legal heresy regarding women, but leaving the confining environment of her parents' home did provide a new degree of freedom. She read, traveled, and thought, and in the decade following her marriage she became the nation's leading proponent of women's rights. Her political philosophy rested on two deceptively simple premises: (1) women, like all human beings, had natural rights and (2) the posited law, legal institutions, and legal faith of the United States denied those rights. Cady Stanton's demands were in her era frequently taken to be shocking and almost unbelievable. Her legal heresy was quite revolutionary.

Shortly after their 1840 marriage, Cady Stanton and her husband Henry left for the World Anti-Slavery Convention in London. The Atlantic crossing was both boring and exciting, and the spirited Cady Stanton raised more than a few eyebrows when she convinced the ship's captain to hoist her high above the deck in a specially rigged chair. After their arrival Henry Stanton addressed antislavery groups throughout the British Isles, and the couple met influential reformers and saw the sights as they toured. However, it was the conference itself that had the most powerful impact on Cady Stanton. She met women delegates to the conference, most notably the Philadelphia Quaker Lucretia Mott, and she took quickly to Mott's argument that women should have the right to vote and participate fully in the conference. She also listened to Mott preach at a London church, the very first time she had heard a woman address in public an audience of both men and women.

At the conference meetings themselves, Cady Stanton was outraged when women were not allowed to speak or even to sit on the convention floor. She steamed when forced to sit in a curtained gallery at one end of the hall. "It was really pitiful," she said later, "to hear narrow-minded bigots, pretending to be teachers and leaders of men, so cruelly remanding their own mothers, with the rest of womenkind, to absolute subjection to the ordinary masculine type of humanity."[14] Her husband spoke against this seating, as did William Lloyd Garrison. The immediatist, soon to be Christian anarchist, was not only an abolitionist but also a strong supporter of women's rights. He actually left his seat on the convention floor to sit with the women in their gentile gender prison, a symbolic act that made a tremendous impression on Cady Stanton.[15] She and Lucretia Mott agreed, when all was said and done, that a women's rights convention was needed when they returned home.

But alas, plans fueled by outrage do not necessarily come to pass—at least not immediately. When Cady Stanton returned, she reconciled with her family. Temporarily putting aside his abolitionist work, her husband apprenticed as a lawyer with Cady Stanton's father and then opened a law office in Boston. Cady Stanton never took to the role of blindly loving helpmate, but she did give birth to her first son in Johnstown and then two more in Boston. In her era she no doubt registered as quite the "alternative" mother, freeing her infants from tight swaddling clothes, throwing open the windows in the name of fresh air, and eschewing the commonly used syrups and medicines laced with opium derivatives. During her babies' naps and when at long last they were in bed, Cady Stanton also read voraciously in theology, history, political philosophy, and law. Especially important works in her continuing self-education included Mary Wollstonecraft's *Vindication of the Rights of Women* (1792), Sarah Grimké's *Letters on the Equality of the Sexes* (1838), and Margaret Fuller's *Women in the Nineteenth Century* (1845), all of which helped her break through the reigning assumptions of male superiority.

Cady Stanton's initial efforts on behalf of women's rights came not in Boston but rather back in New York. She perhaps felt more comfortable making her first public speech in sleepy Johnstown rather than in the more cosmopolitan and agitated Boston. During visits to New York family members she circulated petitions to the New York legislature on behalf of expanded property rights for married women. She also lobbied legislators whom she knew through Albany society connections. Finally, the pull of her New York was too strong, and in 1847 Cady Stanton and her family moved to Seneca Falls, a small industrial town linked to both Johnstown and Albany by train but also far enough away to limit her father's suffocating influences.

Once settled in Seneca Falls, Cady Stanton rekindled her friendship with Lucretia Mott, and along with others they crafted plans for the women's rights convention they had first discussed in London eight years earlier. As was the case with Garrison, the stabilization of a like-minded community helped Cady Stanton achieve political maturity and direction. Legal heretics and radicals in general might emerge from a group of like-minded individuals. They might seem the leaders, the originators, the moving force in and of their charismatic selves. But inevitably, their political demands and philosophies derive from some variety of community and collectivity.

Most of the planning for the convention took place in Mary Mc-Clintock's properly Victorian parlor in nearby Waterloo, and although the women did not feel themselves endangered, they did realize the radicalism of their undertaking. Laughter spiced their discussions—the type of laughter born of tension and anticipation rather than humor and silliness.[16] The most common variety of early nineteenth-century women's reform had involved moralistic ladies' societies. These societies assumed women, *as women*, were well suited to address issues concerning poor relief, orphans, prostitution, and sexual mores. The societies condemned the sexual exploitation of women and the double standard that deplored extramarital sex for women but tolerated it for men.[17] These efforts no doubt helped invigorate Cady Stanton and her Seneca Falls colleagues, and as the prominent women's historian Carroll Smith-Rosenberg has argued, one should not overlook the resentment of male dominance embedded in the campaigns of the ladies' societies.[18] But Cady Stanton did not assume an exclusive women's sphere. She and the other women planning the convention were not prepared to speak only moralistically and leave more formal political authority exclusively to men.[19]

The greatest stroke of genius in discussions for the convention came from Cady Stanton, to wit, the notion of paraphrasing the Declaration of Independence in the declaration of goals and grievances for the convention. Particularly important to her were the first few paragraphs of the Declaration of Independence, the paragraphs speaking not to the posited law and existing legal institutions but rather a natural rights philosophy. The suggestion that all men were created equal and endowed with inalienable rights was powerful for early nineteenth-century Americans. It had rhetorical clout.[20] By playing off of this rhetoric, Cady Stanton could capture the attention and perhaps the support of others. She substituted "men and women" for simply "men" in the classic sentence: "We hold these truths to be self-evident: That all men are created equal; that they are endowed by their Creator with certain inalienable rights; that among these are life, liberty, and the pursuit of happiness. . . ." In the Preamble, she also stated that "women" as opposed to "these colonies" had suffered under an unjust government, and she cast the oppressing tyrant as "man" rather than as King George.

Beyond its rhetorical flourish, Stanton's work for the convention also made changes in the Enlightenment-era political philosophy in which the notion of inalienable rights was so central. While for John Locke and other social contract theorists men could revolt if their governments failed to recognize their inalienable rights, there was no suggestion that women could exercise the same options. Hence, Stanton and her colleagues executed a subtle but crucial change in the philosophy. The issue was not recent injustice that could be corrected by revolt. Women had from the beginning been *denied* their inalienable rights. "By claiming the ideology of natural rights and by appropriating its language while at the same time implying that women's past experience vis-à-vis natural rights was different," the scholar Sylvia D. Hoffert has argued, "early women's rights advocates declared their independence from male experience and history and established a basis for developing their own historical consciousness as women."[21]

Other aspects of the key document for the convention also reflected Stanton's studies and experience. The very title of the document—the "Declaration of Sentiments"—echoed the endorsement of sentiment found in Scottish Enlightenment philosophers such as David Hume and Adam Smith. "Sentiment" was neither flimsy nor unreliable but rather a much needed way to correct the occasional blindness of reasoned self-interest.[22] Women could bring sentiment to bear. Women could appreciate the numerous ways man's laws and legal institutions denied women's rights. Drawing on her command of law, Stanton in the grievance section of the "Declaration of Sentiments" pointed to the denial of suffrage, the denial of property rights for married women, and unequal divorce laws. "He [man] has endeavored, in every way that he could, to destroy her [woman's] confidence in her own powers, to lessen her self-respect, and to make her willing to lead a dependent and abject life."[23]

The actual convention on July 19 and 20 attracted three hundred people, more than the organizers had anticipated. The great majority of those in attendance were women, but forty men also participated. When Cady Stanton addressed the assembled on the first day of the convention, she was so nervous that she felt like "abandoning all her principles and running away."[24] But she persevered, noting how especially frustrating she found the indifference and contempt of other women, how disheartening was their "scornful curl of the lip." "We are assembled to protest against a form of government existing without the consent of the governed—to declare our right to be free as man is free, to be represented in the government which we are taxed to support, to have such disgraceful laws as give men the power to chastise and imprison his wife, to take the wages which she earns, the property which she inherits, and, in case of separation, the children of her love; laws which make her the mere dependent on his bounty."[25]

On the second day of the convention the participants considered a list of resolutions. The natural rights philosophy which Cady Stanton used to challenge the emerging positivism of the American legal faith was again evident, this time in a preface to the resolutions. She invoked the revered British legal commentator Sir William Blackstone to support the argument that a law of nature was everywhere coeval with the law of mankind. "No human laws," Cady Stanton reasoned, "are of any validity if contrary to this [the law of nature], and such of them as are valid, derive all their force, and all their validity, and all their authority, mediately and immediately, from this original. . . ."[26]

All of the convention resolutions except one passed unanimously, but Cady Stanton's resolution demanding suffrage for women caused controversy. Although not opposed in principle, Mott thought the radicalism of the resolution would make the convention seem comical to outsiders. Other Quakers at the convention opposed the resolution because, as pacifists, they refused to participate even as voters in war-making governments. Henry Stanton, Cady Stanton's husband, also backed off, thinking the resolution would be harmful to his political ambitions. But Cady Stanton refused to budge. Radical as the idea might be, the vote, it seemed to her, was crucial in making women full political actors and in toppling the system of legalized male dominance. "To vote," she said later, "is the most sacred right of citizenship—a religious duty"; if women could obtain the vote, the polling booth would be a "temple" and election days "holy feasts."[27] Men, meanwhile, could not be expected to extend voting rights easily. This "stronghold of the fortress," she told women planning a convention in Ohio, was "*the one* woman will find the most difficult to take, *the one* man will most reluctantly give up."[28] In the end, and only after a stirring address by Frederick Douglass, a bare majority of those in Seneca Falls voted for the suffrage resolution.

During the last twenty-five years Cady Stanton's efforts and the convention in Seneca Falls have acquired almost mythic status in American women's history. But immediately after the convention mainstreamers attacked participants, and the inspired "Declaration of Sentiments" could have ended up on history's trash heap of forgotten documents. Of the one hundred men and women who actually signed the "Declaration of Sentiments," a substantial number retracted their signatures. Among the backsliders was Cady Stanton's own sister Harriet, and Daniel Cady also attempted to convince Cady Stanton to remove her name.

The press also attacked the Seneca Falls participants and proceedings, and some editors turned not to criticism, a stance at least implying serious engagement, but rather to ridicule. What better way to diffuse radicalism than to make fun of it? James Gordon Bennett, the rambunctiously successful publisher of the *New York Herald*, penned his own editorial, casting the preamble in the "Declaration of Sentiments" as especially amusing. Bennett, for reasons that reside more in his libido than his politics, delighted in referring to women's undergarments in his journalism, and he could not resist references to women's so-called "inexpressibles" in his mocking commentary on the Seneca Falls convention.[29] In subsequent years, Bennett continued to rail against women's rights advocates, calling them "Amazons" and "hens that crow."[30]

Only the exceptional man such as Frederick Douglass seemed able to respect what had happened in Seneca Falls. In addition to attending the convention and speaking forcefully on behalf of the suffrage resolution, Douglass authored an editorial for the *North Star*. "We are not insensible that the bare mention of this truly important subject in any other than terms of contemptuous ridicule and scornful disfavor, is likely to excite against us the fury of bigotry and the folly of prejudice," he said. "A discussion of the rights of animals would be regarded with far more complacency by many of what are called the wise and the good of our land, than would be a discussion of the rights of women." Cady Stanton's position, Douglass thought, struck many as a "dangerous heresy."[31]

For her own part, Cady Stanton refused to recant her position from Seneca Falls, and in the remaining years before the outbreak of the Civil War she continued her fight for women's rights. She jointly undertook many of her activities with Susan B. Anthony, a daughter of a liberal Quaker family and former schoolteacher who resided on the outskirts of Rochester, New York. The two met in May of 1851 when Anthony came to Seneca Falls to attend antislavery meetings led by William Lloyd Garrison and George Thompson, an English abolitionist. Anthony knew of Cady Stanton and was anxious to meet her, but their first exchange was reportedly an awkward one. Cady Stanton was dressed in the signature bloomers of progressive women, but Anthony was not. Cady Stanton was preoccupied with entertaining Garrison, but Anthony hoped she herself would receive more attention.[32]

Fortunately, despite the initial miscommunications and disappointments, a friendship sprouted and then blossomed. In the years following their first meeting, Cady Stanton and Anthony attempted to establish a women's college in upstate New York, and along with other colleagues the two also formed the New York Women's Temperance Society. As the first president of the organization, Cady Stanton carried the society's demands to the state legislature, advocating a limit on the number of places selling liquor.

The campaign for temperance might seem a curious place to concentrate one's energies, but it helps to remember that the early nineteenth century was marked by truly extraordinary levels of alcohol consumption. Between 1790 and 1840 Americans drank more alcohol per person than ever before or ever since. The average adult man drank a half pint a day, and many greatly exceeded the average. Men drank not only in taverns and privately, but at work, in the military, and during meals. Boys of eleven or twelve drank, often with the encouragement of parents who thought early drinking would guard against drunkenness during the adult years. And through it all the alcoholic beverages were almost always distilled liquors—rum, whiskey, gin, and brandy. On the average, such liquors were 90 proof or, to put things more bluntly, 45 percent alcohol.[33]

For reformers such as Cady Stanton the campaign for temperance related to her quest for women's rights. The cult of male drinking often intertwined with the patronizing of prostitutes, wife abuse, and oppressive conditions for women. If one could limit the amount of alcohol consumed, Cady Stanton reasoned, one might take a step toward liberating women. If an individual man could not bring his drinking under control, Cady Stanton continued, a woman should at least be able to divorce him. In her appeal to the New York legislature Cady Stanton made her general pitch for women's rights, saying women's grievances were "as numerous as those made by our forefathers against their King." But if legislators would not act pervasively to rectify the larger problem, she added, at least they could be "chivalrous knights" and limit the production and sale of liquor.[34]

The temperance campaign met with only partial success, and even within temperance circles themselves many failed to share Cady Stanton's reasoning. In 1853 conservative women not only voted to bring men into the New York Women's Temperance Society but also refused to reelect Cady Stanton society president. From a more conservative perspective, drunken men might be saved with the Lord's help, but gender norms and the overarching patriarchy need not be challenged.

The rejection disappointed Cady Stanton, but it hardly disabled her. She told Anthony "to waste no powder on the Women's State Temperance Society. We have other and bigger fish to fry."[35] Some of the frying could be done in a state women's rights organization which met annually, sent speakers throughout the state, collected signatures on petitions, and lobbied the legislature. The organization continued to demand women's suffrage and also reasserted the demand for liberalized divorce laws that had surfaced in conjunction with the temperance struggle. Cady Stanton and Anthony insisted that marriage was merely a civil contract rather than something handed down from the Heavens and that women should be able to divorce chronically drunken husbands. Such divorce was not anticipated by the posited legal regime, but surely it was consistent with women's natural rights.[36]

Anthony, a single woman of indefatigable energy, carried much of the organizing and traveling load during the 1850s, as Cady Stanton stayed at home tending to her growing family. She gave birth to four more children, the last of whom was born in 1859. She described him as "a great boy," who "weighed at his birth without a particle of clothing 12 1/4 lb."[37] Birthing and nurturing and educating her brood was difficult, and Cady Stanton reported to Anthony that she sometimes paced back and forth in her home "like a caged lioness."[38] But the self-styled lioness continued to growl through her petitions, manifestoes, and speeches written for Anthony and others. "I forged the thunderbolts," Cady Stanton said, "and she [Anthony] fired them."[39]

The most famous speech that Cady Stanton herself delivered during the decade came in 1854 to the New York legislature. She worked on the speech for over two months and consulted lawyers and judges to make sure she had legal references exactly right. The speech demanded that rights of women be fully recognized and outlined what that would entail: the vote, the right to sit on juries, the rights of citizenship, and equality in marriage, parenthood, and widowhood. Countless men, she reported, wanted to know "What do you women want? What are you aiming at?" The answer, Cady Stanton asserted, was simple: "We ask no better laws than those you have made for yourself. We need no other protection than that which your present laws secure to you." The women of the Empire State, Cady Stanton continued, believe that "the rights of every human being are the same and identical."[40]

In 1862, with the cannons of war booming, Cady Stanton and her family moved to New York City, where her husband had secured a custom's house position. More activism would follow the war, but her record during the preceding fifteen years was nothing short of remarkable. Unlike most women in the moral reform societies or temperance movement, Cady Stanton did not assume a separate sphere for women or endorse obedient domesticity. She stood for something bolder. Women had natural rights, and those rights were equal to the natural rights of men. Also, unlike most women in the moral reform societies or temperance movement, Cady Stanton did not assume exemplary conduct or subtle influence were the ways to improve society. She looked to law and legal faith, and appreciated that in a society that did not depend on royalty, rank or class, "Law, the immutable principles of right, are all and everything to us."[41] Since the natural rights were givens, the law would have to change. Americans needed desperately to exorcise the fundamental and pervasive sexism of their legal system.

In the decades following the Civil War Elizabeth Cady Stanton's prominence and stature grew. She lectured widely on the lyceum circuit, led protest rallies over what she considered grotesque miscarriages of justice, and launched a symbolic run for Congress. But in many ways her difficulties only increased as the years went on. Some of her positions on post–Civil War Constitutional amendments seemed nativist and perhaps racist. She became disaffected with the suffrage movement. And she even quarreled with Susan B. Anthony, her most trusted friend and co-leader of the women's rights movement. At the heart of these controversies was Cady Stanton's legal heresy. As the nineteenth century marched toward its end, the national legal faith grew more rigid and elaborated. Women's reform groups grew more cautious and limited in their aspirations. Through it all, Cady Stanton held firm to the political philosophy she had developed in the 1840s. She continued to invoke a natural rights jurisprudence to champion the full liberation and empowerment of women.

More effectively than Garrison before her, Cady Stanton used legal cases to demonstrate the inherent biases of courts and courtroom proceedings. As previously noted, Americans had since virtually the founding of the Republic made the courtroom trial into a special forum for personal and social meaning. Americans did not always agree with what a judge or jury had to say in each individual case, but the courtroom trial itself was the most important ritual of the legal faith. Cady Stanton argued that the ritual was false and misleading when women were involved.

The case of Hester Vaughan, for example, demonstrated how sexist preying on vulnerable women could lead to the horrors of infanticide. Vaughan had immigrated from the British Isles to Pennsylvania expecting to marry, but upon her arrival she learned that the man she expected to marry was already married. She then took up work as a maid, only to be seduced, impregnated, and then fired by her employer. When police found her in Philadelphia in 1868, Vaughan was ill and close to starvation. Her baby was dead. Despite what seemed extenuating circumstances, she was convicted of murder, and the self-righteous judge announced that "some women had to be made an example of."[42]

Cady Stanton and Anthony were outraged, both at the verdict and at the way respectable citizens were supposed to look the other way when something like infanticide muscled its way into the public consciousness. They publicized the case in the *Revolution*, an aggressive feminist journal they had founded in 1868, and also organized a large public protest meeting in New York City. In Cady Stanton's opinion infanticide—and abortion as well—were deplorable, but she did not condemn women for resorting to them. The real problem was that men could not control themselves, and too many women lacked the strength and confidence to fight them off. In part because of Cady Stanton's efforts, the governor of Pennsylvania ultimately pardoned Vaughan, citing the absence of proof that she intended to kill the infant.

In the Albert McFarland trial of 1870, the issue was not seduction but rather divorce reform. McFarland, an attorney in New York City, had killed newspaper reporter James Richardson after discovering the latter's involvement with Abby Sage, McFarland's wife or ex-wife, depending how you looked at things. Sage, it seems, had been abused by McFarland and had gotten a divorce in Indiana, where the grounds were more liberal. Back in New York, meanwhile, the court refused to recognize the Indiana divorce, with the effect being that Sage could not testify against McFarland at trial. Without this crucial testimony, the jury acquitted McFarland, presumably feeling murderous rage was understandable when a husband caught his wife in an affair. In a separate proceeding McFarland even received custody of his child with Sage!

Again, Cady Stanton was outraged. With Anthony's able assistance, she organized a protest rally. Men were not allowed to attend, but two thousand women did. At the rally Cady Stanton called the McFarland verdict the Dred Scott case of the women's rights struggle. Marriage to a "bloated drunkard or diseased libertine," she said, was "the most degraded type of slavery the world knows." Women should not waste time crying over the sufferings of individual women but rather "learn what we can do to day [*sic*] towards an entire revision of the laws of New York on marriage and divorce." Divorce at the will of the parties, in her opinion, was "not only right but it is a sin against nature, the family, the state for a man or woman to live together in the marriage relation in continual antagonism, indifference, disgust." Her idea of freedom, Cady Stanton thundered, was "not to coquette with unjust law, thrust it to one side or try to get beyond its reach, but to fight it where it is, and fight it to the death. Let the women of this state rise in mass and say that they will no longer tolerate statutes that hold pure virtuous women indissolubly bound to gross vicious men whom they loathe and abhor. . . ."[43]

Cady Stanton's run for Congress, by contrast, was less vigorous and inspiring. She realized in 1866 that even though women were ineligible to vote, they could nevertheless run for office. She hastily filed as an independent for the House of Representatives race in New York City's Eighth District and attempted to mount a campaign. But the campaign never took off, perhaps because elected politics as opposed to thoughts of the iconic Constitution, the courtroom ritual, and the rule of law rarely set the stage for contemplation of higher principles. To be sure, Cady Stanton made a symbolic statement by being the first woman in American history to run for Congress, but her larger message about women's rights for the most part went unheard. On election day she received only twenty-four votes out of over twenty thousand cast. Her only regret, she said, was that she had not "procure[d] photographs of her two dozen unknown friends."[44]

If Cady Stanton had somehow been able to win election to the Congress, she might have been able to influence the Constitutional amendments that were ratified immediately after the Civil War. In early 1865, Congress began considering the Fourteenth Amendment, a Constitutional change intended to give freed slaves the full range of rights. Cady Stanton and other women's rights activists had assumed that, even though they could not vote, they were "citizens." But the wording of the amendment contained a rude surprise. Republican leaders in the Congress had added the word "male" to language of the amendment, thereby linking citizenship to gender. One stated rationale was that African American suffrage in and of itself was controversial and did not need to carry the extra baggage of women's rights. More generally, of course, patriarchy and male dominance lurked. Individuals might recognize the equality of other individuals, but it is always more difficult for a group with power—in this case men—to recognize the equality of another group—women—which traditionally occupied an inferior position.

If the Republicans would not support women's rights, Cady Stanton likely thought, at least former abolitionist colleagues would. But again, a disappointing surprise was in the wings. While some former abolitionists supported women's rights, prominent abolitionist figures such as Frederick Douglass, Wendell Phillips, and Charles Sumner made clear that African American rights must come before women's rights and that African American rights for the time being at least meant male rights. Cady Stanton refused to see it that way, and when suffrage was not included for women, she and Anthony opposed the Fifteenth Amendment granting suffrage to African American males. The amendment not only failed to enfranchise women, they argued, but it exacerbated gender inequalities. As a result, even William Lloyd Garrison, who had so inspired Cady Stanton earlier in her life, lost his patience. He castigated her as a "female demagogue" and said he considered her "untruthful, unscrupulous and selfishly ambitious."[45]

The problem seems to have been that Cady Stanton, and Anthony as well, thought victory in the Civil War was an opportunity to eliminate all varieties of undue privilege and to give democracy a new and broader meaning. But alas, their disappointment also led Cady Stanton to denigrate African American, ethnic, and working-class men. "As you go down and down in the scale of manhood," she argued, "the idea strengthens and strengthens, at every step, that woman was created for no higher purpose than to gratify the lust of man." "The great battle for the laborer must be fought for him by the educated classes, just as for the slave."[46] "Saxon women" should stand first in line; certainly they should have their rights before former slaves and "the lower order of men."[47]

Cady Stanton's frustration in seeing an opportunity slip through women's fingers is understandable, but her willingness to use racism, nativism, and class bias for her cause is deeply troubling. Perhaps the biases of her privileged youth just bubbled to the surface in a period of stress. Cady Stanton had, after all, revealed an elitist strain earlier, complaining of "ignorant foreigners" and "the alien and the ditch-digger" in her Seneca Falls address and 1854 speech to the New York legislature, respectively.[48] More generally, the troubling comments illustrate how much she focused on women's rights. Her heresy, like others, could be more intense than it was broad and wide-ranging. Cady Stanton was so determined to obtain for women what she considered their natural rights that she sometimes failed to respect the natural rights of others.

In the 1870s the ugliest of Cady Stanton's statements stopped, but troubles now surfaced in what had become the woman's suffrage movement. After their defeat in the struggle to include women in the Fourteenth Amendment, Cady Stanton and Anthony formed the National Woman Suffrage Association. Centered in New York, the association discussed and lobbied for a wide range of women's economic, social and political issues. However, the work of the association had hardly begun when rivals Lucy Stone and Henry Blackwell formed the competing American Woman Suffrage Association. Boston-based, Stone

and Blackwell were wife and husband. They had been abolitionists before the war and, especially in Stone's case, seemed to resent the way
Cady Stanton and Anthony assumed they were the anointed leaders of
the women's rights movement. According to one scholar, this seemed to
Stone "a blatant ignoring of a large number of workers who had been in
the movement for years."[49]

The split was unfortunate, and in retrospect it revolved around more
than petty differences and jealousies. Cady Stanton believed suffrage
should be coupled with other issues including divorce reform. Her goal
had long been a large-scale restructuring of American law in keeping
with women's natural rights. She constantly put a political charge into
her positions, hoping to jar the public and perhaps the legislatures and
courts into action. Stone, Blackwell, and the American Woman Suffrage
Association, meanwhile, wanted to narrow the issue to simply suffrage
and thought in fact that divorce reform and other issues would complicate things. They wished to work more gradually, politely, and noncon-
frontationally for their goal. This troubled Cady Stanton to no end, and
she thought the "Boston malcontents" were too anxious to preserve
their reputation and social standing.[50]

Anthony much more than Cady Stanton ultimately took the lead in
unifying the women's rights organizations. In 1888 she promoted the
week-long International Council for Women and, in a sign of reconcil-
iation, shared the same platform with Lucy Stone. In 1890, Anthony
agreed to a merger of the National and American suffrage organizations,
with the new organization to be clumsily dubbed the "National American Woman Suffrage Association." For her part Cady Stanton remained skeptical and continued to believe the goal of the movement
must be not the vote in and of itself but rather radical, comprehensive
change to liberate and empower women. She complained that the
wordy constitution of the organization was "very mannish."[51] In her address to the first convention Cady Stanton called the emphasis on just
suffrage "puerile" and said the ballot had to be used for change. She reiterated her longstanding commitment to liberal divorce laws, saying
easy divorce was for women what Canada had been for escaping slaves,
and decried the way "the Bench, the Bar and the Jury"—all men—had
for fifty years turned a deaf ear on women's pleas for justice. It was use-

ful, she thought, to "stir up a whole group of new victims from time to time, by turning our guns on new strongholds. Agitation is the advance guard of education."[52] Lest there be any lingering doubt where she stood, from 1893 to 1902 she wrote an annual grumpy letter to each National American Woman Suffrage Association meeting.

In the course of her post–Civil War battles Cady Stanton even jeopardized her relationship with Anthony. After making one another's acquaintance in 1851, the two had formed one of the most successful and enduring partnerships in all of American history. They met together for days at a time, worked on the same causes, and even shared some of the burdens of raising Cady Stanton's seven children. Part of the reason for the success of the relationship, according to the scholar Lois W. Banner, was the meshing of opposites.[53] Cady Stanton was vivacious and fun-loving, while Anthony was controlled and stern. Cady Stanton was at her best theorizing and speaking, but Anthony was the better organizer and fund-raiser. Nothing suggests the women were sexually involved with one another, but in intellectual and political ways Anthony was much more Cady Stanton's "mate" than was her husband Henry. Indeed, Anthony probably spent more time in the Tenafly, New Jersey home into which Cady Stanton moved in 1868 than did Henry, who maintained separate living quarters in Manhattan.

Stress in the relationship became most evident during the Gilded Age. After the *Revolution* was sold in 1870, Cady Stanton refused to assume any responsibility for its outstanding debts. Anthony, who as the unmarried partner in the enterprise had agreed to sign all contracts, was stuck with the tab and needed six years to pay it. In 1871 when the women toured together in the West, Anthony felt Cady Stanton was a scene stealer. "Whoever goes into a parlor or before an audience with that woman," Anthony said, "does it at the price of a fearful overshadowing" because of the "brilliant scintillations" from her "never-exhausted magazine."[54]

A public breakup never occurred, and even as late as 1890 Anthony insisted that Cady Stanton be named the first president of the merged National and American suffrage organizations. However, there were differences of opinion. To a greater extent than Anthony, Cady Stanton insisted on broad-based women's liberation, was leery of the newly unified women's movement, and was prepared to agitate, agitate, agitate. As with the battles over the Fourteenth Amendment and women's suffrage, the issue might have been at its core Cady Stanton's political philosophy. She subscribed passionately to women's natural rights and believed just as passionately in the need to end the fundamentally gendered nature of the American law, legal institutions, and legal faith.

In the years after their deaths, Anthony was lionized more than Cady Stanton, and this may underscore their differences. Anthony became the great saint of the suffrage movement, complete with preserved homes, honorific books, and eventually, her face on a silver dollar. Cady Stanton has increasingly received her due from scholars in recent years, but during her lifetime and most of the twentieth century her legal heresy was much more difficult for the reigning legal faith to accommodate. While Anthony was by nature a reformer, Cady Stanton was very much a radical.

Elizabeth Cady Stanton lived on until 1902 and, in the words of one of her biographers, became a "deviant old lady."[55] The plumpness of her youth developed into downright obesity and forced her retirement from the lyceum circuit, but she remained spontaneous, clear-headed, and playful. Reflecting on what lawyers had done to her sister Tryphena's last will and testament, Cady Stanton offered a lawyer joke that works even a century later when lawyer bashing has become a refined art form: "I do believe that half a dozen commonplace attorneys could so mystify and misconstrue the Ten Commandments, and so confuse Moses' surroundings on Mount Sinai, that the great law-giver, if he returned to this planet, would doubt his own identify, abjure every one of his deliverances, yea, even commend the very sins he so clearly forbade his people."[56]

During the 1890s Cady Stanton wrote frequently for popular and political journals and completed her autobiography. She also continued to write for others. Anthony, in particular, benefited from the power of Cady Stanton's pen, and indeed, Cady Stanton wrote for her not only speeches but also convention calls, resolutions, and even personal letters. For the Columbia Exposition in Chicago in 1893 alone Cady Stanton drafted five speeches for Anthony. With as much accuracy as wryness, Anthony once remarked that a collection of her speeches would be impossible because the speeches had all been written by Cady Stanton.[57]

The greatest controversy of Cady Stanton's final decade involved her campaign against organized religion and what she took to be religious sexism. In the Christian denominations the growing presence of women had not in Cady Stanton's opinion reduced the power of male ministers or the notion of a masculine, patriarchal God. In her view God was feminine *and* masculine, "the apex of a system of male and female forces which permeated the universe and kept it in equilibrium."[58] Shortly after turning eighty in 1895, Cady Stanton brought her campaign to a head by publishing with a team of other women an extremely controversial work, *The Women's Bible.* The book critiqued those parts of the Bible especially relevant to women and argued that the biblical image of women was the work of biased male authors rather than truly divine.[59]

Added to her previous radical positions, Cady Stanton's opposition to religious institutions and doctrine was more than many women's groups could stomach. The National American Woman Suffrage Association censured *The Women's Bible* in 1896, and Cady Stanton then angered the association even more by including the censure in the next edition of the work. Other women's organizations of the era such as the Women's Christian Temperance Union, the Young Women's Christian Association, and the Women's Educational and Industrial Union were full of bourgeois Christian women and sometimes avowedly religious in orientation. Somewhat like the moral reform societies of the first half of the nineteenth century, these organizations stressed women's special sensitivities and responsibilities, assigning to themselves the care of society's homes, orphans, and children and the policing of American sexual conduct. They looked to Christian values as the antidote for society's woes and took Cady Stanton's antireligious stances to be even more poisonous than a failure to profess the faith.

Most biographers of Cady Stanton have concluded their works with moving accounts of her final scene, one in which she demanded to stand, placed her hands on the table before her, and seemed for seven or eight minutes to be mentally delivering a fiery last address.[60] But notwithstanding the appealing image of Cady Stanton going to meet her maker with her guns blazing, a better concluding indication of her mature political philosophy might be "The Solitude of Self," a speech she delivered three times in three days a decade before her death. She gave it in written form to the House Committee on the Judiciary, as a valedictory to the National American Woman Suffrage Association, and then as a speech to the Senate Committee on Woman Suffrage. Anthony never liked the address, a reaction Cady Stanton wrote off as "a striking example of how the executive and business side of her remarkable make-up overtops the literary and intellectual side."[61] For her own part, Cady Stanton immodestly judged the speech "the best thing I have ever written, at least in my declining years."[62]

Commentators on the speech have rightfully been struck by its libertarian and existentialist features. "The point I wish plainly to bring before you on this occasion," Cady Stanton began, "is the individuality of each human soul." Each individual woman, she argued, was "in a world of her own, the arbiter of her own destiny, an imaginary Robinson Crusoe, with her woman, Friday, on a solitary island." To some extent, being marooned made for melancholy. The "solitary voyager" has an inner life "more inaccessible than the ice-cold mountains, more profound than the midnight sea."

Cady Stanton flirted with socialist thought in her final years, but clearly "The Solitude of Self" does not constitute a collectivist manifesto. The underlying reason for her insistence on individualism and personal solitude is the natural rights of women. As an individual, as a human being who frequently stands alone with herself in the world, woman has natural rights. "Seeing, then, that life must ever be a march and a battle, that each soldier must be equipped for his own protection, it is the height of cruelty to rob the individual of a single natural right." In so many ways, Cady Stanton asserted, the social and legal system denied women what they were entitled to and needed:

> To throw obstacles in the way of a complete education is like putting out the eyes; to deny the rights of property is like cutting off the hands. To refuse political equality is to rob the ostracized of all self-respect; of credit in the market place, of recompense in the world of work, of a voice in choosing those who make and administer the law, a choice in the jury before whom they are tried, and in the judge who decides their punishment. [Consider] . . . woman's position! Robbed of her natural rights,

handicapped by law and custom at every turn, yet compelled to fight her own battles, and in the emergencies of life to fall back on herself for protection.[63]

Cady Stanton tried to cast "The Solitude of Self" as new thinking on her part, as an effort to move beyond older arguments.[64] In reality, the speech illustrates that her political philosophy and concomitant legal heresy had not changed since she creatively rephrased the Declaration of Independence in the Seneca Falls "Declaration of Sentiments" a half-century earlier. "We hold these truths to be self-evident," she had written, "That all men and women are created equal; that they are endowed by their Creator with certain inalienable rights; that among these are life, liberty, and the pursuit of happiness. . . ." Furthermore, "Whenever any form of government becomes destructive of these ends," those who suffer under such a government have a right "to refuse allegiance to it, and to insist upon the institution of a new government. . . ." For Cady Stanton, women were full human beings whose rights were denied by the legal system and by the society in which they lived. She insisted the fundamental flaw of the legal faith be recognized and eliminated.

From our perch at the end of the twentieth century, in an era in which the vote and most of the other legal changes Cady Stanton demanded have been instituted, her arguments and philosophy may not appear heretical. She could be seen as an ameliorative thinker and incrementalist, as someone simply extending the rhetoric and principles of her culture so as to include women. But this would be a misperception. Elizabeth Cady Stanton's emphasis on the natural rights of women was an attack on the fundamentally gendered nature of American law and legal institutions. Failure to appreciate the heretical nature of this stance would in itself be a variety of the gendered blindness that has outlived the specific legal disabilities women faced in the nineteenth century.

4

Eugene Debs
Law-Related Socialist Conversion, Catechism, and Evangelism

The Fourth of July was ideological terrain suitable for both attack and counterattack. While William Lloyd Garrison, Elizabeth Cady Stanton, and others used the nation's birthday as an occasion to promote their legal heresies, self-styled spokesmen for the nation could use the holiday to champion the American legal faith and condemn nonbelievers. An extended illustration of such counterattack appeared in the conservative *Chicago Tribune's* front-page cartoons of July 3–5, 1894. The strike against Chicago's Pullman Palace Car Company provoked the cartoons, and along with various articles and editorials the cartoons made clear the *Tribune* had little taste for the purported lawlessness of the strikers.

The chief target of the cartoons was Eugene Debs, the president of the American Railway Union (ARU) and leader of the strike. In the cartoon of July 3 Debs, a jackass with long ears and hooves, donned a lion's suit, brayed at Uncle Sam, and trampled both train cars and a large volume titled "LAW." On July 4 itself, Debs shed his lion's suit in favor of a crown. Arrogantly smoking a cigar and telling two boys Independence Day had been ended, he plopped his boots on the Declaration of Independence. On the floor in front of him the American eagle was tied to a spittoon, and on the wall above a destroyer of American icons had scratched out a painting of the flag and substituted "ARU" for "Union" in a "The Union Forever" sign. At least on July 5 Uncle Sam got even for all the sacrilege. Using a wand labeled "U.S. Troops," he lit the fuse of a fire cracker which appeared to be the lawless Debs himself![1]

In Chicago itself, real troops and a real legal injunction did succeed in ending the strike, but in a larger sense Debs avoided defeat. He went on to become America's most prominent turn-of-the-century socialist, to run five times for the Presidency, and to speak out dramatically against the nation's efforts in World War I. As a socialist, Debs proffered an alternative to capitalist exploitation. Most importantly for purposes at hand, the nation's law, legal institutions, and professed commitment to a rule of law registered on Debs as highly suspect. In his later years he struggled to tear down the facades of the legal faith.

There were other turn-of-the-century socialists and legal critics, but few melded socialism and legal criticism as fully as Eugene Debs. Bursting through an earlier subscription to the dominant legal faith, he included a vigorous critique of law and legal institutions in his socialist preaching. Especially useful in conveying his message were the trials, including his own, which illustrated the bias of American life, and he invoked these trials to challenge fundamental understandings of legitimacy and illegitimacy. Debs' "conversion" to socialism was law-related. His socialist critique included a large legal "catechism." And his "evangelism" often utilized legal motifs and proceedings. Here, literally, was the premier socialist legal heretic.

Those who encountered the young Eugene Debs on the streets of Terre Haute, Indiana, in the decades immediately following the Civil War would have been surprised to learn that he ultimately became an imprisoned subversive. Born in 1855, Debs was the first son and third of six surviving children of hard-working immigrant storekeepers. His initial speech, delivered to the Occidental Library Society, concerned the heroism of Patrick Henry. He successfully courted Kate Metzel, a woman well above him in station, and the Brotherhood of Locomotive Firemen, a union in which he served as secretary-treasurer, was an elite guild. Enamored with Debs's gregarious optimism, the good burghers of Terre Haute twice elected him city clerk and also sent him off to a term in the state legislature in Indianapolis. Debs's early heroes were Washington, Jefferson, and Lincoln; he believed in liberty and individualism; and he touted law and legal institutions. In the immediate aftermath of the convulsive national railroad strike of 1877 Debs cast the railroad corporation as the "architect of progress" and urged members of the brotherhood not to "disregard the laws which govern our land."[2]

Debs's basic "Americanism" never left him,[3] but eventually he ceased to understand himself as a champion of American ways. In his opinion, it was the 1894 Pullman strike, related legal proceedings, and his own subsequent imprisonment that turned him into a socialist. During his imprisonment, Debs said later, "Socialism gradually laid hold of me in its own irresistible fashion," and "helped me out of darkness into light."[4] Debs's sense of having brought himself over from one belief system to another empowered and invigorated him. Socialist colleagues frequently reiterated the conversion theme, and critics of Debs bemoaned his fundamental transformation. Hardly inconsequential is the fact that Debs's conversion took place in proximity to America's legal institutions. His sense that these institutions—the pillars of the dominant culture's legal faith—were flawed activated the conversion.

At the time of the 1894 Pullman strike Debs held the office of president in the ARU. He had concluded only a few years earlier that the division of railroad workers into various crafts and guilds made effective responses to manipulation and exploitation by railroad bosses exceedingly difficult. As the leader of the ARU, he argued for the organization of railroad workers across employment categories, and in April of 1894 he led the ARU in a victorious strike against James J. Hill's Great Northern Railroad. The victory inspired railroad workers. Approximately two thousand workers joined the ARU daily in the weeks following the Great Northern strike, and with a resulting membership of one hundred fifty thousand the ARU constituted the largest of all railroad labor organizations.[5]

Among those encouraged by the victory over the Great Northern and the emergence of a unified railroad labor organization were the employees of George Mortimer Pullman. The prototype of the self-made man, Pullman had come to Chicago in the early 1850s and made a small name and fortune for himself jacking downtown buildings up from the mud. He then used efficient production processes and sharp dealing to make an even larger name and fortune for himself producing luxurious sleeping cars. The fates seemed to smile on Pullman. After Lincoln's assassination the public was captivated by Pullman's "Pioneer" sleeper which was part of the funeral train. A few months later, General Grant accepted the use of a plush Pullman car for the final legs of his long, slow, and much reported hero's return to Illinois. Once again, the public took notice.[6]

With business booming, Pullman developed a company town to the south of Chicago. His workers labored for the Pullman Palace Car Company, and along with their families they rented Pullman housing, worshiped at the churches Pullman constructed, and buried their dead in Pullman's cemetery. Pullman's company town has fascinated modern scholars, striking one as an intended "cure for Gilded Age Chicago"[7] and another as an "experiment in industrial order and community planning."[8] Actual Pullman workers of the period just knew that Pullman deducted rent, grocery bills, utility charges, and even library fees from their wages. When between September 1893 and May 1894 Pullman reduced wages by 25 percent without reducing rents and utility charges, many of the workers quite simply could not feed and clothe their families in the town of Pullman. The proprietary Pullman acknowledged the workers' difficulties, but he asserted that in hard times labor should expect to suffer since it contributed nothing to the success of a business enterprise. He also, despite the severe wage cuts, paid the usual 8 percent dividend to the company's investors in fiscal 1893 and 1894.[9]

The workers, who could be understood as "railroad workers" by virtue of a few miles of private track in Pullman and had thereby joined the ARU, struck on May 11, 1894. Aware that depression conditions had produced masses of potential strikebreakers, Debs initially withheld full support for the Pullman strike. However, when the ARU held its first annual convention in Chicago in the midst of the strike, the delegates reacted to powerful testimony from Pullman workers with great emotion and support. They voted overwhelmingly to strike Pullman's repair shops and to boycott all Pullman cars. The ARU demanded that individual railroads cut out their Pullman cars. The railroads, tied into the use of the cars by various long-term contracts with Pullman, released switchmen who refused to move trains carrying Pullman cars, and in the space of only a few weeks the whole ARU was on strike.

Rail traffic in and through the sprawling Chicago railroad yards ground to a halt, and truly, the lines were drawn. On one side stood the largest union of the mid-1890s. On the other were twenty-four railroads terminating or centering in Chicago. They held combined capital of $818 million and employed over 220,000 people.[10] The boycott and expanded strike were front-page news not only in Chicago but also across America. *Harper's Weekly* featured on its cover of July 14 a roguish Debs sitting astride a railroad bridge and stopping the entire "Highway of Trade."[11] Events in Chicago had become the "Debs Rebellion" or the "Debs Insurrection." The *Chicago Tribune*, in an editorial of June 30 titled "Assault on the Railroads and the People," said correctly, "[T]he issue has passed far away beyond all that is involved in the labor strike of the Pullman workers for higher wages."[12]

How did the managers of the affected railroads react to the boycott and strike? Nick Salvatore, the leading Debs biographer, has suggested that they actually welcomed it as an opportunity to destroy Debs's brash ARU.[13] Hopes along the latter lines were not far-fetched, especially since the managers had good friends in the right places. United States Attorney General Richard Olney was himself a former railroad lawyer with continuing loyalties to the railroads. He convinced President Cleveland to send federal troops into Chicago. At the suggestion of the railroads' General Managers' Association (a Chicago-based alliance of the railroads), Olney also appointed Edwin Walker, a lawyer for the Chicago, Milwaukee, and St. Paul Railroad, to the position of Special Assistant United States Attorney on matters relating to the boycott and strike. With the help of drafting suggestions from the very judge who would later rule on the petition, Walker alleged in federal court that Debs and other ARU leaders were in violation of the Sherman Anti-Trust Act of 1890 and obtained an order enjoining not only interference with railroad operations but also any efforts to encourage the boycott. Suggestive of how capital, government, and the media worked hand in hand, the injunction was published in Chicago daily papers a day before it was served on Debs and the other defendants.[14]

Fourteen days after obtaining the injunction, Walker confidently returned to court and began reading ARU telegrams to show a violation of the injunction had occurred. William A. Woods, United States Circuit Judge of the Northern District of Illinois, stopped Walker after only a few telegrams. Debs and the others were found to be in contempt of court, and Debs was sentenced to six months in the McHenry County Jail at Woodstock, Illinois.[15]

If plucked out of history and judged by the standards of a century later, the quick and effective intervention of federal authorities in Chicago might seem almost unbelievable. However, in late nineteenth-century America many others also found their strikes, boycotts, and militant labor actions enjoined. Earlier in American history, courts had been receptive to the prosecution of striking workers as "conspirators," but in the later decades of the nineteenth century courts relied less on conspiracy prosecutions and more on injunctions.[16] Scholars in the 1940s found that between 1880 and 1931 more than eighteen hundred injunctions were issued against strikes, a good number originating from *ex parte* proceedings, that is, proceedings in which the unions and workers' organizations received no notice or opportunity to be heard in court.[17] More recently, historian William Forbath has upped the count. He estimates that courts issued at least forty-three hundred labor injunctions between 1880 and 1930. According to Forbath, fully 15 percent of the recorded sympathy strikes of the 1890s (strikes comparable to the Pullman boycott) were enjoined.[18] The decade was one of pronounced friction between labor and capital, and the type of injunction which stymied Debs and the ARU was, quite simply, common.

Although genuinely stunned by the speed with which the federal courts had accommodated the railroads' requests, Debs nevertheless petitioned the Supreme Court of the United States for a writ of habeas corpus. In the habeas corpus proceeding Edwin Walker and others filed briefs for the government, but even lengthier and more numerous briefs were filed on behalf of Debs by Stephen Gregory, Lyman Trumbull, and Clarence Darrow. Gregory was a prominent attorney and served at another point in time as president of the American Bar Association, and Trumbull was an eighty-year-old former United States Senator who was largely responsible for the drafting of the Thirteenth Amendment. Darrow's days as the renowned champion of unpopular causes and individuals were still ahead of him, but, interestingly enough, he actually resigned a position as the attorney for the Chicago and North-Western Railway in order to represent Debs.[19]

All of the Debs briefs are intriguing, and especially so is the ninety-seven-page opus from Darrow. He argued that the Sherman Anti-Trust Act was inapplicable to the case at hand and also that Debs had committed no acts which could be enjoined. The pronounced concentration of capital, Darrow insisted, was radically changing social life:

> The whole industrial world has been made over in the last fifty years. It has practically been made anew in the last quarter of a century. And rules and regulations which concerned the interest and welfare of the small communities of the middle ages, with their isolated farms, their small shops and mills and their primitive tools can not equally conserve the changed industrial conditions of today. Those rules and regulations that once prevailed might even exist up to the last quarter of a century, but since man learned to use the forces of nature, and invented cunning machinery to do his work, all industrial conditions, all methods of production and distribution, the whole relation of employer and employed, has been completely changed.[20]

Dismissing a telegram from Debs which urged ARU members to "save your money and buy a gun" as merely a "playful statement or a joke," Darrow argued that workers' ability to organize and to strike was part of their fundamental freedom. To deprive workingmen of the right to strike, he wrote, "would be to strip and bind them and leave them helpless as the prey of the great and strong. It would be to despoil one army of every means of defense and aggression while on the field of battle, and in the presence of an enemy with boundless resources and all the equipments of warfare at their command."[21]

Despite the force of Darrow's legal logic and rhetoric, a unanimous Supreme Court of the United States rapidly upheld the contempt citation. Justice Brewer framed what he took to be the central questions of the case: "First. Are the relations of the general government to interstate commerce and the transportation of the mails such as to authorize a direct interference to prevent a forcible obstruction thereof? Second. If authority exists, as authority in governmental affairs implies both power and duty, has a court of equity jurisdiction to issue an injunction in aid of the performance of such duty?" Brewer then answered his own questions affirmatively, and, lest anyone doubt his patriotic zeal, he went on to offer "a lesson which cannot be learned too soon or too thoroughly." The lesson was that in America, the courts and the ballot box are the ways to seek redress and that "no wrong, real or financial, carries with it legal warrant to invite as a means of redress the co-operation of a mob, with its accompanying acts of violence." After all, Brewer pontificated, even the workers in the case at hand, once the question was decided by the courts, "unhesitatingly yielded to their decisions." Even the workers shared the conviction that the courts should decide "questions of right and wrong between individuals, masses, and states."[22]

His appellate possibilities exhausted, Debs served his six-month sentence, and the strike and boycott collapsed. Presumably, Pullman, the railroads, and assorted titans of industrial capitalism beamed at the sight of Debs behind bars, and the actual type of injunction which *In re Debs* allowed remained a powerful weapon for industry until precluded by the Norris-La Guardia Act of the 1930s. But the time in the Woodstock jail by no means disabled the industrious Debs. He reported in a letter to his parents that he was in "the best jail in the state, out in the country where we ate with the sheriff's family, have clean, comfortable beds, lots of room and everything we care for." In another letter to just his father he insisted, "No disgrace attaches to the family. You need not blush."[23] Most importantly, Debs used his imprisonment to reflect and to read. This self-education was critical in Debs's eventual legal heresy.

This is not to say, meanwhile, that Debs exited prison and jumped right onto the proper political path. Real lives are rarely that tidy. Upon his release from the Woodstock jail, Debs traveled to Chicago on a special train and arrived in pouring rain to the cheers of one hundred thousand. Later on the same day Debs addressed a smaller assembly in the Chicago Armory on Michigan Avenue.[24] Laden with heavy-handed metaphors and cadenced repetition, the Chicago Armory address is typical of turn-of-the-century public speaking. It also manifests the type of "labor republicanism" which recent American historians have found within not only early nineteenth-century artisan movements but also late nineteenth-century unions battling the lords of industrial capitalism. Some have quarreled with the use of "republicanism" to construct a coherent tradition in American labor history, but Debs's address surely drips with the images and sentiments taken to be identifying badges of "labor republicanism." With typical vigor he invokes his rights as "a free-man" and as "an American citizen," defends the United States Constitution, and vigorously lionizes Thomas Jefferson.[25]

Even a year later in 1896 Debs's political alignment remained somewhat unclear. He supported the Presidential candidacy of William Jennings Bryan, the nominee of both the Democratic Party and the Populist Party. While the Democratic Party's platform included planks denouncing government injunctions against strikes as judicial "oppression" and opposing life tenure for federal district and circuit court judges, there is no indication that these law-related planks had been what drew Debs to the Bryan campaign. When the Bryan candidacy sadly devolved into one for the free coinage of silver, Debs was largely uninterested in reviving more fundamental issues.[26]

Only on January 1, 1897, did Debs formally announce his socialist conversion. Writing in an open letter in the *Railway Times*, Debs stated that he had never truly taken the free coinage of silver as a panacea for social ills or, indeed, been totally committed to the Bryan's platform and campaign. The 1896 election, Debs said, showed that the ballot in and of itself was unlikely to produce emancipation from wage slavery. He cast the economic system as "cannibalistic, with men set one against another," and he left no doubt as to where he stood:

> The issue is Socialism vs. Capitalism. I am for Socialism because I am for humanity. We have been cursed with the reign of gold long enough. Money constitutes no proper basis of civilization. The time has come to regenerate society—we are on the verge of universal change.[27]

While scholars continue to debate the extent and precise date of Debs's socialist conversion, more intriguing is the way Debs's contact with legal institutions prompted it. Debs insisted over the years and his comrades increasingly concluded that it was the Pullman legal proceedings and subsequent imprisonment that led to the conversion. He was shocked by what had happened in America's courtrooms, but while in prison he profitably withdrew into contemplation and study. He reported being particularly impressed by the writings of Karl Kautsky, whom he found "so clear and conclusive that I readily grasped, not merely his argument, but also caught the spirit of his Socialist utterance. . . ."[28] Victor Berger, the leader of Milwaukee's socialist movement, visited Woodstock, gave Debs a copy of *Das Kapital*, and, in Debs's words, "delivered the first impassioned messages of Socialism I had ever heard—the very first to set the wires humming in my system."[29] Debs had his shattered faith, his ascetic withdrawal, his guiding saints, and even his new holy book. The archetype for his experience might be Saul on the road to Damascus,[30] but uniquely present in the legalistic dominant culture of the United States were the legal themes and institutions against which the convert could construct his conversion narrative.

What's more, fellow socialists found great resonance in Debs's law-related conversion. Socialist publications routinely lionized Debs, making him into a veritable cult figure, and Debs's fabled conversion was central in the portrayals and idolizing.[31] In nominating Debs for President at the Social Democratic Party convention in 1900, Frederick Mac-Cartney excessively evoked the prophetic Christian conversion experience:

> When he entered the tomb, he had completed one cycle of his life. There it was that, like a John of Patmos, he had revealed to him a vision of the things that were to be, of the new kingdom, of the new era. There it was [the Woodstock jail] that there came to him a message which was the completion of the Pilgrim's Progress of labor. When he came forth from that tomb it was to a resurrection of life and the first message that he gave to his class as he came from his darkened cell was a message of liberty. He became the liberator.[32]

According to legend, "in a flash of overwhelming insight, Debs understood the systematic problems with capitalism and the promise of Socialism and emerged from jail a changed and charged man."[33] Other Americans who had become socialists in quieter and less avowedly dramatic ways could revel in this mythic narrative. They could anticipate that more and more countrymen and women, like Debs and themselves, would see the light.

After his imprisonment and conversion to socialism, Debs articulated not only a general critique of capitalism but also a pointed critique of the legal faith. The latter did not rise to the level of "jurisprudence" in a refined, academic sense.[34] Nor does Debs deserve placement among the leading socialist legal theorists of his era. Among Debs's American socialist contemporaries, Daniel De Leon surpassed him as an intellectual and systematic thinker, Morris Hillquit reigned as the Socialist Party's leading theoretician, and Frank Tannenbaum was more renowned as a radical criminologist. In Europe in the early twentieth century, the Austrian Karl Renner published a significant socialist legal treatise, and William A. Bonger, a Dutch socialist and criminologist, authored the impressive *Criminality and Economic Conditions* (1905). However, Debs did think long and hard about law, asking what seemed to him the most important questions and providing his best answers. His critique of capitalist law constitutes a veritable socialist legal catechism.[35]

In terms of origins, Debs's legal catechism grew generally out of the anger and pain prompted by industrial capitalism and a sense that law was part of the problem. In the decades following the Civil War, a wide range of progressive and radical spokespeople criticized the legal system. Debs might have been influenced by the Knights of Labor, a Gilded Age workers' organization which often cast the courts' intricate legal reasoning in labor disputes as subterfuge and went so far as to deny lawyers membership in the organization.[36] In 1886 George McNeill, the Knights' executive officer, said, "Recent decisions of judges upon the question of conspiracy and boycotting are new revelations of an old fact, that the interpretation of law rests largely upon the public sentiment of the wealthy part of the community."[37] Debs might also have heard Johann Most, a Bavarian who immigrated to the United States in 1882 and lectured widely. Influenced by the works of Bakunin, Dave, Kropotkin, and other anarchists, Most offered a radical criminology which argued that all crime was the result of private property. If workers combined in order to obtain better wages, Most argued, the propertied classes decry it as conspiracy and use the law to prosecute.[38]

Especially likely to have influenced Debs's legal thought were the Gilded Age writings of the radical ex-lawyers Edward Bellamy and Laurence Gronlund. The former's *Looking Backward* (1888) was an immense best seller and prompted the formation of "Bellamy Clubs" from coast to coast. Bellamy imagined a utopian future in which the elimination of private capital had spelled the end of crime, lawsuits, and even law schools.[39] Gronlund's *The Cooperative Commonwealth* (1884) described the law as an amoral war over property and confidently predicted the abolition of the legal profession in the socialist future. Gronlund's work was influential among socialists well into the twentieth century, and Debs formally stated at one point that he believed "in a cooperative commonwealth upon the principles laid down by Laurence Gronlund."[40]

Debs's legal thought also of course derives from the ultimate texts of Marxism, the actual writings of Marx and Engels. For short periods at the universities of Bonn and Berlin, Marx himself, when not drinking and dueling, studied law. Although he never went on to write an extended treatment of law, many of his writings touch on legal concerns. The "Manifesto of the Communist Party," a document which Marx and Engels authored in 1848 and which was perhaps more widely read and translated than any other nineteenth-century Marxist tract, told bourgeois interests their jurisprudence was: "[B]ut the will of your class made into a law for all, a will whose essential character and direction are determined by the economic conditions of existence of your class."[41] Marx and Engels also devoted considerable attention to the English Poor Law and Corn Laws, and the first volume of *Capital* (1867) characterizes law as "the reflex of the real economic relations."[42] Perhaps most discussed from a theoretical perspective is Marx's "A Contribution to the Critique of Political Economy" (1859), which in the context of presenting the base/superstructure model casts the economic base as "the real foundation on which rise legal and political superstructures and to which correspond definite forms of social consciousness."[43]

After Marx's death in 1883 and even more so after the death of Engels in 1895, many Marxists adopted a crude economic determinism.[44] This reductive sense that economics dictated everything else no doubt influenced Debs's postconversion thought. As previously noted, Debs acknowledged an indebtedness to Karl Kautsky, a popularizer of Marx and Engels's arguments. More generally, he belonged to a generation of turn-of-the-century Marxists who critiqued government institutions as extensions of capitalist power. Debs's legal tenets seemed to grow out of his era's economic determinism and the Marxist understanding of the state as a protector of capital.

As was also true for his Marxist contemporaries, Debs emphasized the failures of existing legal institutions and said relatively little about the presumably more appealing socialist legal institutions of the future.[45] Debs came to see legal proceedings and institutions as instruments of the ruling class. Powerful capitalists, in Debs's opinion, could use law to continue their exploitation and manipulation of workers. The ruling class could also call on the military to keep workers in line, as in the use of the state militias in the American railroad strikes of 1877 or in the use of federal troops in the Pullman boycott itself. But the legal system was in a sense an even more useful method of repression, blessed as it was with a veneer of neutrality. In his writings and speeches, Debs, as a catechist, repeatedly summarized Marxian legal dogma, asked probing questions about legal proceedings and institutions, and gave his catechumens formulaic training in socialist legal heresy.

Indeed, Debs's legal catechism began to develop even before he announced his conversion to socialism. Writing in Chicago's *Evening Press* while still in jail after the Pullman boycott, he deplored the appointment of judges based on "their willingness to do the bidding of those who are able to pay the price. . . ."[46] Speaking in Terre Haute in November 1895, shortly after his release from the Woodstock jail, he deplored the way Henry C. Payne of the Northern Pacific and George Pullman himself were able to garner special dispensations from judges when, in the midst of legal proceedings, they left their home mansions to travel, respectively, to Europe and New York. What is an injunction? In the same speech Debs answered forcefully:

> It has all of the force and vital effect of a law, but it is not a law in and by the representatives of the people; it is not a law signed by a President or by a governor. It is simply the wish and will of the judge. A judge issues an injunction; serves it upon his intended victim. The next day he is arrested. He is brought into the presence of the same judge. Sentence is pronounced upon him by the same judge, who constitutes the judge and court and jury and he goes to jail and he has no right of appeal.[47]

Reflecting on the way courts served the rich but not the poor, Debs chose a fishing metaphor: "There is something wrong in this country;

the judicial nets are so adjusted as to catch the minnows and let the whales slip through. . . ."[48]

With friends and former employees of the railroads such as Attorney General Richard Olney and Special Assistant United States Attorney Edwin Walker pulling most of the strings in the Pullman trials, Debs was not off target in his criticism of that particular affair. Corporate owners and capitalist interests, in Debs's opinion, could count on their judicial friends, and labor could find no justice in the American trial courts.

Loftier legal institutions were equally biased. From Debs's perspective, the United States Senate seemed a pawn of big business. He called the nation's first legislative chamber "[t]he diseased vermiform appendix of the decadent political state of capitalism. There is no more need of it than there is for a tail to an oyster or a wart to a clam."[49] His rhetorical antilegalism in good form, Debs said the Senators were a "bunch of burnt-out corporation humpty dumpties," and he suggested some hobos from the nation's capital "turn the hose on the bunch and sweep them into the Potomac where they might display their senatorial courtesy and talk themselves to death."[50] The United States Supreme Court, meanwhile, seemed to Debs not the highest, grandest court of the land but rather something especially repugnant. When the Court by a five to four vote declared early child labor legislation unconstitutional, Debs criticized the process as "a kind of craps game—come seven, come 'leven." The net effect of the decision, he said, was to allow capitalists "to grind the flesh and blood and bones of puny little children into profits for the junkers of Wall Street. . . ."[51]

Many of Debs's comments on American legalism are short, pungent, and chiefly rhetorical; Debs uttered them on the stump or in short essays and editorials in socialist publications. But in one law-related area Debs authored a more sustained and subtle critique. Based primarily on the four years he had spent in three county jails, one state prison, and two federal penitentiaries, Debs, with the help of socialist journalist David Karsner, shared his thinking in criminology and penology. When Karsner arrived in Debs's beloved Terre Haute in March of 1922, he found Debs in poor health from his incarceration in the Atlanta

Penitentiary. Though pale and fatigued, Debs nevertheless dictated his agonized thoughts and memories as he strode back and forth in his study. The redrafted dictations were to be twelve articles for the Bell Syndicate. The Syndicate only released nine and in some cases deleted sections thought to be too radical or propagandistic. In 1927, after Debs's death, the Socialist Party published the uncensored versions of the articles along with three additional and amplifying chapters as *Walls and Bars*, Debs's only book-length work.[52]

Eschewing the era's popular assumptions that genetic flaws produced criminals, Debs argued in *Walls and Bars* for an understanding of crime grounded in social structure and history. In particular, he stressed poverty as the greatest cause of crime, both in the sense that poverty might prompt acute instances of theft and more generally because of the degradation and dysfunctionality poverty entailed. "The most casual examination of the inmates of the jails and prisons," he observed, "shows the great majority of them at a glance to be of the poorer classes."[53]

Imprisonment for crime, meanwhile, struck Debs as uncivilized in and of itself and impractical because it led to more criminal conduct.

> The process is slow, by degrees, like polluted water trickling from the slimy mouth of a corroded and encrusted spout—but it is a sure process. When a man has remained in prison over a certain length of time his spirit is doomed. He is stripped of his manhood. He is fearful and afraid. He has not been redeemed. He has been crucified. He has not reformed. He has become a roving animal casting about for prey, and too weak to seize it. He is often too weak to live even by the law of the fang and the claw. He is not acceptable even in the jungle of human life, for the denizens of the wilderness demand strength and bravery as the price and tag of admission.[54]

During his own time in prison Debs found himself face to face with the blighting, disfiguring, destroying effects of capitalism. "I saw here," Debs wrote soberly, "accentuated and made more hideous and revolting than is manifest in the outer world the effects of the oppression and cruelty inflicted upon the victims of this iniquitous system." Socialism was the solution. Because of its respect for human dignity and cooperative ethos, a socialist system would replace the prison with the hospital and the asylum. This triumph would be a matter of "taking the jail out of man as well as taking man out of jail."[55]

Throughout Debs's extended oral and written catechism, one finds an overarching determination to counter the assertion that labor activists and socialists were the unlawful "other," that is, a negative referent for the purportedly just and legitimate system. As the law professor Dianne Avery has shown, appellate labor law opinions in Debs's era and also more recently portray strikers as foreign, shiftless, irrational and, most notably, prone to violence. These images, she suggests, inevitably affect the role workers' organizations might play in workplace governance.[56] In commenting on essentially the same aspect of legal characterization, William Forbath coins the term "semi-outlawry." Labor activists, especially those of a socialist stripe, allegedly resemble hooligans, outlaws, lawbreakers, criminals.[57]

For concrete examples of this attempt to place labor activists and socialists outside the legitimate mainstream, Debs had only to look at the way he himself had been characterized. The negative referencing began even before the Great Northern strike and Pullman boycott. In 1893 Debs found himself cast as criminal and lawless when he supported Illinois governor John Altgeld's pardon of the surviving Haymarket inmates.[58] Similar characterizations continued to appear during the subsequent labor actions. In the Pullman hearing for contempt, much was made of a telegram in which Debs appeared to urge violence. Sent to an ARU officer in Montana, the telegram was greatly outnumbered by those in which Debs urged officers to "commit no violence." The suspect telegram, as Clarence Darrow argued in his appellate brief, appeared in fact to be a joke. But still, it could be used to suggest Debs was a violent lawbreaker.[59]

Prominent ministers declared that the injunction was nothing less than an act of God,[60] and newspapers and periodicals facilitated a feeding frenzy worthy of supermarket tabloids of a century later. The *Chicago Tribune* ran an article on its front page of June 30, 1894, titled "Law Is Trampled On—Riotious Operations of Emissaries of Dictator Debs." Lest the title left any doubt regarding the labels being attached, the article reported, "With the coming of darkness last night Dictator Debs' strikers threw off the mask of law and order and began the commission of acts of lawlessness and violence."[61] *Harper's Weekly*, having already editorialized against "reckless damagogues" and "blackmailers" determined to injure the nation, published a cover with a bug-eyed "King Debs" riding in a litter carried by Governor Altgeld and others dressed as clowns. Trailing the litter was a banner reading "ANARCHY" and a menacing menagerie of man-beasts carrying torches and guns.[62]

Later, when Debs composed his frequently cited conversion to socialism essay, the many images of his own purported lawlessness were clearly grating. Twice in the essay he makes a special point not merely to defend his own fundamental lawfulness but also to turn the tables, that is, to deplore the lawlessness of the legal system and its champions. He writes first of how the "lawful" authorities in the midst of the Pullman strike sacked and destroyed his offices, of how they gave thugs and murderers badges, and of how they harassed and attacked the members of the ARU. Against the backdrop of this state terrorism, he then reflects wryly, "the press volleyed and thundered, and over all the wires sped the news that Chicago's white throat was in the clutch of a red mob." In a second law-related reflection in the same essay, Debs recalls his days in the Cook County jail immediately following his arrest in the Pullman controversy. A jailer, apparently appointing himself informal tour guide, showed Debs the bloodstained rope used in the recent execution of a murderer and provided a detailed account of the affair. So this, Debs reflected, is how "lawful murder" is committed.[63]

Debs's implication, of course, was that the legal system was not truly and fundamentally lawful. The system—and not the activists and socialists, the thieves and inmates—was the penultimate lawbreaker. Time and again during his long, determined career as a socialist spokesperson, Debs attempted to reverse the negative referencing, to cast the purportedly legitimate as illegitimate. Those who privately appropriated natural resources, he argued, had committed crimes against humanity, but "far from being viewed as criminals meriting punishment," these individuals are treated as "the exalted rulers of society."[64] Crime—true crime—was evident in the factories as well as in the coal fields and the pineries:

> Multiplied thousands of men, women and children are killed and maimed in American industry by absolutely preventable accidents every

year, yet no one ever dreams of indicting the capitalist masters who are guilty of the crime. The capitalist owners of fire traps and of fetid sweating dens, where the lives of the workers are ruthlessly sacrificed and their health wantonly undermined, are not indicted and sent to prison for the reason that they own and control the indicting machinery just as they own and control the industrial machinery in their system.[65]

This stance was truly radical. Debs was not prepared, as were other early labor leaders such as Samuel Gompers, to take on the trappings of patriotism and Americanism. Capitalism, in Debs's opinion, was the criminal, and the legal system was its accomplice.

In his often personal analysis of twentieth-century American socialism, Irving Howe comments on the socialist movement's "evangelicism." Having taken up the socialist creed, American socialists carried their beliefs to the American people with a crusading and militant zeal. They also bifurcated human conduct into the recognizably good and distressingly evil and called on Americans to make a choice between one or the other. One could hear the phrases of Marxism in this call, but according to Howe, "Anyone with an ear for the native accent could detect a deeper note—the preacher's call to salvation, the Emersonian prod to self-fulfillment."[66] Eugene Debs not only shared this evangelical trait with his socialist brethren but also served as the socialist preacher *par excellence.* He stood above party squabbles, spoke to the largest concerns, and tried to bring Americans an alternative faith. "His mission was to evangelize socialism."[67]

To some extent, Debs's forums and style are predictable. He wrote numerous essays and editorials for labor and socialist publications, and, more importantly, he delivered an estimated six thousand speeches at rallies, encampments, and picnics. On average the speeches lasted two hours, and many are noteworthy for their passion and emotional appeal.[68] By all accounts, the bald and slender Debs was an absolutely riveting public speaker. According to Elizabeth Gurley Flynn, herself a traveling lecturer for the Industrial Workers of the World: "Debs paced back and forth on the platform, like a lion ready to spring, then leaned far over the edge, his tall gaunt frame bending like a reed, his long bony finger pointing—his favorite gesture. His deep blue eyes appeared to look searchingly at each one in the audience, he seemed to be speaking to each individual."[69]

Often Debs's speeches were delivered as part of a political campaign, and Debs indeed conducted what was in effect a continuous campaign for the Presidency from 1900 to 1920. With the exception of 1916, he was the Socialist Party candidate in each quadrennial election, often campaigning from a small train which allowed him to tour extensively and to pick up particular socialists for a local stop or two. Perhaps most famous was the three-car "Red Special" from which he campaigned in 1908. It carried Debs, his entourage, a brass band, and bundles of campaign literature to over three hundred communities in thirty-three states.[70] Even in 1916, when he did not seek the Presidency, Debs ran for Congress and in the process delivered hundreds of speeches from the porches and cabooses of his Terre Haute district. Debs knew he would not win at the polls, but he looked upon his campaigns as an opportunity to educate workers in the evils of capitalism and in the virtues of socialism.[71]

Beyond the rallies and campaigns, Debs also carried his evangelistic message to the people in a more surprising way, one which was consistent with the legal heresy which was so central in his larger critique of capitalist America. Time and again during the final thirty years of his life, he used the arrest, trial, or imprisonment of a socialist to call attention to the intertwined injustices of American life and legal process. These law-related pronouncements echoed Debs's sense of what had transpired in the Pullman trials and were consistent with his more abstracted critique of capitalist law and legal institutions. To be sure, Debs sometimes found egg on his face, as in the 1910 trial of the McNamara brothers, officials of the Structural Iron Workers Union who were charged with dynamiting the *Los Angeles Times* building and killing twenty. Debs vigorously defended the McNamaras both in print and on the lecture circuit, only to learn that they had confessed.[72] But episodes of this sort notwithstanding, Debs's numerous law-related commentaries served to inspire and unite the socialist camp and also to educate and perhaps convert the unconverted.

The trials of socialists which provided Debs with the greatest and most extended opportunities to educate and preach involved militant labor leader Big Bill Haywood in 1906 and socialist editor Fred Warren in 1911. Haywood, the fiery spokesman of Industrial Workers of the World (IWW), was arrested along with Charles Moyer, another founder of the IWW, and George Pettibone, a Denver businessman. All three were then extradited from Colorado to Idaho to stand trial for the murder of Idaho governor Frank Steunenberg. Police arrested the suspects on a Saturday night when it was impossible to seek an extradition stay and used a private train to sneak them back to Idaho. Debs was outraged, and in articles and speeches he cast the indictment as an attack on the entire labor movement. "It is a foul plot," he wrote, "a damnable conspiracy; a hellish outrage." He compared the proceedings to the discredited trial of the Haymarket anarchists twenty years earlier, and he predicted that a conviction would prompt revolution.[73]

The accuracy of this bold prediction went untested when the defendants were found innocent, but the passion and power of Debs's criticisms were striking. "Arouse, Ye Slaves," a front-page article in the socialist weekly *Appeal to Reason*, was perhaps Debs's most important statement in the matter. It launched a series of articles, and in addition Debs also gave hundreds of speeches from coast to coast.[74] A grumpy President Theodore Roosevelt himself entered the fray, deploring not only Haywood but also Debs, "the so-called labor leader who clamorously strives to excite a foul class feeling on behalf of some other labor leader who is implicated in murder."[75] Protest parades were held in many cities, including one in Boston with an estimated fifty thousand participants.[76] Within the socialist movement, James P. Cannon reports, the campaign for Haywood, Moyer, and Pettibone was: "[t]he biggest socialist action of the time. All the agitation seemed to center around that one burning issue and it really stirred up the people."[77]

Not long after his spirited writing and speaking on behalf of Big Bill Haywood, Debs joined the permanent staff of Fred Warren's *Appeal to Reason*. He and Warren were close friends and mutual admirers, and Warren had echoed Debs's claim that Haywood had been illegally extradited in still another article concerning extradition policies. In this second article Warren pointed out that former Governor Taylor of Kentucky was residing in Indiana, but the Governor of Indiana would not allow him to be extradited to Kentucky in conjunction with a murder investigation. In Warren's opinion, the government extradited labor leaders automatically but would not extradite capitalist leaders.[78] Therein, of course, lay the critique of the biased character of legal institutions which Debs had offered so many times in so many ways.

Providing proof for the polemical pudding, the federal government indicted and convicted Warren of sending defamatory and threatening literature through the mails, an allegation strengthened somewhat by Warren's published offer to give one thousand dollars to any Hoosier who seized Taylor and turned him over to Kentucky authorities. Due to various postponements, two years passed before Warren's trial was completed and Warren was sentenced to six months in prison. Two more years passed before appeals to higher courts and for an executive pardon were finished.

During this lengthy period Debs campaigned vigorously for Warren's release, managing in 1910 alone to give a remarkable two hundred speeches on Warren's behalf.[79] Warren, in Debs's rhetorical framework, was comparable to both the early persecuted Christians *and* to John Peter Zenger, who had been tried one hundred seventy years earlier for violating British censorship laws. More generally, Americans had before them still another example of how the courts were used to suppress dissent and criticism of the capitalist system. Samuel Gompers, whom Debs disliked intensely, was also swept up in Debs's ire. While Warren bravely condemned the courts and legal authorities, the early labor leader Gompers, in Debs's opinion, "has been mumbling his apologetic excuses like an old woman in the hands of a constable, fearing to utter a word of protest, or sound a note of challenge, lest he give offense to the corporation attorneys who have been put upon what is called the bench to declare the crimes of capitalists lawful and the lawful works of workingmen crimes."[80] On January 7, 1911, Debs devoted the entire front page of the *Appeal to Reason* to a "Declaration of Revolt" against the courts. His outrage was greatest with the federal courts and, in particular, the United States Supreme Court, which he described as "the most irresponsible and lawless body in the land."[81]

Perhaps Debs's conscientious campaign had some impact. On February 2, 1911, President Taft struck the six-month prison term from Warren's sentence, reduced his fine to one hundred dollars, and had a formal pardon delivered to his editorial offices in Kansas. When the puckish Warren received the pardon, he noted that it did not bear a union printing label and immediately slapped on a "Demand the Label" sticker. He also offered to pay his fine in *Appeal to Reason* subscription cards, an offer which the courts presumably declined.[82]

Throughout the extended Warren affair Debs had once again used a specific trial to further his indictment of capitalism and socialist legal heresy. More an orator than a theorist, Debs used the plights of Big Bill Haywood and Fred Warren to personalize oppression. More an agitator than a philosopher, he used specific legal proceedings as telling morality plays to carry forth his message of capitalist injustice.

In his final years Debs found still another trial which could be used to dramatize the socialist cause and expose the capitalist legal system. Troubled by the unprecedented repression of dissent in the midst of World War I and especially by the arrests of socialists who had opposed American policy, Debs decided to jeopardize himself. During the first two weeks of June 1918 he began to deliver speeches critical of the war effort. He told Noble Wilson, his 1916 campaign manager, "Of course, I'll take about two jumps and they'll nail me, but that's all right."[83] Debs wanted to goad the federal government into arresting and trying him. He was consciously taunting the government in hopes of prompting, at great sacrifice to himself, a well-publicized legal proceeding.

At first his efforts were unsuccessful, as a dozen speeches in Illinois and Indiana failed to produce the desired effect. Then, on June 16, he addressed an audience of twelve hundred in Nimisilla Park in Canton, Ohio. While his listeners laughed, cheered, and pushed excitedly toward the wooden platform, Justice Department agents circulated through the crowd collecting evidence that draftable men were present, and a government stenographer recorded the speech. The resulting transcript became the basis of Debs's indictment.[84]

Of the thousands of speeches Debs delivered in his lifetime, the Canton, Ohio speech might be the most famous. Even from just the published page which has come down to us in the present the reader senses

Debs's evangelical zeal. His commitment is palpable when he speaks of a socialist movement which has taught him

> how to serve—a lesson to me of priceless value. It taught me the ecstasy in the handclasp of a comrade. It has enabled me to hold high communion with you, and made it possible for me to take my place side by side with you in the great struggle for the better day; to multiply myself over and over again; to thrill with a fresh-born manhood; to feel life truly worthwhile; to open new avenues of vision; to spread out glorious vistas; to know that I am kin to all that throbs.[85]

His use of notions such as "ecstasy" and "communion" seems more than casual, and at several points in the speech he refers to socialism as a "faith." Socialists, Debs assured his listeners, "are moving toward democracy and the dawn; marching toward the sunrise, their forces all aglow with the light of the coming day." "Join the Socialist Party," he urged his listeners. "Not only will you lose nothing but you will find something of infinite value, and that something will be yourself." "If you would be respected you have to begin by respecting yourself. . . . How would you like to sleep in a room that had nobody in it? It is an awful thing to be nobody. That is certainly a state of mind to get out of, the sooner the better."[86]

Ironically in light of Debs's subsequent indictment for undermining the war effort, the speech had relatively little to say about America's role in World War I. Debs argued that throughout history, wars have been declared and promoted by the ruling classes but fought and suffered through by the lower classes. "The master class," he said, "has had all to gain and nothing to lose, while the subject class has had nothing to gain and all to lose—especially their lives." The issue in Debs's mind was not the autocratic rapaciousness of the German junkers. As far as he was concerned, there were junkers on Wall Street as well. It also made no difference whether the Republicans or Democrats were in power in the United States. He described the two parties as the "gold-dust lackeys of the ruling class." In essence, he argued that war and its disastrous effects derived from socioeconomic systems of grotesque inequality.[87]

At many points in the speech Debs's criticism of war-making in a capitalist epoch is strikingly paralleled and even overwhelmed by his socialist legal heresy. Like other popular orators, he routinely recycled images and pleas in his addresses, and even in a speech designed to attack the war-makers, his legal critique comes through loud and clear. Hence, the government is condemned for, in the midst of pro-war frenzy, unfairly arresting and prosecuting radicals, such as Max Eastman, Kate Richards O'Hare, Rose Pastor Stokes, and Alfred Wagenknecht, each of whom Debs discusses separately. He alleges that the San Francisco trial of Tom Mooney was nothing but a ruling-class effort to muffle a friend of the working class, and he casts the on-going trial of 122 IWW "Wobblies" in Chicago as still another instrumentalist exercise of ruling-class power. In the legal system of the Pacific Coast or of the Midwest—anywhere for that matter—the wealthy call the shots; "their will is the supreme law." The United States Supreme Court is "a body of corporation lawyers, with one exception," and of 121 federal judges:

> [E]very solitary one holds his position, his tenure, through the influence and power of corporate capital. The corporations and trusts dictate their appointment. And when they go to the bench, they go, not to serve the people, but to serve the interests that place them and keep them where they are.[88]

Capitalists, Debs reminded his Canton listeners, appear to proceed legally for the reason that the class which has the power to rob upon a large scale also has the power to control the government and legalize their robbery. Striding about the wooden platform in Canton's Nimisilla Park, Debs made the need to demystify the legal system virtually his core theme.

E. C. Wertz, the United States Attorney for the Northern District of Ohio, was outraged by what he took to be the seditious thrust of Debs's words. Wertz sent a copy of the speech to the Attorney General in Washington. The latter studied it for three days but, fearing the embarrassment of an acquittal, advised against prosecution. Undeterred, Wertz took the case before a Cleveland grand jury and obtained an indictment for violating the Espionage Act. How many of the government officials remembered Debs's legal travails and imprisonment of the 1890s is unknown, but for Debs the Cleveland developments echoed his indictment almost twenty-five years earlier. When he was arrested on

June 30, 1918, and taken to the Federal Building in Cleveland, he recalled for the assembled reporters his leadership of the ARU and his indictment in Chicago during the Pullman strike.[89]

If Debs hoped actually to be found innocent, the identity of his judge and the makeup of the jury should have discouraged such thinking. The judge was the stern D. C. Westenhaver, who had been a law partner to Secretary of War Newton D. Baker and who during his term on the Cleveland School Board voted to discharge teachers who organized a union.[90] Contrary to more modern procedures, the panel of possible jurors came not from voter or taxpayer lists but rather from nominations made by county judges in the federal Northern District of Ohio. The panel from which Debs's jury was drawn was unrepresentative of the citizenry. In the first day of jury selection the defense quickly exhausted its peremptory challenges, and the actual jury which was sworn in during the early afternoon averaged seventy-two years of age and had individual assets averaging what was by 1918 standards a staggering fifty to sixty thousand dollars.[91] Surveying the wealthy graybeards who had been chosen to judge him, Debs commented on their "dressed-up faces" and "smug bodies." "If they had been dressed in rags," he said, "it would have been all right."[92]

The proceedings themselves were dramatic and featured a stirring dénouement. In his opening statement prosecutor F. B. Kavanaugh cast Debs as "the palpitating pulse of the sedition crusade," and he then called a half dozen witnesses. Two were newspaper reporters, clad in khaki as if they were at the battlefront, and one was the government stenographer who had transcribed the speech. The defense, led by four leading socialist lawyers, decided not to deny allegations or to fight over legal technicalities. It rested without calling a witness and requested only that Debs be allowed to make his own closing argument to the jury. Judge Westenhaver granted the request, and for two hours Debs addressed the jury. He admitted giving the speech in Canton. He invoked the likes of Washington and Jefferson as well as William Lloyd Garrison, Elizabeth Cady Stanton, and Susan B. Anthony. There is a bigger issue at hand than the defendant's guilt or innocence, Debs reminded the jurors as he concluded. "American institutions are on trial here before a court of American citizens."[93]

The next morning Judge Westenhaver directed a verdict of not guilty on those counts in the indictment concerned with ridiculing the government but left to the jury the question of whether Debs had obstructed the draft and military recruitment. Later on the same day the jury filed back into the courtroom, and chairman Cyrus Stoner—at 58, the youngest juror—reported a guilty verdict on three of the four remaining criminal counts. Two days later, after deploring Debs for his "remarkable self-delusion and self-deception" and announcing that those who violate the law must suffer, Judge Westenhaver sentenced Debs to ten years in prison on each count, the terms to run concurrently.[94]

After sentencing, Debs remained free to speak and write in either Terre Haute or the Northern District of Ohio while his attorneys crafted an appeal to the United States Supreme Court. The appellate attorneys for Debs—technically speaking, the plaintiff in error—were Morris Wolf of Cleveland, Joseph Sharts of Dayton, and Seymour Stedman and William Cunnea of Chicago. In their eighty-seven-page appellate brief they asked the court not to take their arguments about errors at trial as an abandonment of Debs's fundamental argument that he was free under the First Amendment to say what he had said. They argued further that protection for Debs was necessary if discussion of the war was not to be restricted to exclusive circles of government officials. In particular terms, Debs's lawyers specified eleven errors involving the failure of the original indictment to charge a crime, the admissibility of the Socialist Party's St. Louis platform and the records of other criminal proceedings, and the definition of various terms in the Espionage Act.[95]

John Lord O'Brian, Special Assistant to the Attorney General for War Work, signed the ninety-one-page brief for the government. The brief countered the specific allegations of error in the brief for Debs and also addressed seriously the constitutional dimensions of the case. Against a backdrop of blanket rejection of civil liberties by many leading members of both the legal community and the Wilson administration during U.S. involvement in World War I, this willingness to argue in constitutional terms is in itself noteworthy and perhaps representative of O'Brian's repressed civil libertarian sensitivities. The Debs position, O'Brian argued in awkward prose, advocated a "field of immunity from Federal interference for all exercise of the vocal organs." O'Brian admitted that the First Amendment provided protection for legitimate political speech and dialogue, but in his opinion Debs's speech went beyond constitutionally protected bounds. When Debs took his stand in Canton, he had intentionally incited violations of the law, and this was the violation for which Debs had been charged and convicted.[96]

Justice Oliver Wendell Holmes, at work on both the cases coming before the Supreme Court and the immense edifice of his own augustitude, spoke for the unanimous Court and affirmed Debs's conviction on March 10, 1919. Placed in the context of well over two thousand World War I Espionage Act prosecutions in which even vague criticism of the war or government set the stage for convictions,[97] the opinion in *Debs v. United States* was hardly surprising. Indeed, it marked something of a culmination of several decades of opinions in which the Supreme Court routinely found against free speech claimants.[98] As for Holmes himself, scholars agree that at this point in his career the self-conscious jurist was still relying on conventional common-law criminal attempts doctrine in the freedom of speech area. Debs's lawyers may have carefully preserved their client's First Amendment arguments, but the Supreme Court, Holmes included, demonstrated scant respect for such arguments.[99]

If the result of Debs's appeal was predictable, the actual content and tone of Holmes's opinion were less so. Even though both the brief for Debs and the government brief discussed at length First Amendment issues, Holmes virtually ignored these issues, stating simply that speech intended to impede conscription was not protected. Almost all of the opinion summarized and interpreted Debs's original speech in Canton. Holmes plucked from the speech those statements which might conceivably have been designed to obstruct military recruitment. He disregarded "considerable discourse that it is unnecessary to follow." And he reassembled a speech most supportive of the government's claims. "The main theme of the speech was socialism, its growth, and a prophecy of its ultimate success," Holmes admitted. "With that we have nothing to do, but if a part or the manifest intent of the more general utterances was to encourage those present to obstruct the recruiting service and if in passages such encouragement was directly given, the immunity of the general theme may not be enough to protect the speech."[100]

Willing to accept and even aspiring to the role of martyr, Debs received the decision calmly and even invoked a familiar theme. "The decision is perfectly consistent with the character of the Supreme Court as a ruling class tribunal," he said. "It could not have been otherwise."[101] Holmes, meanwhile, was troubled by criticism of his decision, and he allowed his true colors to show in private correspondence. He wrote to Sir Frederick Pollock, "I am beginning to get stupid letters of protest against a decision that Debs, a noted agitator, was rightly convicted of obstructing the recruiting service so far as the law is concerned." In a letter to Harold Laski, Holmes was even blunter and more condescending: "I wonder if Debs really has any ideas. What I have read of his discourse has seemed to me rather silly and what he said about the judgment against him showed great ignorance, if as I am ready to believe he is not dishonest."[102]

A month later Debs received a telephone call ordering him to report at once for imprisonment. In poor health and nearing his sixty-fourth birthday, Debs could have been excused if at this point he chose to cease his socialist evangelism. But compassion and commitment were part of Debs, not things he could put aside. After entering prison, Debs began advising his fellow inmates and writing letters for them, prompting the warden to describe Debs as the kindest man he ever met, "forever thinking of others, trying to serve them, and never thinking of himself."[103] Debs also agreed to be the Socialist Party's nominee for President in 1920, the first time a man in prison had run for the nation's highest office. For obvious reason, Debs was unable to take his message directly to the voters, but he nevertheless found a way to make his law-related heresy a part of the campaign. He ran as "Prisoner #9653," thereby calling attention to the alleged miscarriage of justice in his own case and class-based bias in the legal system generally. On election day Debs received 919,799 votes, the highest total in his five campaigns for President.[104]

On December 23, 1921, President Warren Harding announced that the imprisonment of Debs and twenty-three others would be commuted on Christmas Day, and shortly thereafter Debs returned to his home in Terre Haute. The remaining five years of his life involved more battling of illnesses than of the capitalist power structure. But even in his final debilitated years he continued to express outrage whenever the legal system seemed in his mind to be biased. When Communist Party leader William Z. Foster was arrested before a scheduled Colorado speech, taken across the state line, and dumped in the Wyoming desert, Debs deplored the outrages perpetrated on Foster "in the name of capitalist law and justice."[105] When in 1926 the Massachusetts Supreme Court denied Sacco and Vanzetti a new trial, Debs said, "the decision of this capitalist tribunal is not surprising. It accords perfectly with the tragical force and the farcical tragedy of the entire trial of these two absolutely innocent and shamefully persecuted working men."[106] Debs was an evangelistic socialist and a legal heretic, and this combination made a critique of the capitalist legal system a pronounced part of his work and rhetoric to his dying day.

The enduring value of Debs's legal heresy is not its designation of exploitive laws, catalogue of biased trials, or theoretical sophistication. As noted, Debs's legal heresy does not for the most part reach theoretical or jurisprudential levels, and academic jurisprudes, comfortably at work in their sealed worlds, have given no attention to what Debs had to say. Down the hall, legal sociologists acknowledge that law and legal institutions cannot be fully autonomous from social and economic power, but credit Debs with no particular insights. Most damning, even contemporary Marxist theorists, at least by implication, reject much of Debs's thought as simplistic class analysis and economic determinism. The editors of the leading anthology of Marx and Engels's writings on law, for example, say "the tendency to elevate the simple class reductionist thesis into the substance of Marxist social theory" is "the major problem in the history of Marxist theory."[107] In Alan Stone's opinion, "[T]he simple (if not simple-minded) view that law is nothing more than a capitalist confidence game designed solely to cover up the exploitation of the masses" deserves nothing less than disdain.[108] Marxist theorists have virtually expunged the general thesis that law is merely superstructural, and leading Marxist scholars now grant that law has some degree of independent history and logic.[109]

But still, there are aspects of Debs's legal heresy which merit admiration. He recognized that law had become the primary discourse for social relations in the United States. While for Garrison the discourse was only establishing itself, by Debs's time judges, politicians, journalists, and others had fully promoted law into the ultimate American belief, sometimes allowing legal principles to grow rigid and fetishlike in the process. While for Cady Stanton the chief problem with law was its gendered character, Debs perceived the ways law, legal proceedings, and legal institutions shielded and perpetuated immense economic inequalities. Law had the capacity, Debs realized, to inscribe inequality on the American scene. He was determined to demystify the system of legal domination.

Debs did not become President. He did not succeed in converting capitalist America into a socialist republic. But in a personally draining and amazingly dogged way, he broke through the legal faith, enunciated a biting legal critique, and carried his message far and wide. Debs prioritized a concern with legal bias, and his legal heresy was a mechanism which many, both in Debs's era and the present, could use to imagine and structure a more egalitarian world.

5

The Black Panther Party
A Study in Legal Cynicism

West Oakland is a depressing place. Wine bottles and trash fill the empty lots. Ramshackle houses and run-down projects constitute the housing stock. There are few trees to shield the residents from either the sun or their poverty. But at 1454 9th Street, near the huge Acorn Public Housing Project, there is a surprising shrine to a fallen hero. Constructed by neither the government nor a well-meaning foundation, the shrine comes from the people and adds a spark to at least one neighborhood block.

The shrine honors Huey P. Newton, the one-time leader of the Black Panther Party, and it marks not his birthplace, his adult home, or burial site, but rather the spot where on August 23, 1989, he was killed from three shots to the head. Plastic flowers surround the site, and a careful stencil on the sidewalk shows Newton with his jaw set and his famous beret at a jaunty angle. According to official reports Newton met his end in a drug deal gone awry, but the words painted alongside the stencil declare, "The Pigs killed Huey."

The story of how this shrine came to be began in the same neighborhood in the late 1960s when Newton, Bobby Seale, and others reimagined their pasts in ways which led to the founding of the Black Panther Party. Joined by Eldridge Cleaver after his release from prison, the Panther leaders went on to confront government officials, mount rallies, publish broadsides, and even author substantial autobiographical works.[1] Their liberationist efforts, contrary to media portrayals of the Panthers as lawless, were surprisingly legalistic. However, the legalism which the Panthers made part of their activism and ideology and delighted in turning back on their perceived white oppressors was itself fundamentally cynical. This cynicism contrasted with the American legal faith and made Panther legalism heretical.

The primary target of Panther anger and distrust was law enforcement, in particular the urban police department, and the designation of specific instances and extended patterns of police misconduct was central in the Panthers' legal heresy. The best evidence, perhaps, of the coherence and potential of the Panther critique of law enforcement was the police response to it. Both in the Panthers' Oakland home and at a national level, the police suppressed the Panthers and muffled their heresy. A study of the Panthers illustrates the type of legal heresy which might be generated by an African American underclass, but the ultimate fate of the Panthers also illustrates the dangers of articulating a legal heresy that challenges law enforcement and the legal faith too effectively.

Huey P. Newton, Bobby Seale, and Eldridge Cleaver were the three most important leaders of the Black Panther Party during the late 1960s. Newton, working with Seale as his chief and sometimes only lieutenant, founded the party in Oakland in October 1966, and Cleaver joined the party in 1967 shortly after his parole from Soledad Prison. Within the year, Newton and Seale were incarcerated, and Cleaver became the party's most visible spokesman.[2] Tensions eventually developed among the three and led to Cleaver's dismissal from the party in 1971,[3] but for almost five years Newton, Seale, and Cleaver directed party activities and rankled the power structure. In addition to recording events in their authors' lives, their autobiographical writings underscore the moments when the authors were able to seize control of the directions and meanings of their lives. Their narratives in this sense include thematic attention to an author's very ability to narrate.

When the two decades of greatest African American migration from the South began in 1940, the Newton, Seale, and Cleaver families become part of this massive movement of people. In particular, the three families were attracted to what must have seemed at the time the great promise of California, the "Golden State." But this promise went unfulfilled, depositing the three families onto the mean streets of

California ghettos. As youths, Newton, Seale, and Cleaver knew deprivation and began to rebel.

In Newton's case the road ran from Louisiana to Oakland. His parents had met originally in Arkansas and then moved to Louisiana, where Newton's father worked in a sobering archipelago of gravel pits, mills, and factories. Newton himself was one of seven children and was born on February 17, 1942, in Monroe, Louisiana. Evidencing the Kingfish's appeal to southerners of both races, Newton's parents named him after Huey Long, Louisiana's blustering and demagogic Senator of the Depression era.[4] After moving to California, the Newtons lived in a two-bedroom apartment in Oakland's "flatlands," and Newton himself slept in a small cot next to the refrigerator. He recalled later his daily fare of "cush" (day-old bread mixed with leftovers and gravy) and the amusement of trapping and igniting neighborhood rats. He also recalled in more detail his boyhood fighting, drinking, and burglarizing of homes in more affluent Berkeley. Although he graduated from Oakland Technical High School, he took no pride in this accomplishment:

> My high school diploma was a farce. When my friends and I graduated,
> we were ill-equipped to function in society, except at the bottom, even
> though the system said we were educated. Maybe they knew what they
> were doing, preparing us for the trash heap of society.[5]

Seale was born in Dallas on October 22, 1936, the son of an often unemployed carpenter. His parents' marriage was unstable, and Seale lived in various familial arrangements in Port Arthur, San Antonio, and other Texas cities, with Seale himself sometimes being terrorized by his father.[6] When Seale was seven, his family relocated to California and lived for a while in Cordonices Village, a federal housing project which was built in Berkeley for workers in the war industries and came in the early 1950s to house ten thousand people. "My mother never really had any money," Seale recalled in his most important autobiographical work. "I ran around with a couple gangs in my younger days, when I was fourteen, fifteen and sixteen."[7] After dropping out of school, Seale enlisted in the air force, initially deriving some satisfaction from his work as a mechanic but ultimately receiving a bad conduct discharge. When he returned to Oakland, Seale recalled in his memoirs, hiding his discharge greatly complicated his search for satisfactory employment.[8]

While Newton and Seale flirted with prison terms during their early adulthoods, Cleaver served several. He had been born in Wabaseka, Arkansas, on August 31, 1935, and then moved at the age of eleven to Los Angeles. His mother worked as a cleaning lady, and his father disappeared. Cleaver was first arrested at the age of twelve for bicycle theft, and he spent a good portion of his youth and early adulthood in penal institutions. He served time at three reform schools and then a long, almost unbroken stretch between 1954 and 1966 in Folsom, San Quentin, and Soledad, adult prisons which set the standards for penal violence and degradation. His offenses included selling drugs, attempted rape, and assault with intent to kill. While as outraged and humiliated by prison as Newton was by the Oakland Public Schools and Seale by the United States Air Force, Cleaver at least used his lengthy incarceration to learn to write and to think critically.[9]

We know from their subsequent autobiographies that Newton, Seale, and Cleaver were unable to put their earliest rebellion into any kind of political framework; all report stumbling about during their youths in an underclass rage and stupor. Newton was a master of petty crime and street-level machismo, and his early falling out with his family over the surface issue of whether he should wear a beard betrayed a deeper need for self-definition.[10] During his court-martial from the air force, Seale's interrogators asked him to comment on the civil rights movement, and Seale, struggling to articulate anything at all, said civil rights activists were communists.[11] During his teenaged years in Los Angeles, Cleaver never stopped to take personal stock and lived in "an atmosphere of novocain."[12] When in 1954 the United States Supreme Court handed down its decision in *Brown v. The Board of Education*, just one month before Cleaver entered prison, he did not have "even the vaguest idea of its importance or historical significance."[13] Predictions made circa 1960 that these men would shape a movement with political acumen and forcefulness would have seemed foolhardy indeed.

Fortuitously, the Panther leadership's autobiographies not only record personal travails but also describe how the subjects were themselves able to begin making sense of the lives they were leading. In keeping with Jean-Paul Sartre's prescription for good autobiography, the Panthers were able to objectify themselves and comment thereon. In particular, they highlight in their stories moments and periods during which they become aware of and increasingly competent at the practice of narrative.[14]

For Newton and Seale, enrollment at Merritt College was crucial. A community college housed during the early 1960s in an old Oakland high school, Merritt College offered remedial and higher education for poor and alternative students. Newton himself, known for his theorizing and impassioned rhetoric, became a striking, albeit unconventional, "big man on campus." He and Seale moved through various student and black nationalist groups and came eventually to see themselves as friends and comrades. Looking back on these relatively innocent times, Newton remembered fondly his friendship with Seale:

> Our conversations with each other became the most important thing. Brothers who had a free hour between classes and others who just hung around the campus drifted in and out of Bobby's house. We drank beer and wine and chewed over the political situation. . . . In a sense, these sessions were our political education classes, and the Party sort of grew out of them.[15]

While Newton and Seale politically educated themselves in and around Merritt College, Cleaver learned his initial political lessons in the harsher academy of Soledad Prison. He fell in with a group of young African Americans who were rebelling against everything they perceived as white and American. In one of his first attempts to define himself vis-à-vis the law, he willingly accepted the label which the system had earlier attached to Debs and others; Cleaver declared himself an "outlaw." He was proud to be someone who "had stepped outside of the white man's law. . . ."[16] Indeed, his diatribes against whites became so pronounced that prison authorities declared he had suffered a "nervous breakdown" and placed him in a padded cell. Only when he ceased decrying everything white did the prison authorities allow him to leave the hospital and return to the general prison population.[17]

External events as well fueled the future Panthers' developing ability to see their history and present condition differently. At the same time that the civil rights movement won apparent success with the passage of federal civil rights legislation, unabated frustration led to rioting in African American ghettos beginning in the summer of 1964 and continuing for several years. Particularly important for African Americans in California were the riots in Watts during the summer of 1965. After noting the ironic fact that "Watts" was once used in the African American community as a term of derision (much as "country" was used in the white community), Cleaver reported that it had now become a source of pride. "I'm from Watts . . . ," Cleaver brayed, "and I'm *proud* of it. . . ."[18]

More generally, pasts in the ghetto, the housing project, or the prison ceased being merely something to forget or overcome. They could be reimagined and represented narratively as a source of special self-awareness and an inspiration to struggle. Newton and Seale characterized their early Panther comrades as "brothers off the block," hailing from "the nitty gritty and the grass roots." "You could look at their faces and see the turmoil they'd lived through."[19] They were not "house niggers" who had been pampered and somewhat privileged but rather "field niggers" who were fully denied, oppressed, and ultimately, more determined to demand their rights. If the master's house caught on fire, house niggers worked harder than even the master to put the fire out. Field niggers—and by extension the members of the Black Panther Party—prayed that the house would burn down.[20] Humble origins and deprivation notwithstanding, the Panther leadership was able in the 1960s to construct personal and collective narratives which could lead to liberationist activity. They had retold and reimagined themselves superbly well.

During the period of their greatest success and prominence the Panthers were not immune to reductive outbursts of anti-intellectualism of the sort which has plagued many populist movements in American history.[21] Seale, for example, castigated a Panther arts program as "damn shit artwork,"[22] and there is the even more distressing record of Cleaver's vicious, homophobic attacks on the essayist and novelist James Baldwin.[23] But generally, the Panther leadership respected ideas and theoretical writings and eagerly used them to shape the Black Panther Party's ideology. Newton in particular wanted to use the theoretical and political literature of revolutionaries and oppressed people to articulate "principles and methods acceptable to brothers on the block,"[24] and Cleaver was quite determined to raise ideological labor to the level of consciousness in hopes of gaining proficiency at it. In the first pamphlet in what was supposed to become a series exploring party ideology, Cleaver defined ideology:

> Ideology is a comprehensive definition of a status quo that takes into account both the history and the future of that status quo and serves as the social glue that holds a people together and through which a people relate to the world and other groups of people in the world. The correct ideology is an invincible weapon against the oppressor in our struggle for freedom and liberation.[25]

As was the case with Debs's ideology, the Panthers' ideology would ultimately derive sharpness and strength through its focus on law and legal institutions.

The previously mentioned distinction between "house" and "field niggers" is itself an illustration of how the Panthers borrowed from other sources in developing their ideology. The distinction was not original but rather came from Malcolm X, who perhaps more so than any other figure supplied the Panthers with perspective and "attitude." Malcolm, of course, was widely recognized in African American communities of the 1960s, and Seale was able to collect Malcolm's speeches and editorials from both the *Militant* and *Muhammad Speaks*. Malcolm also attracted significant attention in the mainstream media in the 1960s, just as the Panthers were launching their ideological project. Articles about Malcolm appeared in *Reader's Digest*, the *Saturday Evening Post*, and *Playboy*. C. Eric Lincoln published a book-length study, and Mike Wallace put together a network special.[26] Malcolm and his thoughts were available to the Panthers, and they were not blind to the resource.

Indeed, the assassination of Malcolm in 1965 led the Panthers to invoke him as not only a hero but also a martyr. In an especially poignant section of *Seize the Time*, Seale recalled learning of Malcolm's assassination and then running down the street in a rage, throwing bricks at passing police cars, and putting his fist through a window. When his son was born, he named him for Malcolm.[27] Cleaver, meanwhile, was among the many African American inmates who had a special admiration for Malcolm because the latter had himself survived prison with dignity and direction. Cleaver had in the early 1960s been a leader of Elijah Muhammad's Nation of Islam (Black Muslim) community in the California penitentiaries, but when Malcolm split with Elijah Muhammad, Cleaver followed Malcom's lead. When he learned of Malcolm's assassination while watching a movie in a prison mess hall, Cleaver thought, "For a moment the earth seemed to reel in orbit."[28]

What made Malcolm X so tremendously appealing and important? It was not his religion. Neither the Nation of Islam faith which Malcolm espoused for many years nor the orthodox Muslim faith which Malcolm accepted at the end of his life appealed to the Panthers. They have in fact been singled out by at least one scholar for their particularly secular orientation.[29] Nor was it the social doctrine of black separatism which Malcolm emphasized during and after his service in Elijah Muhammad's church.[30] It was instead Malcolm's call for an aggressive black political party and his general invocation of black personhood.

When Newton, Seale, and Cleaver progressed from coming to terms with their own lives to proffering an ideological line for the party, they all cast the latter as the embodiment of what Malcolm had envisioned.[31] And as for the more fundamental notion of personhood, one finds in the Panthers' lionizing of Malcolm a prefiguring of contemporary African American youths who wear caps and shirts with giant X's. The Panthers related positively, indeed almost desperately, to Malcolm's promise of fuller personhood. Cleaver cited approvingly Ossie Davis's sense that, "Malcolm was our manhood, our living black manhood!"[32] "I do not claim that the Party has done what Malcolm would have done," Newton said. "Many others say that their programs are Malcolm's programs. We do not say this, but Malcolm's spirit is in us."[33]

Malcolm was not the only external resource on whom the Panthers drew as they constructed their ideology, and the greatest goldmine of rhetoric and conceptualization for the Panthers, as is true for Debs and many other radicals in the West, was Marxism. From the surface of this mine the Panthers took some of their images and slogans. The Marxist revolutionary, Che Guevara, for example, inspired Cleaver with his complete and total commitment to liberationist struggle:

> Wherever death may surprise us, it will be welcome, provided that this, our battlecry, reach some receptive ear, that another hand reach out to pick up weapons, and that other fighting men come forward to intone our funeral dirge with the staccato of machine guns and new cries of battle and victory.[34]

The same notion of a life-sacrifice in the name of revolution inspired Newton so much that he gave the title *Revolutionary Suicide* to his most important autobiographical work.[35] Mao Zedong's *Red Book*, meanwhile, originally captured Newton's imagination only as something which could be sold for a profit to the liberals and radicals clustered at the University of California in Berkeley. He, Seale, and other Panthers hawked copies outside the university's Sather Gate at the northern end of Telegraph Avenue and used the money to buy shotguns.[36] But then, the hustling salesmen were taken by their own product, and Newton memorized the book and adopted one of Mao's sayings as the Panthers' motto: "We are advocates of the abolition of war; we do not want war; but war can only be abolished through war; and in order to get rid of the gun it is necessary to pick up the gun."[37]

The Panthers' penchant for quoting Guevara, Mao, and other Marxist liberationists may seem superficial, and indeed, the leading historian of Berkeley in the 1960s has dismissed the Panthers as shallow Marxists.[38] However, the Panthers' variety of Marxism went deeper than sloganeering. During his lengthy imprisonment, Cleaver sought and read works by Marx, even though they left him with a standing headache.

> I took him for my authority. I was not prepared to understand him, but I was able to see in him a thoroughgoing critique and condemnation of capitalism. It was like taking medicine for me to find that, indeed, American capitalism deserved all the hatred and contempt that I felt for it in my heart.[39]

Newton, always the most philosophical of the Panthers, was enamored with the Marxist understanding of dialectical materialism, and this method of analysis more so than anything else led him to declare proudly that the Panthers were a Marxist-Leninist party.[40] Also important to Newton, Seale, and Cleaver were certain fundamental Marxist conceptualizations and premises, and they peppered their writings and speeches with the key words and phrases of Marxism. There was, for example, the familiar "base" and "superstructure" and the suggestion in keeping with conventional Marxist thought that the ideas and attitudes of the latter be understood with reference to the material and economic realities of the former. History was pulled forward, meanwhile, by a "class struggle," and in the present epoch that struggle pitted the capitalist ruling class against the proletarian working class. The latter needed a "vanguard" which included the Panthers, and the vanguard must remember that its "theory," in order to be valuable, must always be translated into a "practice." Ultimately, the working class and its vanguard would bring about a revolution, the dénouement of the grand Marxist narrative—a narrative with more worldwide popular appeal than any claims to a Marxist "science."

In addition to Malcolm and Marx, other political thinkers helped inform and shape the Panther ideology. As noted previously, the Panther leadership looked always for ideas which could be adapted to the situation of twentieth-century African Americans, and they were prepared to critique even the ideas they essentially accepted, Marxism included.[41] In part because lengthy prison terms afforded ample opportunity to do so, the Panther leaders read extensively. We have in the Panthers' writings frequent citations to books they found noteworthy as well as lists of books in their personal prison libraries.[42] Newton and Cleaver in this regard independently invoked Robert Williams and his *Negroes with Guns* (1962). An NAACP worker in North Carolina, Williams had organized African American self-defense units, used foxholes and sandbags to repulse the Ku Klux Klan, and argued that it was necessary to meet violence with violence. Cleaver also took the writings of the anarchist Mikhail Alekandrovich Bakunin to be his prison bible, and he later authored an introduction to the party's republication of a work by Bakunin.[43] In citing these authors and mentioning these books, the Panthers were consciously and subconsciously sharing important ideological building blocks.

Especially influential in Panther thought was Frantz Fanon, a Martinique-born psychiatrist who became associated with the Algerian struggle for independence. In Cleaver's opinion, Fanon was the first major Marxist-Leninist theoretician who was primarily concerned with blacks.[44] Seale claimed to have read Fanon's *The Wretched of the Earth* no fewer than six times and then steered Newton toward the work.[45] Beginning in his earlier *Black Skin, White Masks*, Fanon had insisted that the black psyche must be understood in a social context and particularly with reference to white racist colonization of blacks. In this context, Fanon argued, blacks develop a pathological inferiority complex and even a third-person consciousness of their own bodily schema.[46] In *The Wretched of the Earth*, Fanon not only observed that colonized blacks frequently directed their pent-up rage against their own people but also provided griping clinical studies from his medical practice in Algeria.[47] As a psychiatrist, Fanon counseled individual men and women, but he then moved beyond from his clinical work to articulate a brilliant and surprisingly lyrical critique of colonialism.

The Panthers were not the first to apply insights regarding colonialized Africans to ghettoized African Americans,[48] but they were especially enamored with the analogy. Newton used the title of Fanon's most famous work to designate his people. "Penned up in the ghettos of America, surrounded by his factories and all the physical components of his economic system," Newton wrote in 1967, "we have been made into 'the wretched of the earth,' relegated to the position of spectator while the white racists run their international con game on the suffering peoples."[49] In his formal commentary on the ideology of the Black Panther Party, Cleaver asserted that a "Black Colony" existed in the United States.[50] Indeed, Newton added, certain of the pathologies which were familiar in colonial societies were also distressingly evident in African American ghetto men:

> He [the African American ghetto male] may attempt to make himself visible by processing his hair, acquiring a "boss mop," or driving a long car even though he cannot afford it. He may even father several "illegitimate" children by several different women in order to display his masculinity. But in the end, he realizes that his efforts have no real effect. . . .

He is confused and in a constant state of rage, of shame, of doubt. This psychological state permeates all his interpersonal relationships.[51]

Worst of all, the residents of the American ghetto appeared to perpetrate violence against one another as did the victims of the colonial societies which Fanon analyzed. Angry and miserable, oppressed people struck out not against the true oppressor but rather against more defenseless brothers and sisters.[52]

Perhaps the most intriguing Panther derivation from Fanon's writings involved the notion of a "lumpenproletariat." Marx had used the term in passing to refer somewhat negatively to a small subclass of vagabonds and petty criminals,[53] but Fanon had put a different twist on the term in his writings. For Fanon, the "lumpenproletariat" was the mass of Third World people who came from the villages to the city, lived in shanty towns, and circled tirelessly hoping for incorporation into the developed world. The "lumpenproletariat," in his opinion, was one of "the most radically revolutionary forces of a colonized people."[54] Inspired by the latter usage, the Panthers recast any African American ghetto dwellers who lacked a secure relationship with the means of production and other institutions of capitalist society as "lumpenproletariat." The Panthers concentrated, in Seale's words, on organizing "the brother who's pimping, the brother who's hustling, the unemployed, the downtrodden, the brother who's robbing banks, who's not politically conscious—that's what lumpenproletariat means. . . ."[55]

Furthermore, the Panthers saw their party and a politicized "lumpenproletariat" as a "vanguard" which might lead the way to liberation. Cleaver gave credit to Newton and said the latter had transformed the black lumpenproletariat from the forgotten people at the bottom of society into the vanguard of the proletariat. The traditional working class had become a new industrial elite without any revolutionary fire, but the Panthers and the African American lumpenproletariat could continue the fight against capitalism. "O.K. We are Lumpen. Right on," Cleaver snorted.[56] When she joined the Los Angeles chapter of the party, Elaine Brown was told explicitly by her party instructor that affiliation with and endorsement of the lumpenproletariat was a significant break with Marxism.[57] A group of Black Panther Party singers even dubbed themselves "The Lumpen," and as sodden as their sobriquet might seem in the present, the singers gave concerts, performed at rallies, and recorded an album titled "Seize the Time."[58]

Marx himself might have blanched at all this, and during the late 1960s more hidebound Marxist-Leninists did indeed criticize the Panthers' theoretical deviations. The era's Progressive Labor Party, for example, challenged Newton whenever possible, but hardly afraid of a fight, be it physical or intellectual, Newton did not back down.[59] Nor did Seale and Cleaver. Marx and Lenin would turn over in their graves, Seale said, "if they could see lumpen proletarian Afro-Americans putting together the ideology of the Black Panther Party."[60] "Some blind so-called Marxist-Leninists accuse the Lumpen of being parasites upon the Working Class," an irritated Cleaver said. "This is a stupid charge derived from reading too many of Marx's footnotes and taking some of his offhand scurrilous remarks for holy writ."[61] The Panther leadership believed in the importance of ideology, but they built up their own ideology rather than taking it on already packaged.

Overall, Newton, Seale, and Cleaver over the course of five years spectacularly shaped various theoretical and political materials into the party's ideology. Rarely sterile or abstract, this ideology often drew on the personal experiences of the Panther leadership. It also borrowed from Malcom X, Marx, Fanon, and other relevant theorists. The ideology of the Black Panther Party conveyed the oppression of African Americans and, more importantly, projected liberation through the concentrated efforts of a boldly politicized lumpenproletariat of color.

The Black Panthers prowled through the popular mind of the late 1960s and early 1970s as particularly lawless beasts. To a certain extent, they instigated and intentionally promoted this perception, what with their menacing bearing, berets, and leather jackets. They also ostentatiously displayed their weaponry, and the most famous photograph of Huey Newton showed him with a rifle in one hand and a spear in the other.[62] Police reports, inflammatory media portrayals, and white racism in turn inflated the popular perception of Panther lawlessness. The Panthers at the peak of their prominence were viewed by many as thugs, terrorists, and mad killers.

It is therefore surprising when a careful review of the Panthers' personal accounts and ideology reveals the Party to be extremely legalistic. In their earliest years, the Panthers adopted a rights consciousness, endorsed legal education and law-abiding conduct for members, and addressed statutes and ordinances with a picky hypersensitivity. To some extent, this was called forth by the legalistic character of the culture in which the Panthers lived. The American legal faith had lost the earnestness of Garrison's era and the rigidity of Debs's time, but the faith lived on. By the last third of the twentieth century, it seemed to give everyone, Panthers included, a legal ax to grind.

In addition, the Panthers stood for something more distinctive. Pervading their interests in law, its origins, and its uses was a searing distrust. While Garrison, Cady Stanton, and Debs remained committed and genuine, the Panthers were profoundly contemptuous and mocking. Their legal hypersensitivity was an example of legal heresy grounded in cynicism.

The initial source of Black Panther legalism was perhaps Huey Newton himself. He had contemplated legal rules and procedures in his criminal justice classes at Merritt College, remained interested in law while he worked in the Oakland antipoverty program, and even attended classes for one semester at the San Francisco Law School. Newton reported in his autobiography that he had first studied law in order to further the criminal career with which he flirted in the early 1960s:

> I first studied law to become a better burglar. Figuring I might get busted at any time and wanting to be ready when it happened, I bought some books on criminal law and burglary and felony and looked up as much as possible. I tried to find out what kind of evidence they needed, what things were actually considered violations of the law, what the loopholes were, and what you could do to avoid being charged at all. They had a law for everything. . . .[63]

Later, Newton reveled in defending himself in the courtroom after he had been charged with a crime. He saw these efforts as a way to show his contempt for the system, but his eager commentaries on legal definitions and issues also betray an actual engagement with legal discourse. "Each law has a body of elements, and each element has to be violated in order for a crime to have been committed," he announced in *Revolutionary Suicide*. "That's what they call the 'corpus delicti.' People think that means the physical body, but it really means the body of elements."[64] Here and elsewhere, the legally trained hears echoes of his or her own first-year law school notes. Strange as might seem, Newton had the categorizing and differentiating aptitude of a fine lawyer.

Seale aspired as a young man to be an engineer and, it seems, came to his own fascination with law largely through Newton, but Cleaver was directly engaged by legal issues in the way that many inmates are. Dreaming of their release from prison and holding onto that dream to preserve their sanity, inmates continually draft and mail their postconviction legal petitions. Cleaver was no exception. He studied the ratty law books in prison libraries. Frustrated, he also realized that these books had limited usefulness for an inmate seeking postconviction relief:

> Of the law books, we [California inmates] can only order books containing court opinion. We can get any decision of the California District Court of Appeals, the California Supreme Court, the U.S. District Courts, the Circuit Courts, and the U.S. Supreme Court. But books of an explanatory nature are prohibited. Many convicts who do not have lawyers are forced to act *in propria persona*. They do all right. But it would be much easier if they could get books that showed them how properly to plead their cause, how to prepare their petitions and briefs. This is a perpetual sore point with the Folsom Prison Bar Association, as we call ourselves.[65]

Besides longing for more useful legal literature during his lengthy incarceration in Folsom, San Quentin, and Soledad, Cleaver had another early "legal experience" of quite a different sort: He fell in love with Beverly Axelrod, his lawyer. Bemused and playful, Cleaver asks in *Soul on Ice*, "But can a convict really love a lawyer? It goes against the grain. Convicts hate lawyers."[66]

After the formal establishment of the Black Panther Party in the fall of 1966, the legal sensitivities which the leadership had reported in their writings began to manifest themselves in the party's documents, organizational norms, and activist practice. As noted, a grand Marxist-Leninist narrative was present in the party's ideology, but the Panther leaders also articulated, in a somewhat contradictory vein, a belief in inviolable human rights. On one level, these articulations were merely evidence of the vague and generalized "rights consciousness" which the legal historian Lawrence Friedman has found so pervasive in American society.[67] "Every man is born, therefore he has a right to live, a right to share in the wealth," Newton wrote. "If he is denied the right to work then he is denied the right to live."[68]

However, the Panthers' claims to their "rights" also had a sharper, more piercing tenor. In the latter regard, one of the more frequently used motifs in their earlier writings was that of the American colonial patriots throwing off the British. Like Garrison, Stanton, Debs, and other dissenters and radicals before them, the Panthers invoked images of the patriots with an eye toward making something other than a lionizing or conventionally patriotic point. Yes, beginning with the Declaration of Independence of July 4, 1776, and continuing through the Revolutionary War, the patriots were justified in demanding their rights.[69] But alas, the patriots had stopped short. "I emphasize that this was 1776 when white people of America gained Human Rights," Newton wrote. "Unfortunately, Blacks because of racism in the country and the fact of Slavery were not included in these rights."[70] Furthermore, Cleaver added, it was necessary "to transform the American black man's struggle from a narrow plea for 'civil rights' to the universal demand for human rights. This . . . was Malcolm's dying legacy to his people."[71]

As is often the case in American political discourse, talk of human rights melded quickly into talk of constitutional rights, a more recognizably "legal" tack. Nothing less than the party platform, which Newton and Seale drafted, was rife with a variety of constitutionalism. Three of the ten basic demands were law-related: the end of police brutality against black people, the release of black men from jails and prisons, and black juries for cases involving black defendants. Each of these demands was buoyed by a prescriptive paragraph citing amendments to the United States Constitution. Concluding the platform and supporting its final demand for a United Nations-supervised plebiscite on independence in America's "black colony" was the very Preamble to the Declaration of Independence that Cady Stanton had so effectively parodied![72]

Beyond the party's platform, Newton, Seale, and Cleaver frequently asserted constitutional rights, most commonly in the midst of conflicts with authorities. The Panthers insisted seriously on their constitutional right to bear arms and their freedoms of assembly, speech, and the press.[73] Failure to respect the Panthers' rights, they themselves were sure, indicated that fascism was on the rise.[74] Even the infamous fiasco in Judge Julius Hoffman's Chicago courtroom in 1969, after Seale was indicted for conspiracy, related to perceived constitutional rights. His fellow "Chicago Eight" defendants, especially Abby Hoffman and Jerry Rubin, may have intentionally converted the proceedings into a circus in order to attract media attention. But the outbursts by Seale, which led to him being bound and gagged in the courtroom and ultimately sentenced to four years for contempt, appear to have derived from other concerns. Seale wanted Charles Garry, the regular Panther lawyer who was at the time facing a gall bladder operation, to represent him. That being impossible, Seale then wanted either a postponement of the trial or the right to represent himself. When Judge Hoffman refused both requests, Seale continually disrupted the proceedings, not only calling Hoffman "a fascist dog" and "a son-of-a-bitch" in open court but also invoking his Sixth Amendment constitutional rights. "Anyone can read the court record," Seale wrote later, "and see that I wasn't trying to sabotage the trial, but that I was only trying to get my constitutional right—to either defend myself, or to have my lawyer present—recognized, but Judge Hoffman wouldn't recognize it."[75]

Intellectually speaking, the greatest problem with the Panthers' understanding of constitutional rights involves its static positivism. They seemed to think, almost like William Lloyd Garrison and his colleagues in the Boston Clique, that the meaning of constitutional rights could be unambiguous. Instead of marching about, occasionally falling over, and even changing right before your eyes, rights were supposed to stand still. But this type of jurisprudence, while rhetorically useful, is simplistic and constitutes a historical reductiveness.

Given the way the Panther leadership was so certain of constructs as fluid and complex as a constitutional rights, it is hardly surprising to find the leadership comparably certain concerning the meaning of statutes. While on trial in Chicago and indignantly asserting his Sixth Amendment rights, Seale "got hold of material about an old Reconstruction law, Section 1941 of the U.S. Government Code, that says a black man cannot be discriminated against in any manner in any court in America, concerning 'legal defense.'" "When I got hold of that, man," he thought. "Oh, man! It was the real thing with me, because I knew I was right by the laws."[76]

References to the violation of their extant constitutional rights and statutory protections gradually drained from the Panthers' work, and in 1970, speaking in "Washington, D.C., Capital of Babylon, World Racism and Imperialism," Cleaver called for a revolutionary people's convention to draft a new constitution.[77] However, distinct sensitivity to legal concerns remained central in the party's internal educational program. The mandatory instruction for admission to the party included "thirteen points of basic, legal first aid, legal and constitutional rights." Senior Panthers often repeated the thirteen points in political education classes and also in weapons training sessions.[78]

In addition, the Party established twenty-six rules for members and required that members commit them to memory. Reflecting the ghetto parlance which was so much a part of the Panthers' collective persona, one rule read, "No party member can have a weapon in his possession while drunk or loaded off narcotics or weed." "No party member will commit any crimes against other party members or BLACK people at all, and cannot steal or take from the people not even a needle or a piece of thread," read another.[79] To be sure, rules in and of themselves, even if memorized, neither guarantee law-abiding conduct nor protect radicals from being cast as lawbreakers. Allegations that the Panthers were merely a criminal gang tailed the party throughout the period of its greatest prominence, and even twenty years later spokesmen for the system were anxious to attach the lawbreaker label to the Panthers. Speaking after Newton's 1989 death, Alameda County District Attorney Tom Orloff said: "I'm not surprised he ended up meeting a violent death because violence was so much a part of his life. He was nothing more than a gangster."[80] Riding into the ground the cultural habit of constructing the odious other, the conservative Center for the Study of Popular Culture even attacked the 1995 movie *Panther* because, contrary to the positive celluloid images, the real Panthers were "cocaine-addicted gangsters who turned out their own women as prostitutes and committed hundreds of felonies."[81]

In the late 1960s themselves, instances of unlawful conduct by Panther initiates were common, but rather than endorsing such lawbreaking, the Panther leadership expelled lawbreakers from the party.[82] Newton, Seale, and to a lesser extent even Cleaver genuinely wanted their comrades to keep their activities within legal bounds. The strategy had two goals: (1) to deny the police reasons for acting against the Panthers and (2) to win the confidence of the African American population.[83]

This rigorous legalism, meanwhile, did not connote a deep and genuine respect for the law, lawmaking process, or law enforcement. The Panthers did not worship in the legal faith. Manifesting a belief in the same type of economic determinism that Eugene Debs championed, Newton said, "The laws exist to defend those who possess property. They protect the possessors who should share but do not."[84] In late 1962 in his very first conversation with Seale, and long before the founding of the party, Newton argued that there were plenty of laws on the books to protect blacks and that contributing to Martin Luther King, Jr., and others who wanted additional civil rights legislation was a waste of money.[85] When after the founding of the party conservative California state assemblyman Donald Mulford attracted support for a bill that would limit the Panthers' brandishing of weapons, Newton saw the development as predictable. "We knew how the system operated," he said. "If we used the laws in our interest and against theirs, then the power structure would simply change the laws."[86] As for law enforcement, Cleaver perceived a similar bias:

> If the capitalists are in power, they enforce laws designed to protect their system, their way of life. They have a particular abhorrence for crimes against property, but are prepared to be liberal and show a modicum of compassion for crimes against the person—unless, of course, an instance of the latter is combined with an instance of the former. In such cases, nothing can stop them from throwing the whole book at the offender.

For instance, armed robbery with violence, to a capitalist, is the very epitome of evil. Ask any banker what he thinks of it.[87]

In response to this perceived bias, the Panthers both brandished weapons and spouted law. These legal pronouncements came in predictable areas such as probable cause or the carrying of guns.[88] They came as well in areas more peripheral to their liberationist struggle: the rules for renting the Oakland Coliseum, the safety requirements for passengers in police vehicles, even ordinances regarding U-turns on residential streets. The Panthers were frequently hypersensitive to law. At times, their awareness of precise legal prescriptions and proscriptions seemed almost manic.

This cynical legal hypersensitivity contrasts strikingly with the genuine faith in law so evident in the dominant culture and even among reformers and civil rights leaders. From the perspective of James M. Nabrit, Jr., the former president of Howard University writing in the 1960s, "As has been stated many times, ours is basically a society of laws, and it is through the enactment of laws and their enforcement that much of the progress in the future must be made just as has been done in the past."[89] To be sure, American history includes separatist movements and impassioned commitments to the culture of black Africa. Yet, in the words of two prominent scholars of American culture and racial diversity, "The overwhelming number of American Blacks have concentrated on using the law to obtain equal rights and access to the resources of the larger society."[90]

No less a figure than Martin Luther King, Jr., is illustrative. In the last two years of his life—when he led open housing marches in Chicago, denounced American imperialism in Vietnam, and organized the Poor People's Campaign—King had in fact become radicalized. But during his earlier years of greater prominence, King's ideology was quite different than that of the Panthers. He looked to the federal government in the form of the President, the Congress, and the Supreme Court for help in achieving black civil rights. He expected legislation to play a positive role, and as his often cited letter from the Birmingham jail indicates, he deeply respected law and its potential to be righteous. Speaking from a Christian natural-law perspective, King proffered in the letter a vision in which the law could and would be reformed to more fully correspond to the just and the moral.[91]

The Panthers' legal thought, by contrast, manifested no deep respect for law or abiding belief in a warming parable of legal change. The Panther leaders sang paeans early in their history to constitutional rights. They insisted that the poor, unrepresented, and oppressed had the right to equal treatment under the existing laws. Yet Newton was also on record that "trying to get more laws was only a meaningless diversion from the real issues."[92] With thoughts of law reform foisted upon him, Panther leader David Hilliard said, "As though we give a fuck about pig laws."[93] Most fundamentally, the Panthers wanted to know the law and abide by it in order to protect themselves and to thumb their noses at the system. In their writings and action the Panthers withheld respect from law and legal institutions, and in doing so they disavowed the legal faith. In the context of American culture and in contrast to others who demanded equality for African Americans, the Panthers' cynical legalism truly distinguished them as indigenous radicals.

During the late 1960s the Black Panther Party's often heard chant of "Off the Pigs" seemed to many just a burst of superficial, albeit menacing, rhetoric. In reality, the criticism of law enforcement which the chant represented grew out of the Panther leadership's experiences as young African Americans on the streets of the nation's cities. An attempt to "retell" these experiences led directly to the formation and programs of the party, and criticism of law enforcement played a central role in the Panther program.

While they were growing up in the ghettos of California, the men who would become the leaders of the Black Panther Party had personally degrading encounters with the police. Cleaver recalled during a 1968 interview conducted by Nat Hentoff that the police, all of whom were white, frequently stopped and wrote up his boyhood friends and himself for no apparent reason:

> We'd just be walking down the street and the pigs would stop us and call in to see if we were wanted—all of which would serve to amass a file on us at headquarters. It's a general practice in this country that a young black gets put through this demeaning routine.[94]

Newton was equally rankled, and years later in *Revolutionary Suicide* he gleefully recalled his exhilaration the first time he faced down a white policeman.[95] Cleaver's lingering and searing anger is evident in "Domestic Law and International Order," an essay casting the police department and the army as the domestic and international arms of the power structure. The policeman and the soldier, he wrote, "will shoot you, beat your head and body with sticks and clubs, with rifle butts, run you through with bayonets, shoot holes in your flesh, kill you. . . . They will use all that is necessary to bring you to your knees."[96]

The writings of Frantz Fanon and Malcolm X were useful to the Panther leadership in characterizing and criticizing the police. For Fanon the police were "the official, instituted go-betweens" in a world of colonial oppression; the policeman spoke "the language of pure force" and was "the bringer of violence into the home and into the mind of the native."[97] In *The Autobiography of Malcolm X*, a work today recognized as the joint product of Alex Haley's writerly skills and Malcolm's recollections, Malcolm recalled an incident that brought the Nation of Islam to the public's attention. Malcolm and others had established Temple Seven in Harlem, but the Black Muslims had attracted little attention. Then, two white policemen, in the aftermath of breaking up a street scuffle, encountered several Black Muslims who would not "move on" and beat one with their nightsticks. When the injured Black Muslim was taken to the nearby precinct station, fifty Black Muslims stood in "ranks-formation" outside the station, and Malcolm himself formally demanded that the bloodied brother be given medical attention. The nervous precinct commander consented, and the Black Muslims, still in formation, followed the ambulance to Harlem Hospital, using busy Lenox Avenue as a route. The next day, "in Harlem, the world's most heavily populated black ghetto, the *Amsterdam News* made the whole story headline news, and for the first time the black man, woman, and child in the streets was discussing 'those Muslims.'"[98]

Newly able to see police conduct in a politicized narrative and perhaps sensing what such a focus might yield, Newton and Seale began contemplating the use of a police critique as *the* idea of a new organization. In deference to the people they considered "field niggers" and "street brothers," Newton and Seale began comparing their thought to that of Oakland's ghetto residents. They wanted to learn if their emerging police-related narratives had resonance in the larger community. "We asked them if they would be interested in forming the Black Panther Party for Self-Defense, which would be based upon defending the community against the aggression of the power structure, including the military and the armed might of the police." When the response was positive, Newton and Seale formally established the party.[99]

Almost immediately the focus paid significant organizational dividends. When a Contra Costa County deputy sheriff killed the young Denzil Dowell in the horrid ghetto in North Richmond, the Panthers revealed inconsistencies in the police reports, held rallies on the spot of the killing, and attracted both media attention and new members. "The police murder [of Dowell] is outright and not justifiable homicide," Newton argued. "They always cook up a story, but simple investigation will expose their lies. That is why we must disarm and control the police in our communities if we want to survive."[100]

Shortly thereafter, in May of 1967, thirty Panthers, twenty of whom were visibly armed, visited the State Capitol building in Sacramento. They received a chilly, bordering on frozen, welcome from the legislators, but Newton used the occasion to issue "Executive Mandate Number One":

> As the aggression of the racist American government escalates in Vietnam, the police agencies of America escalate the repression of black people throughout the ghettos of America. Vicious police dogs, cattle prods, and increased patrols have become familiar sights in black communities. City Hall turns a deaf ear to the pleas of black people for relief from this increasing terror.[101]

Always eager for scenes of racial confrontation, the media provided extended coverage, including television footage in which the Panthers called the police "motherfuckers." For their own part, the Panthers had again attracted both attention for their complaints against police and more new members.

Less dramatically, but perhaps more significantly in terms of life in the ghetto, the Panthers also began patrolling the police. At first, in

December of 1966, the patrols according to Seale were informal and sporadic:

> Sometimes we'd just be high, going to a party. We might not have guns. Other times, we'd have guns. Still other times we weren't even going to a party. We'd just be going to a meeting. We'd have our shit with us, and while we were going to the meeting, we'd patrol those pigs, trying to catch them wrong. We'd see a pig, we'd get keyed off the meeting. We'd just forget about the meeting, and patrol that pig, just drive around behind him, a long time.[102]

Before long, the patrols grew more systematic, especially on Friday and Saturday nights. Two to five cars, each full of Panthers, spent several hours following a squad car as its occupants cruised the Oakland ghetto. Often, the patrolling Panthers brandished pistols, rifles, and shotguns. According to radical sociologist Robert L. Allen, "This was perfectly legal, and the Panthers scrupulously avoided violating the law."[103] Newton even made a point of carrying a rifle or a shotgun because, in keeping with his reading of the law, it was illegal for a man on probation to carry a handgun.[104] Furthermore, the guns were carried openly in hopes of "educating the masses of black people about the necessity for guns and how self-defense was politically related to their survival and their liberation."[105]

While the weapons were no doubt the most striking aspect of the Panthers' patrols, the Panthers carried other items as well: cameras, tape recorders, and lawbooks. When the Panthers perceived a policeman harassing a citizen, one member of the party patrol would stand off to the side and read relevant sections of the lawbook in a loud and righteous voice. The goals were to deter harassment and also to educate and politicize others who invariably gathered at the scene. "[W]e were proud Black men," Newton said recalling these police encounters, "armed with guns and a knowledge of law."[106]

Sometimes, of course, the police arrested either the person they had originally confronted or a Panther on patrol, but even in these situations the Panthers had a plan. They followed the squad car to the police station and posted bail as soon as possible. The Panthers were especially determined to police the police, but their thoughts on the incarceration of a "brother" were almost as strong. To some extent, they saw jails and prisons as simply an extension of the police department. Newton in particular was dedicated to using bail to get "brothers" out of jail as quickly as possible. He also realized that when the Panthers posted bail, "Many citizens came right out of jail and into the Party."[107]

More so than any other aspect of their personal lives, police encounters offended the Panther leadership, and more so than any other concern, police control became central in their ideology and critique of legal institutions. Internal divisions and state suppression ultimately cut short their efforts, but as the 1960s gave way to the 1970s, the Panthers were developing plans for community-based policing as an alternative to white policing of the ghetto. According to Seale, the stage would be set for community-based policing by amendments to city charters which decentralized police departments and required that policemen who patrol a community live in that community. Neighborhood councils would then elect community police commissioners, and these commissioners would supervise and discipline individual policemen. "The people throughout the city," Seale said, "will control the police, rather than the power structure, the avaricious businessmen, and the demagogic politicians who presently control them."[108]

In the era itself, virtually no one in the dominant white community took the Panthers' ideas for police reform seriously, much less Cleaver's demand for "autonomous black departments of safety in black communities."[109] However, as the physical and bureaucratic brutalization of Rodney King makes clear, the root problem which prompted Panther demands for police reform has hardly disappeared. Nothing in the entire range of the Panthers' writings and activism has greater lasting importance in public discourse than their determination to control and redirect the police.

The Panthers' police patrols, legalistic confrontations, and cynical legalism perhaps reduced the incidents of police harassment of the ghetto population and also brought some degree of empowerment to the party members and others.[110] But whatever the Panthers' initial success, it cost them dearly. They had articulated a variety of legal heresy, but now they were being heard. Bristling in their tight uniforms and—on higher levels in the structure of command—in their business suits, the police retaliated against the Panthers and their patrols. From its base in Washington, D.C., the federal government also struck back. This retaliation was not the type of subtle cooptation which theorists have underscored in ostensibly electoral and legalistic regimes. It was direct, violent and, in the end, effective.

The retaliation was perhaps most evident locally. In the East Bay area, Berkeley police patrolled constantly in front of the Panther headquarters, and in Oakland police charged people with felonious extortion for selling Huey Newton buttons on the street. More significantly, the Oakland police carried the license numbers of vehicles belonging to the Panthers and never missed an opportunity to make an inspection or, even better, an arrest. These matters seem indisputable.[111]

How much further did the retaliation extend? How complete was the resolve of the Oakland police to eliminate the party? Cleaver asserted that the efforts of the Oakland police were systematic.[112] Perhaps he engaged in overstatement, but it is true that local strings of events that led to Newton's imprisonment and Cleaver's self-exile both began with what appears to be instances of calculated police harassment.

In Newton's case, he was stopped in the middle of the night on October 28, 1967, and, according to his own account, asked to get out of his car. As he did so, he reached for a lawbook and began to read aloud the section on reasonable cause for arrest. One investigating police officer snarled, "You can take that book and shove it up your ass, nigger." A gun battle ensued which left patrolman John Frey dead, patrolman Herbert Heanes injured, and Newton wounded from a gunshot to the stomach.[113] An indictment and trial followed, with the latter prompting frenetic rallies outside the stark and massive Alameda County Courthouse on the shore of Lake Merritt in downtown Oakland. While as many as five thousand protestors chanted "Free Huey" and "Set Our Warrior Free," Newton offered a more precise analysis: "The Black Panthers' activities and programs, the patrolling of the police, and the resistance to their brutality had disturbed the power structure; now it was gathering its forces to crush our revolution forever."[114]

Cleaver was prepared to make Newton's trial a "showdown case" regarding police harassment and brutality,[115] but he had only a limited opportunity to agitate on Newton's behalf. In April 1968, according to Cleaver, the Oakland police decided to sabotage a Panther picnic, rally, and fund-raiser on behalf of Newton. On the night of April 6 a squad car pulled up to a vehicle in which Cleaver and Bobby Hutton were riding. The police and the Panthers exchanged fire, and after leaving a shed in which he had taken refuge, Hutton was killed by police fire. Cleaver was wounded, arrested, and sent temporarily to the State Medical Facility at Vacaville. When it was ruled that he would have to return to prison for parole violation while awaiting trial on his new charges, Cleaver fled first to Cuba and then to Algeria.[116]

Despite the incarceration of Newton and self-exile of Cleaver, the Black Panther Party continued to grow in prominence and notoriety in 1968 and 1969. Bobby Seale, although lacking Newton's charisma and Cleaver's command of words, emerged as a strong party leader. Judge Julius Hoffman, one suspects, never understood how powerful an image of state oppression he created by binding and gagging Seale in his Chicago courtroom. The trial of Seale and co-defendant Ericka Huggins for the alleged murder of party infiltrator Alex Rackley in New Haven, Connecticut, also led to large rallies on the venerable New Haven Green in the shadow of Yale University and widespread national and international attention. After a hung jury, the state dismissed charges, but between the time of the indictment and the dismissal, white campus radicals adopted and lionized the Panthers.[117] The chants of "Free Bobby" in Cambridge, Ann Arbor, Madison, Berkeley, and elsewhere were as loud as those of "Free Huey" had been earlier on the steps of the Alameda County Courthouse.[118]

Perhaps these struggles carried the Panthers too far from their Oakland home and from a focus on police control, but during the period of the Panthers' greatest prominence a tremendous tension continued to exist between the party and law enforcement. In February 1970, *The Black Panther*, the party's sporadic newspaper, listed no fewer than 410 instances of harassment, raids, shootings, and arrests by local, state, and federal police.[119] Some of the arrests might have been justified, but justification for the brutal murders of Mark Clark and Fred Hampton (chairman of the Illinois Black Panther Party) by the Chicago police in December 1969 is difficult to muster.[120] Firm evidence in fact exists that the federal government acting through the FBI egged on the police in this particular episode and also had a extensive program to divide and undermine the party.[121] The program even grew so absurdly excessive as to include surveillance of an uptown Manhattan wine-and-cheese party hosted by the composer Leonard Bernstein in 1970 *and* subsequent attempts to discredit him with damaging news leaks.[122] The Black Panther Party, in the words of one scholar, "became targeted as the 'Number One Threat' to the internal security of the United States by the FBI."[123]

Even those who think the reality of America does not measure up to its promise might find this direct suppression hard to believe. It seems foreign and old-fashioned. The system might co-opt and incorporate the poor and minority groups. The system might find ways to persuade subordinate groups that their subordination is a "normal" reality. But rarely, if ever, does the system use all its might to control its dissidents.[124] Yet this is what happened with Newton, Seale, Cleaver, and the Black Panther Party. The Panther leaders found ways to meaningfully present their individual lives, to construct a liberationist ideology, and to critique legal institutions including the police. Their speeches and writings were cogent and appealing to many African Americans in urban ghettos; the Panthers offered a legal heresy that made sense of present-day oppression and that offered perspectives and strategies for a better future. They found ways to express their resistance and to offer shaped radical alternatives.

However, not only African Americans but also agents of the system heard the Panthers' legal heresy. The heresy had clout. It constituted resistance. The police were often the ultimate villains in the Panthers' speeches and writings, and the FBI appreciated this clout and sensed heretical power. Direct coercion and suppression resulted, and the Panther legal heresy, briefly coherent and effective, grew less and less audible. In a nation with a legal faith, radicals in command of their legal heresies run the risk of being forced to be quiet.

6

Legal Heresy Today

Militia, Anti-Abortion Activists, and Beyond

After years of contemplating individual legal heretics, I cannot resist imagining them assembled as a group—perhaps even on the Twentieth of September, the day William Lloyd Garrison proposed as an alternative to the Fourth of July. At such a get-together, Garrison and Elizabeth Cady Stanton might rekindle the affection they had known for one another before conflicting perspectives on African American and women's liberation pulled them apart in the post–Civil War years. Cady Stanton might enjoy hearing from Eugene Debs how he himself stepped forward after the Terre Haute literary society refused to host Susan B. Anthony. Both Garrison and Cady Stanton might be honored to learn that Debs cited them in his stirring remarks to the jury in his trial following the Canton address. Eldridge Cleaver could report that he lionized the abolitionists and Debs in *Soul on Ice*, and with some extended coaching, Cleaver might perhaps see that Cady Stanton as well belonged on his list of heroes. Ranging from politics to literature, Huey Newton and Debs might be surprised to learn that both loved Hugo's *Les Misérables*.[1]

In the book at hand, I imagine such a gathering not merely as one of prominent outsiders and dissidents in American history. The goal is not another "beatification of the subversive," to use the wonderful phrase employed by Harvard professor Sacvan Bercovitch to underscore a tendency among American cultural historians.[2] Instead, one wants somehow to hear Garrison, Cady Stanton, Debs, Cleaver, and Newton discuss law and the legal faith. One wants to hear them stitch together the tradition of legal heresy in American history and culture.

The legal heretics under consideration all broke through the legal faith that historically speaking has been so central to American ideology. Countless others, in quieter, more private ways, also refused to believe in the rule of law, the courtroom trial, and the Constitution. There is a mountain of heretical gestures and feints from Americans whose names do not appear in history books. But the specific men and women considered in this book went further to articulate and publicly shape heretical stances vis-à-vis the dominant legal faith. They are major figures in what might be thought of as the tradition of American legal heresy.

Does the heretical tradition continue today? Who might be welcomed to the fanciful get-together of legal heretics? Ted Kaczynski, the "Unabomber," embodied what he considered a principled lawlessness. But his infamous manifesto rejected not a legal faith but, more concertedly, a technological and managerial one. While the manifesto employed the plural "we," Kaczynski lived quite alone, literally as a hermit. Dr. Jack Kevorkian has effectively used his own prosecutions and trials to almost single-handedly awaken public consideration of the so-called "right to die." But his efforts are an individualized, sometimes manic, quest and do not constitute a fully developed legal heresy. Eventually, the legislatures and courts seem likely to sort out Kevorkian's demands.

Better contenders for the mantel of contemporary legal heretic are the members of the militia and the anti-abortion movements. To be sure, these movements are ongoing, and commentary on phenomena of the present must always be cautious. Yet some version of legal heresy is evident in both. To what extent are the militia and anti-abortion movements embodiments of legal heresy? An answer to the question might help clarify the tradition of American legal heresy. What distinguishes this tradition? What is the tradition's place in American life, and how does it contribute to Americans' ability to see themselves in the world?

The militia movement is hardly the first movement of its sort in American history. The distinguished historian Richard Hofstadter wrote in the late 1960s of a populist paranoia that frequently manifests among

Americans. It arises from a seemingly perennial American discontent and feeling that things are out of control. Eventually, the paranoia coalesces into a conspiratorial vision, a sense that certain individuals or groups have plotted to grab America by the throat. This "paranoia" is not a matter of clinical pathology. It constitutes instead a political style of mind with normative ramifications. Surely McCarthyites of the 1950s showed this tendency, but it surfaced in the nineteenth-century anti-Masonic and anti-Catholic movements and even in the late eighteenth-century movement against the supposedly nefarious Bavarian Illuminati. Who were the Bavarian Illuminati? They were anticlerical rationalists who never established the tiniest toehold in the United States, a fact apparently irrelevant to those imagining the subversion of their new nation.[3]

In the post–Vietnam War era a self-styled patriot movement began blaring and listening to its own variety of populist paranoia. Patriots drew stylistically on the paramilitarism that emerged in the 1980s. In the realm of popular culture, for example, paramilitarism was evident in the likes of Dirty Harry and Rambo, both fictional heroes for many. More ominously, *Soldier of Fortune*, a periodical for self-styled independent warriors, found a large readership, and, even more ominously, purchases of military-style weapons by private citizens skyrocketed.[4] Patriots identified an enemy clutching the American throat, and that enemy was none other than the federal government. The latter, patriots concluded, not only overtaxed and overregulated but also manipulated and at times even killed its citizens. Speaking on the *MacNeil-Lehrer News Hour*, Missouri patriot Harold Sheil said:

> One of the things the people really fear from the government is the idea [that] the government can ruin your life, totally destroy your life. I don't mean kill you. But they can totally destroy your life, split your family up, do the whole thing and walk off like you're a discarded banana peel, and with a ho-hum attitude.[5]

During the 1990s, the militia, the branch of the larger paramilitiaristic patriot movement most likely to be armed, sharpened the edges of its paranoid antigovernment sentiments on specific events and developments. The FBI's killing of survivalist Randy Weaver's wife and son during a 1992 siege at Ruby Ridge, Idaho, was "proof" that the government would not tolerate a man's wish to live apart from bureaucracy and control. The government's 1993 siege and destruction of the Branch Davidian compound in Waco, Texas, indicated just how much force could and would be marshaled to suppress dissenters. Even the passage of the Assault Weapons Ban and the modest Brady Bill, with its requirement of a five-day wait for handgun purchases, evidenced a government plot to disarm independent men and women. Others would of course see these events in a different light, but once in place, paranoid perceptions of persecution and grandeur can invest selected events with particular meaning. For the militia movement, Ruby Ridge, Waco, and the passage of gun-control legislation fit together as parts of a far-reaching government plot.

While other heretical movements discussed in this book generated recognizable organizational structures and leaders, the militia movement has not. Organized into small cell-like groups, often quite secretive, and prone to at least imaginary and perhaps actual guerrilla activity, the militia take pride in a lack of national structure and endorse a "leaderless resistance."[6] The phrase itself originated with Louis Beam, a one-time Grand Dragon of the Texas Knights of the Ku Klux Klan and founder of the Texas Emergency Reserve, a militia group that mounted an ugly terrorist campaign against Vietnamese shrimp fishermen in Galveston Bay.[7] The militia draw some sense of security from their "invisibility," and membership in loosely organized, leaderless cells reinforces the militia's populist paranoia.

Overall, there are hundreds of individual militia cells in the nation, and estimates of total membership range from ten thousand to forty thousand. The goal of most members is not the overthrow of the government, but media emphasis on this possibility might help plant the seed of that idea in some cells. The cells which overlap with various right-wing and racist groups such as the Posse Comitatus, the Order, the Minutemen, the Ku Klux Klan, Aryan Nation, and the American Nazi Party might be especially prone to revolutionary fantasies.

If the militia movement is secretive and in some ways "leaderless," it nevertheless possesses and distributes the images, labels, and narratives necessary for a degree of cohesion and community. Especially intriguing in this regard is *The Turner Diaries*, a 1978 novel by neo-Nazi William Pierce, which is sold only at gun shows and in the militia underground but which has still attracted a large readership. The title page lists not Pierce but one "Andrew Macdonald" as the author, and the distancing strategies continue as the fictional foreword by the fictional Macdonald cites the fictional Earl Turner as "author" of the diaries. The "diaries" begin with mention of the "Cohen Act," federal legislation outlawing the private ownership of firearms, which not only prompted "gun raids" but also allowed blacks to force "their way into White homes to rob and rape. . . ."[8] A freedom-loving "Organization" takes shape to fight the "System," and bombing of a federal building launches a full-scale Aryan revolt. The struggle continues from 1989 to 1999, and in the fictional 1994 "tens of millions perished," with the white population reaching a low of only 50 million.[9] Blacks, meanwhile, "lapse into cannibalism," and Jews and blacks go on a "wild rampage of mass murder reminiscent of the worst excesses of the Jew-instigated Bolshevik Revolution in Russia, 75 years earlier."[10] In the end, the "Organization" triumphs and establishes an all-white regime. If one can somehow stomach the racism and anti-Semitism of *The Turner Diaries*, the novel has a readability to it, comparable perhaps to Edward Bellamy's *Looking Backward* of a century earlier.[11]

Beyond this "if wishes could come true" narrative, Chuck Harder's "Peoples Radio" talk show is especially popular with the militia, and the previously mentioned *Soldier of Fortune*, founded in 1975, is probably the most read magazine in militia circles. Other more modest periodicals and newsletters supplement *Soldier of Fortune*. For example, *Media Bypass*, a monthly published in Evansville, Indiana, saw its subscriptions soar when it secured a rare interview with Oklahoma City bomber Timothy McVeigh. The Militia of Montana, one of the most active and visible militia groups, makes available a sixteen-page mail-order catalog that offers for sale fifty-one videotapes, forty-eight books, and eighteen audiotapes. Also available is a seventy-five-dollar training manual with instructions on how to conduct guerrilla warfare in the United States.[12] A patriot matchmaker in Frederick, Colorado, even publishes a monthly bulletin for militiamen and women hoping to locate mates with similar politics.[13]

The militia also connect to one another through shortwave radio, public-access television, and especially the Internet. Indeed, electronic communications have in many ways supplanted in importance the types of periodicals that were so crucial for abolitionists, socialists, and African American radicals of earlier eras. Members of the militia not only read one another's thoughts but also have and eagerly use the opportunity to respond. The Internet provides much more room for actual politicized dialogue than did conventional print publications.

As it did with the Black Panthers thirty years earlier, the general public routinely equates the militia and "lawlessness." There is little wonder at this impression. Timothy McVeigh and Terry Nichols, convicted for their roles in the bombing of the Oklahoma City Federal Building, had ties to the militia movement,[14] and their alleged conduct even creepily mimics the bombing of a federal building at the beginning of *The Turner Diaries*. There are also such groups as the West Virginia Mountaineer Militia, which has been indicted for planning to blow up federal buildings; the Viper Militia, which allegedly discussed the destruction of federal buildings in the Phoenix area; and the 112th Georgia Militia, which stockpiled pipe bombs for ultimate use against the federal government. While prosecutors have concluded that McVeigh and Nichols acted largely on their own, the acts of the other groups appear to have been more collective and more directly a product of militia cells.[15]

On a less immediately violent level, militia "lawlessness" has also involved attempts to sever legal connections to the government. Militia members have overtly disobeyed gun laws, refused to pay taxes, turned in their Social Security numbers, disdained drivers' licenses and motor vehicle registration, and even occasionally renounced their citizenship.[16] The most determined practitioners of these varieties of "lawlessness" might be the Freemen, who declared their 960-acre Montana wheat farm the independent "Justus Township" and then established their own currency and system of laws, the latter derived from the Bible, Magna Carta, United States Constitution, Montana Constitution, *and* assorted sections of the Uniform Commercial Code.[17] The surrender of sixteen Freemen in June 1996 after an eighty-one-day siege averted what some feared could become a "second Waco." However, when the Freemen made their first formal courtroom appearance, several remained defiant by refusing to accept court-appointed "Bar Association" lawyers and the legitimacy of the judge and court.[18]

Despite these expressions of "lawlessness," however, the militia, once again like the Black Panthers before them, might also be seen as "legalistic." When brought into court, many actually assert a variety of legal rights to defend their positions. Militiamen and women can be self-styled lawyers of a sort.

Cases in point are Terry Nichols and his brother James. When sued in a Michigan court for not paying the $19,739 due on his Chase Manhattan Bank credit card, Terry Nichols said, "For the record, I appear here as a common law individual. Should the court insist that I answer any questions, I will do so under duress, threat and intimidation."[19] James Nichols, meanwhile, went even further in his attempts to articulate a type of legalistic sovereignty. After being arrested for speeding and driving without a license on a Michigan country road, he said motor vehicle laws did not apply to a sovereign citizen. When pulled into court for failure to pay child support, he argued that as a sovereign citizen he had revoked his marriage license. Judge James A. Marcus, who heard the case involving James Nichols's motor vehicle violations, said of the militia-generated jurisprudence, "You can't follow their arguments because they're listening to a different music no one else hears."[20]

But there is a music and, as understandably elusive as it might be for good jurists such as Judge Marcus, the music is actually legalistic. It begins in almost all militia circles and communications with a commitment to law and the United States Constitution. The law in which militia believe is not statutory law and certainly not statutes enacted by the United States Congress. Instead, militiamen subscribe to what they take to be the "common law," certain basics that seem obviously to control social life.[21] Even more pronounced is the commitment to the Constitution, the ultimate legal construct from a militia perspective.

On occasion, the militia commitment to the United States Constitution even approaches the rabid. Most militias require new members to take a vow of allegiance to the Constitution,[22] and several active militia groups announce their commitments to the Constitution in the very names of their organizations, to wit, the Oklahoma Constitutional Militia, the Texas Constitutional Militia, North Carolina Citizens for the Reinstatement of Constitutional Government, and the Constitution Defense Militia of New Hampshire.[23] The problem from the militia perspective is that the federal government and particularly federal government bureaucrats do not respect the Constitution. Federal officials violate, abuse, and trash the Constitution. According to Mark Koernke, an influential disseminator of militia beliefs:

> The usurpation on the part of the regime—not a government—but the regime that is in place . . . is about to unfold into a very evil flower. . . . It is the ambition of our enemy and in fact it is their sworn oath, to destroy the Constitution and the Bill of Rights.[24]

To what end? According to one publication of the Militia of Montana, "Those power hungry individuals have corrupted our government and are working on sabotaging our freedom by destroying the Constitution of the United States in order to establish the 'New World Order.'"[25] This freedom-denying constellation of socialists and others is so ominous for some militiamen that military resistance is appropriate. In fact, even the chilling words that Dan Shoemaker's *U.S. Militiaman's Handbook* proposes be said before killing a member of the enemy suggest a belief in the Constitution: "You (call the prisoner by name, if you know his name) have committed treason against the United States Constitution and against your fellow citizens and members of the United States Militia. You are executed."[26]

The most developed constitutional law interpretation in militia circles involves the Fourteenth Amendment. In the view of some militia members, the amendment, ratified in 1868 and the source of so much consternation for Elizabeth Cady Stanton, recognized two varieties of citizenship. One is extended by the amendment itself, involves all federal rules and regulations, and is decidedly inferior to the primary "natural" citizenship in one's state and national republic. Individual Americans, the argument continues, can rely only on their primary citizenship and thereby with impunity eschew any of the obligations to obey federal laws, pay taxes, or abide by speed limits on interstate highways—obligations that only come along with secondary Fourteenth Amendment citizenship.[27] To say historians and scholars of the United States Constitution lend no credence to this theory does not even rise to the level of understatement, but for Terry and James Nichols and for militia members that only makes the theory more believable.

The militia also serve up a striking interpretation of the Second Amendment. That amendment reads in full: "A well-regulated militia, being necessary to the security of a free State, the right of the people to keep and bear arms, shall not be infringed." Starting with the independent rather than the preceding dependent clause, militia members find in the amendment an unambiguous protection of their right to their weaponry. The Assault Weapons Ban or the Brady Bill fall obviously and quickly away, as do any infringements on the right to bear arms. This right is so fundamental in the opinion of Norman Olson—Baptist minister, gun store owner, and leader of the Michigan Militia—that "[T]he Second Amendment is really the First in our country because without guns for protection from tyrants, we would have no free speech."[28] Furthermore, there is the amendment's dependent clause. In the eyes of militiamen, the clause links guns and freedom to the militia itself. As true citizens, as armed protectors of the nation and its Constitution, the militiamen take themselves to be "necessary to the security of a free State."[29]

The militia movement's interpretation of the Second Amendment is not as acrobatic and bizarre as its interpretation of the Fourteenth Amendment, but here, too, legal scholars are disdainful.[30] More importantly for purposes at hand, the militia movement's intense involvement with and commitment to the Second Amendment reveal the self-absorption of the movement. Militiamen and women find in the Second Amendment an appealing self-image. The same is true to a certain extent of their understanding of the Fourteenth Amendment. Listening to militia rhetoric, one hears a voice raised not on behalf of others but out of a burning desire to be somebody.

While the militia movement seems sometimes to have arrived overnight on America's doorstep, the anti-abortion movement has publicly evolved over a span of several decades. Modern anti-abortion activism began in the 1960s as a reaction to the movement to make abortion legal, with the 1967 establishment of the Committee on Family Life by the National Bishops' Conference being an early benchmark. The 1973

United States Supreme Court decision in *Roe v. Wade* greatly energized the movement, and more and more anti-abortion groups made their voices heard during the late 1970s and early 1980s. Beginning in the mid-1980s, anti-abortionists began to picket abortion clinics and sought to convince those seeking abortions to change their minds. In addition, clinics were bombed and otherwise menaced. During the 1990s these actions and campaigns continued, and many struggled to comprehend the assassinations of abortion-performing doctors, clinic workers, and, in one case, a doctor's bodyguard.

Who are the anti-abortion activists and what drives their opposition to abortion? No simple answer is available, and one scholar has rung his hands and said it might actually be better to speak of "anti-abortion movements."[31] Yet the complexity and diversity of the anti-abortion movement notwithstanding, one can point to the most important philosophical and political motivations for this variety of activism.

Starting with the 1960s, the majority of anti-abortion activists were Catholics, whose anti-abortion beliefs derived from the Catholic Church's teachings regarding the beginning of life at conception and the more general sanctity of life. Then, in the 1970s and subsequently, fundamentalist Protestants came increasingly to participate, and the movement ceased to be in any sense a "Catholic" movement. Some of the fundamentalist Protestants shared the Catholic belief that life began at conception, but so-called "Christian Reconstructionists" and others also saw opposition to abortion as a way to reassert a Christian religious hegemony they took to be withering. By the 1980s, there was no single, unified Christian position regarding abortion, with variations abundant both between and among anti-abortion Catholics and Protestants.[32]

In addition, beginning in the 1980s individuals increasingly came to anti-abortion activism from political rather than religious premises. Some sectors of the political Right cited abortion along with sexual promiscuity, the rise in single motherhood, the decline of the traditional family and gender roles, the devaluation of children, the ready availability of contraception, and the sanctioning of euthanasia as signs of decline in a liberal America. Republicans more so than Democrats opposed abortion, and antifeminists saw in the anti-abortion activism one way to speak back to feminists. Anti-abortion activism has also come, like the militia movement, to include a variety of populism. Anti-abortion activists, in general, have less income, education, and socio-economic status than do pro-choice counterparts, and, strange as it may seem, for some anti-abortion politics constitute an expression of anti-elitism.[33]

Anti-abortionists at different points in the movement's history and with different philosophical and political agendas have time and again reacted to law and legal decisions. The primary legal expression to which the anti-abortion movement reacts is the previously mentioned United States Supreme Court opinion in *Roe v. Wade*. By virtue of a 7–2 vote, the Justices recognized a limited constitutional right to choose an abortion. The thinking of the majority was not unitary, and Justice Blackmun admitted in the lead opinion that the precise location of a right to abortion in the Constitution is difficult to indicate.[34] Nevertheless, for anti-abortionists the thrust of *Roe* was clear. American women now had a right to choose abortion, at least until the fetus reached viability. Attempts to criminalize abortion, such as in the Texas statute that was at issue in the case, were henceforth to be unconstitutional.

In the quarter century since the United States Supreme Court ruling, anti-abortionists have never accepted *Roe v. Wade* as truly the law of the land. Reacting to popular concerns and pressures, state and local governments have repeatedly enacted laws and put into place procedures that shape, restrict, and attempt to discourage abortion choices. A dozen major cases have then worked their way up on appeal to the United States Supreme Court, with the Court for the most part finding the state and local laws to be unconstitutional invasions of the right to choose abortions.

If there is any change in this pattern, it came with the decision in *Webster v. Reproductive Health Services* in 1989. Reflecting the growing power of conservative appointments, the United States Supreme Court upheld features of a Missouri statute limiting the abortion choice that previous Courts would most likely have found unconstitutional.[35] Ecstatic over the decision, Randall Terry, the head of Operation Rescue, announced: "The energy is now with the pro-life movement. We'll continue to blockade killing centers. This decision will give us the political clout to become a serious political force."[36] In addition, *Webster* included a concurring opinion from Justice Scalia explicitly urging that *Roe v. Wade* be overruled.[37] Yes, shouted the anti-abortion movement, and it appeared that with one more sympathetic appointment to the Supreme Court, *Roe* would fall. However, in 1992 the Court decided *Planned Parenthood of S.E. Pennsylvania v. Casey*, and although in the process the Court upheld important aspects of a Pennsylvania statute restricting abortion, the Court also upheld *Roe*.[38] For anti-abortionists and indeed for most of the general public, the latter feature of the decision was the most significant.

If *Roe v. Wade* inspired the anti-abortion movement, decisions such as *Webster v. Reproductive Health Services* and *Planned Parenthood v. Casey* have produced both higher expectations and anger. The *Webster* decision contributed to rising expectations that *Roe* really would fall, and Justice Scalia himself put that hope and demand at the forefront. As with other significant movements in American history, the civil rights movement of the 1960s included, rising expectations led to greater demands and less patience. But, at least from the anti-abortionist perspective, the explicit upholding of the *Roe v. Wade* right to choose abortion in *Planned Parenthood v. Casey* dashed expectations, denied demands, and exhausted patience. Wanda Franz, president of the National Right to Life Committee, thought the Supreme Court had in *Planned Parenthood v. Casey* caved in to pro-choice pressure. "It's an appalling thing for pro-lifers to realize," she said, "that 1.6 children died last year as a result of abortion and that this is going to continue to happen simply because five members of the Court are concerned about the integrity of the Court."[39]

Much more aggressive forms of anti-abortion activism ensued. While in the 1960s and 1970s anti-abortion activism took the form of educational campaigns and lobbying, after *Webster* anti-abortion activists also began to picket and block abortion clinics, to discourage woman seeking abortions, to bomb and torch clinics, and to shoot abortion doctors. One anti-abortion group, the Chicago-based Pro-Life Action League, even began giving "Protector of Life" awards to those convicted and sentenced to prison for clinic violence.[40] Although Operation Rescue, another prominent anti-abortion group, formally rejected the notion that killing abortion doctors was justifiable homicide, disgruntled members of Operation Rescue in 1995 formed the American Coalition of Life

Activists and published the list of the "Deadly Dozen," thirteen physicians frequently performing abortions. Within a year, five of the physicians on the list had either been shot at or subjected to some form of violence or physical intimidation.[41] Groups such as the Lambs of Christ, local Operation Rescue chapters, and Missionaries to the Unborn grew bolder and more numerous. While more moderate anti-abortion groups with programs including issues other than abortion were troubled, the single-issue groups and their aggressive actions have brought about a degree of radicalization in the anti-abortion movement.

The radical anti-abortionist role of honor or dishonor, depending on one's perspective, continues to grow. Rachelle Shannon, who shot but did not kill abortion doctor George Tiller in Wichita in 1993, hoarded a copy of a 125-page document titled "The Army of God," which outlined anti-abortion tactics. Shannon is currently serving an eleven-year sentence in a Kansas prison. Michael Griffin in March of 1993 became the first assassin of an abortion doctor, when he shot and killed Dr. David Gunn outside a clinic in Pensacola, Florida. Griffin is now serving a life sentence. In 1994, John Salvi, III, pulled a rifle from his duffle bag in two separate suburban Boston clinics and killed two receptionists and wounded five others. The aspiring hairdresser who envisioned an immense anti-Catholic conspiracy later killed himself in a Massachusetts prison by crawling under a bed with a plastic garbage bag tied tightly around his neck.

Especially noteworthy among the violent anti-abortionists is Paul Hill. He had previously haunted the Griffin trial and garnered for himself both an excommunication from the church in which he had served as pastor and a featured guest appearance on the *Phil Donahue Show*. At the time Hill ambushed both a Florida abortion doctor and his volunteer bodyguard with a twelve-gauge shotgun, Hill supported his wife and three children by running an auto-detailing business out of his home. He believed that killing abortion doctors would save children and told a television reporter a few days before his trial that, "Justice has already been served on a man who killed multitudes of innocent children."[42] At the trial itself, Hill attempted to use a justifiable homicide defense, that is, to argue that killing an abortion doctor saved lives. Representing himself at trial, Hill asked no questions of government witnesses but chose instead in opening and closing statements to speak the same two sentences: "This government is unjust because it does not protect human life. To the extent that we take part in this evil, we will answer to God, and may God have mercy on all of us."[43] A conviction followed.

Shannon, Griffin, Salvi, and Hill take us into the angriest heart of the anti-abortion movement. But all offer thoughts that are only fleeting and partial. As was the case with John Brown in the abolitionist movement or Bill Haywood of the Wobblies in early twentieth-century radicalism, we do not have a substantial comment on legal theory. We do not have the basis to gauge the existence of legal heresy.

Less intensely dramatic but perhaps comparable to the words of Garrison and Debs in their contexts are the commentaries of Joseph M. Scheidler and Randall Terry. One a Catholic and the other a Protestant fundamentalist, Scheidler and Terry represent the two major religious bases of the anti-abortion movement. Scheidler's Pro-Life Action League, which he founded in 1980, exemplifies the numerous groups that came to the fore in the 1970s and early 1980s following the *Roe v. Wade* decision.[44] Terry's Operation Rescue, which he founded in 1986, represents the subsequent mini-generation of even more radical groups. Operation Rescue refined the process of blockading one or more clinics in a given area over a period of weeks or months.[45] Scheidler and Terry have both personally been active in the courts and at the clinics, and both have also authored book-length commentaries on abortion. If contemporary anti-abortion activism is to be placed in an American tradition of legal heresy, Scheidler and Terry perhaps merit the most attention.

Scheidler is himself a former Benedictine monk, who lives with his wife and seven children in Chicago. Bearded and fond of broad-brimmed hats, he strongly supported picketing at clinics during the 1980s, sometimes displaying full-color pictures of aborted fetuses and marching with buckets of baby-dolls drenched in red paint. He also championed picketing the homes of abortion doctors, confronting and embarrassing them in airports and restaurants, calling on possible patients at their homes, and jamming clinic telephone lines. With good reason, he became widely known as a networker of aggressive anti-abortion groups. In 1985 President Reagan welcomed Scheidler at the White

House and thereby confirmed the latter's position as an anti-abortion leader.[46]

Scheidler's thinking—and usually his picture too—is available on every page of *Action News*, the newspaper distributed by the Pro-Life Action League, but a more sustained example of his thought is *Closed: 99 Ways to Stop Abortion*.[47] Published first in 1985 and then issued in a second edition in 1993, *Closed* is the unofficial Bible of the anti-abortion movement. The book literally offers ninety-nine ways to impede, complicate, or stop abortion, and Scheidler discusses each in a three to four-page essay. Essays such as "Expose Planned Parenthood" and "Adopt an Abortionist" identify the enemy, and others such as "Infiltrate Abortion Groups," "Use Private Detectives," and "The Bullhorn" offer serious tactical advice. Scheidler is focused, intense, and sometimes personal. A tedious assignment for anyone so dogged as to read the work cover to cover, *Closed* nevertheless serves well a manual.

But does *Closed* offer a coherent law-related philosophy? Scheidler begins the book by announcing that "abortion equals murder" and is also an "unjust, premeditated taking of an innocent life." "Pro-life activists," Scheidler insists, "cannot wait for the legislative and judicial process that will make abortion illegal. The activist has to save lives now."[48] But on the very next page Scheidler also suggests that, "If you have any questions about the legality or advisability of any of the methods of protest discussed in this book, we suggest that you consult a competent attorney before you engage in them."[49] Subsequent essays also advise finding a lawyer not only for taking depositions and defending oneself at trial but also to qualify for tax-exempt status under 1983 federal legislation. Scheidler speaks repeatedly of his and the unborn's constitutional rights. He says activists should not have contempt for the legal process but rather for lawyers and other helpmates of abortionists. "Many of these arrests and even convictions are unconstitutional," he says in the essay "Counter Charges for False Arrest," and such arrests must be challenged in the courts to preserve constitutional rights to free speech and assembly.[50] On one level, he is a champion of the law:

> We are fighting the Supreme Court's 1973 ruling on abortion. We are fighting the law insofar as it is bad law, but we are not fighting law en-

Legal Heresy Today | 149

forcers who are supposed to keep order. We are trying to improve society and make it better for people to live in. We are trying to protect lives, and this is essentially what laws are supposed to do.[51]

Much of the same inconsistency marks the thought of Randall Terry. The latter had been a member of the Pro-Life Action League's board and was the first to propose "rescues" to Scheidler's group. According to one observer, Terry was at first so enamored of Scheidler that he mimicked his dress and even his hairstyle.[52] But as Frederick Douglass's break with Garrison suggested, protégés often must sever ties with mentors. Terry eventually developed his own organization based in Binghampton, New York, where he lived with his wife and four children. He began launching clinic blockades in 1987, with blockades in Wichita and in Atlanta during the 1988 Democratic Party National Convention attracting the most attention. Terry also in 1991 began using children in Operation Rescue blockades in hopes of both winning more sympathy and complicating police efforts to remove the self-styled "rescuers." If Scheidler's White House meeting with President Reagan had the effect of canonizing him, Terry turned to an even higher source. On November 15, 1991, he met with the Pope in Vatican City.[53]

However, Terry is not a Catholic. He grew up in a Protestant family in Henrietta, New York, a suburb of Rochester, and dropped out of high school in hopes of becoming a rock star. He became a born-again Christian when "saved" at the age of seventeen. With a high school equivalency certificate in hand, he then attended the 275-student Elim Bible Institute in Lima, New York, but this led not to the pulpit but rather to a string of lousy jobs flipping hamburgers, pumping gas, and selling used cars.[54] Operation Rescue became his church, and he brought to it his Christian Reconstructionism. This faith, echoing the teachings of Francis Schaeffer, takes Western culture to be a multifaceted display of moral decay and calls for a "rechristianizing." Christian Reconstructionists want a Kingdom of God on Earth.[55] Abortion, in Terry's mind, is one example of the moral decay, and closing the abortion "mills" and thereby preserving the lives of the unborn would be a major step toward rechristianization.

In 1989 in Los Angeles and Atlanta Terry attempted to use his trials to rally anti-abortionists, but in neither case could he muster the popular support and media attention he wished. This failure derived in part from his own inconsistencies. He on the one hand purported to be above the world of man-made laws and courts, but he on the other hand employed a whole range of technical legal defenses. In Los Angeles Terry was acquitted of trespass and resisting arrest, but in Atlanta he was convicted, sentenced to a year in jail, and fined—with the jail sentence to be suspended if the fine was paid and Terry agreed to stay out of Atlanta. Reminiscent of the young William Lloyd Garrison in Baltimore a century and a half earlier, Terry allowed a supporter to pay his fine and left town.[56]

The contemporary political scientist Charles Hersch has argued convincingly that the narratives of anti-abortionists grow tamer in the courtroom. Operation Rescue's dramatic, moral, and spiritual rhetoric, perhaps inevitably, becomes relatively "lifeless" when lawyers reshape it for judges and juries.[57] Yet Terry's writings as well as his courtroom arguments betray an inconsistency. The official motto of Terry's Operation Rescue is "If abortion is murder, why not act like it?"[58] and Terry has said explicitly that a "Supreme Court decision does not override the laws of God."[59] At the same time Terry refers to man-made legal documents such as the Constitution to assert his rights to speak and believe as he sees fit.[60] Terry's thinking, despite the potential of Christian Reconstructionism to lend coherence, is surprisingly inchoate.

The militia and anti-abortion movements suggest that the possibility of legal heresy continues to exist in contemporary America. Neither group stands for the full expression of a legal heresy, but both could ultimately offer such. How do the movements measure up and how do they fail? To what extent do they embody the tradition of legal heresy?

As did other heretics before them, both the militia and anti-abortion movements have a crucial degree of community or collectivity. The "leaderless" militia share their shortwave broadcasts, electronic mail messages, and pet narratives in only a loose, weblike way. But as the frightening presence of *The Turner Diaries* in Timothy McVeigh's car in Oklahoma suggests, militia members have materials that unite them and fuel their paranoid populism.[61] The anti-abortion movement is more diverse, but it, too, has its messages and narratives, its martyrs and prophets. Reminiscent of the abolitionists in another era, some anti-abortionists even name their children after other anti-abortionists.[62] The social foundations and connectedness of both movements greatly facilitate their distinctive articulations of radical thought.

Projecting from their communities and commitments, the militia and the anti-abortionists have routinely brushed up against the law, with arrests galore for stockpiling weapons, bombing clinics, and a range of other plots and violent acts. Members of both movements and, indeed, the two movements *in toto* have been labeled "lawless." Righteous Americans have called for the control and suppression of both movements, and Congressional committees have undertaken investigations of both.[63] Abolitionists, women's rights activists, turn-of-the-century socialists, and African American radicals of the 1960s knew well the same charges and also were investigated by the United States Congress. Against the backdrop of a powerful legal faith, the charge of "lawlessness" is a common and serious one in American life.

Facing such charges, certain members of the militia and anti-abortion movements have done their best to confirm them. They have thumbed their noses at the system so anxious to cast them out. They have on some level attempted to secede from the system. Recall in this regard the refusal of militia members to pay taxes, possess Social Security numbers, or register their motor vehicles. More dramatic is the Montana Freeman with their purportedly independent township and subsequent rejection of the local court's jurisdictional authority. Recall the anti-abortionists' civil disobedience and also the violence at the abortion clinics they call "mills." Most striking is the image of Paul Hill, on trial for murder in a Florida court, asserting the government was unjust because it did not protect human life, seceding, if you will, from an ungodly man-made institution.

In all of these ways and others the militia and anti-abortionists appear to be legal heretics. They can be seen as standing in a line stretching from Garrison to Cady Stanton and from Eugene Debs to the Black Panthers. But emergence from the dominant legal faith is no simple matter. The faith itself is complex, including as it does not only a belief in the rule of law but also cultural icons and rituals such as the United States Constitution and the courtroom trial. The faith to some extent adjusts and alters itself as one era gives way to another. Furthermore, the American legal faith has never been so all-encompassing as to preclude all feints and gestures of resistance. Many have questioned the law without lifting themselves completely out of the faith and without articulating a fully heretical position.

Hence, we see among the militiamen and the anti-abortionists an arm and a leg and a part of consciousness still caught in the dominant faith. For the militiamen, the Constitution—its whole edifice and in particular the Second and Fourteenth Amendments—impedes full heretical development. With great difficulty, William Lloyd Garrison eventually fought off an inclination to find answers in the Constitution. With great anger, the Black Panthers concluded the Constitution left them out and called for a convention to draft something new. But in the words of militia-watcher Richard Abanes, the militia movement continues to represent a variety of constitutional "fundamentalism." Militiamen insist on interpreting the provisions of the Constitution literally and rigidly. "Each word and phrase of America's founding document means neither more nor less, than its precise dictionary meaning. No judge, government official or politician may place any restriction upon, or make any addition to, the document's simplest reading."[64] The chief icon of the legal faith is still meaningful for the militia movement, and, in fact, militiamen outdistance the judges of a century ago in their tendency to fetishize the Constitution.

Constitution worship is less pervasive or important among anti-abortionists, although as noted, the likes of Joseph Scheidler and Randall Terry are not above vigorously asserting their constitutional rights. Then, too, the festering, rankling "constitutionality" of abortion also illustrates most anti-abortionists have not put aside the Constitution as either text or icon.

Also complicating any characterization of the anti-abortion movement as a variety of legal heresy is the diversity of the movement. "Mainstream" abortion opponents remain wedded to law reform in the legislatures and test cases in the courts—hardly heretical stances. More radical anti-abortionists, meanwhile, seem to be "one-issue" people, and it is in fact the "one-issue" anti-abortionists who are most likely to commit themselves to greater degrees of activism and perhaps violence.[65] As Garrison's development from an abolitionist to a Christian anarchist or the Black Panthers' evolution from police watchdogs to legal cynics suggest, it is possible for outrage over one issue to spawn larger philosophies. Yet more frequently "one-issue" critics remain just that. One scholar has even suggested that "one-issue" anti-abortion activism has predominantly personal meaning for many. That is, opposition to abortion chiefly serves recognizable emotional and material needs.[66] Movement beyond this variety of involvement with anti-abortion activism would be necessary for a fuller expression of legal heresy.

Overall, one might perhaps cast the militia and anti-abortion movements as "pre-emergent" or only "partially emergent" vis-à-vis the legal faith.[67] There is no bright line that must be crossed in order to be a legal heretic. There is no magical moment when feints and postures, ideas and attitudes, add up to legal heresy. But stated simply, the militia and anti-abortion activists are still evolving, and while they may not as yet be welcome at the fanciful meeting of legal heretics with which this chapter began, they may eventually find their way through the door.

While scholarly work remains to be done on the law-related thought of William Lloyd Garrison, Elizabeth Cady Stanton, Eugene Debs, and the Black Panthers, we already know a great deal. The attitudes and positions of these individuals and groups regarding law were not private. They not only lived but also loudly preached within America as a temple of the legal faith. Through their broadsides and newsletters, their journals and letters, these men and women gave us a huge public record. Through their political campaigns and symbolic trials, their arrests and imprisonments, the legal heretics passionately attempted to bring their messages to the American public, to be "educators" in the profoundest sense of the term.

Thought of as a group, the legal heretics share certain characteristics. In various ways they championed underprivileged groups—slaves, women, workers, the African American underclass—all of whom had reason to question America's faith in law. The legal heretics also moved beyond nationalism, beyond an assumption in particular that America's self-congratulatory excellence through law was the be all and end all of political modeling.[68] On the domestic and international stages, the legal heretics have been anti-elitist.

More generally, the legal heretics embody a distinctive counterculture, one that attempts to knock a major part of the nation's dominant culture—the American legal faith—from its pedestal. The legal heretics, in this sense, reflect a large but overlooked strain of Americanism as a whole. Despite the significant variations in the way they rejected law and articulated other things in which to believe, the legal heretics as a group embody articulate American antilegalism. They express an alternative jurisprudential tradition that parallels the much touted American confidence in law and legal institutions.

All countercultures and alternative traditions, regardless of whether one admires them, are useful illuminators of the dominant culture and reigning tradition. The heretics therefore superbly clarify the American legal faith. Reading indictments of *and* by the heretics brings the major components of the American legal faith into clear sight. Most Americans invest the United States Constitution with great iconic power. They find meaning in the ubiquitous courtroom trial convention and use it to construct and reinforce their civic and cultural connectedness. And even in the complicating and cynical present, Americans still subscribe to a rule of law. In these ways and others, our culture remains the most "legalistic" in the world. We, as a people, continue to shape and direct our world with reference to law.

Yet like any major part of a culture, the American legal faith can become brittle and artificial. The legal heretics, regardless of our receptiveness to their specific and general heresies, invite critical contemplation of law as a source of value and meaning. They remind us to probe, doubt, and scrutinize law. They give us ways to keep law fresh and alive. In the context of the nation's legalistic culture and more generally, America's legal heretics remind us that we are not only culturally constituted but also, as human beings, culturally constituting.

Notes

NOTES TO CHAPTER I

1. Thomas Paine, *Common Sense,* in Philip S. Foner, ed., *The Complete Writings of Thomas Paine* (New York: The Citadel Press, 1969), 29.

2. Peter Charles Hoffer, *Law and People in Colonial America* (Baltimore: Johns Hopkins University Press, 1992), 62–63, 96–121; Christopher L. Tomlins, *Law, Labor, and Ideology in the Early American Republic* (Cambridge: Cambridge University Press, 1993), 19–34.

3. Robert A. Ferguson, *Law and Letters in American Culture* (Cambridge: Harvard University Press, 1984), 53.

4. Peter Charles Hoffer, *The Law's Conscience: Equitable Constitutionalism in America* (Chapel Hill: University of North Carolina Press, 1990), 71–79.

5. Ferguson, 61. Speaking of the Constitution, the scholar James Boyd White says, "It is not a battle-cry but rather a charter for collective life." *When Words Lose Their Meaning: Constitutions and Reconstructions of Language, Character and Community* (Chicago: University of Chicago Press, 1984), 20.

6. E. L. Doctorow, "A Citizen Reads the Constitution," *Nation,* February 21, 1987, 211.

7. Bertell Ollman, "Introduction," in Bertell Ollman and Jonathan Birnbaum, eds., *The United States Constitution: 200 Years of Anti-Federalist, Abolitionist, Muckraking, Progressive, and Especially Socialist Criticism* (New York: New York University Press, 1991), 1.

8. James Madison, *Notes of Debates in the Federal Convention of 1787* (New York: W.W. Norton, 1969), 654. In reality, Franklin's motion was a bit craftier and more ambiguous. Knowing the majority of each delegation was for approval, he moved that the Constitution be approved "by the unanimous consent of the States present." Certain individual delegates had withdrawn earlier because of unhappiness with early drafts of the document, and such leaders of the convention as Edmund Randolph, Elbridge Gerry, and George Mason refused to sign the final document. Robert A. Ferguson, "'We do Ordain and

Establish': The Constitution as Literary Text," *William and Mary Law Review*, 29 (1987), 6.

9. Doctorow, 211–12.

10. Quoted in Maxwell Bloomfield, "Constitutional Values and the Literature of the Early Republic," *Journal of American Culture*, 11 (1988), 56.

11. Quoted in Sanford Levinson, *Constitutional Faith* (Princeton: Princeton University Press, 1988), 10.

12. Id., 13.

13. Quoted in Michael Kammen, *A Machine That Would Go of Itself: The Constitution in American Culture* (New York: Alfred A. Knopf, 1986), 15.

14. Quoted in Levinson, 9.

15. Kammen, 3, 14.

16. Max Lerner, "Constitution and Court as Symbols," *Yale Law Journal*, 46 (1937), 1298–99.

17. Quoted in Ferguson, *Law and Letters in American Culture*, 208.

18. Quoted in Brooks D. Simpson, "Daniel Webster and the Cult of the Constitution," *Journal of American Culture*, 15 (1992), 15–16.

19. Id., 17.

20. Id., 16.

21. Ferguson, 236–40.

22. Alan Ira Gordon, "The Myth of the Constitution: 19th Century Constitutional Iconography," in Ray B. Browne and Glenn J. Browne, eds., *Laws of Our Fathers: Popular Culture and the U.S. Constitution* (Bowling Green: Bowling Green State University Popular Press, 1986), 88. Michael Kammen, 22, quarrels with the notion that Constitution worship reached its peak in the early nineteenth century, noting that overt criticism was common between 1788 and 1860. In my opinion, Kammen's engagement with formal rhetoric and politics leads him to underestimate the immense positive popular sentiment regarding the Constitution during the Early Republic.

23. James D. Richardson, ed., *A Compilation of the Messages and Papers of the Presidents, 1789–1897* (Washington, D.C.: Governing Printing Office, 1896–99), vol. 4, 22. Kammen quotes early nineteenth-century Presidents, Harrison included, in *A Machine That Would Go of Itself*, 15–16, 61–62, 70–71.

24. Stephen Botein, *Early American Law and Society* (New York: Alfred A. Knopf, 1983), 31–36; Hoffer, 25–40. Samuel Walker, *Popular Justice: A History of American Criminal Justice* (New York: Oxford University Press, 1980), 13.

25. Botein, 37–38; David Thomas Konig, "Country Justice: The Rural Roots of Constitutionalism in Colonial Virginia," in Kermit J. Hall and James

W. Ely, Jr., eds., *An Uncertain Tradition: Constitutionalism and the History of the South* (Athens, Ga.: University of Georgia Press, 1989), 64–74.

26. Ferguson, *Law and Letters in American Culture*, 23, 69–70.

27. Quoted in Jackson Turner Main, *The Social Structure of Revolutionary America* (Princeton: Princeton University Press, 1965), 200.

28. Ferguson, *Law and Letters in American Culture*, 78–84.

29. Daniel A. Cohen, *Pillars of Salt, Monuments of Grace: New England Crime Literature and the Origins of American Popular Culture, 1674–1860* (New York: Oxford University Press, 1993), 26–31.

30. David Ray Papke, *Framing the Criminal: Crime, Cultural Work, and the Loss of Critical Perspective, 1830–1900* (Hamden, Conn.: Archon Books, 1984), 37–40.

31. *Herald*, September 1, 1935, 3.

32. Frank Luther Mott, *American Journalism: A History, 1690–1960*, 3rd ed. (1941; reprint New York: MacMillan, 1962), 233.

33. George Wilkes, *The Lives of Helen Jewett and Richard Robinson* (New York: George Wilkes, 1867).

34. Maxwell Bloomfield, "Law and Lawyers in American Popular Culture," in Commission on Undergraduate Education in Law and the Humanities of the American Bar Association, ed., *Law and American Literature: A Collection of Essays* (Chicago: American Bar Association, 1980), 11–16, 22.

35. For an interesting treatment of the dramatic features of the courtroom trial, see Milner S. Ball, "The Play's the Thing: An Unscientific Reflection on Courts Under the Rubric of Theater," *Stanford Law Review*, 28 (1975), 81–115.

36. Carl Smith, "American Law and the Literary Mind," in Commission on Undergraduate Education, *Law and American Literature*, 12.

37. Michael Grossberg, *Governing the Hearth: Law and the Family in Nineteenth-Century America* (Chapel Hill: University of North Carolina Press, 1985), 12–16.

38. William E. Nelson, *Americanization of the Common Law: The Impact of Legal Change in Massachusetts Society, 1760–1830* (Cambridge: Harvard University Press, 1975), 2.

39. Tomlins, 16.

40. Albert Venn Dicey, *Introduction to the Study of the Law of the Constitution* (New York: Macmillan, 1908), 179–92.

41. Grant Gilmore has observed that since the late eighteenth century American law was supposed to make some overall sense; it was not supposed to grow and be applied in a disorganized, unplanned, eccentric way as was tolera-

bly the case in England. *The Ages of American Law* (New Haven: Yale University Press, 1977), 10.

42. David Dudley Field, "Magnitude and Importance of Legal Science," reprinted in Stephen B. Presser and Jamil S. Zainaldin, *Law and Jurisprudence in American History*, 2nd ed. (St. Paul: West Publishing, 1989), 712–17.

43. Abraham Lincoln, "Address Before the Young Men's Lyceum of Springfield, Illinois," reprinted in John G. Nicolay and John Hay, eds., *Complete Works of Abraham Lincoln*, vol. 1 (Cumberland Gap, Tenn.: Lincoln Memorial University, 1894), 42–43. Emphasis in original.

44. Richard Ruland and Malcolm Bradberry, *From Puritanism to Postmodernism: A History of American Literature* (New York: Viking, 1991), 101.

45. James Fenimore Cooper, *The Pioneers* (1826; reprint New York: Signet Classic, 1964), 13–14.

46. Id., 153.

47. Id., 343.

48. Id., 364–65.

49. Alexis de Tocqueville, *Democracy in America* (1835; reprint London: Oxford University Press, 1946), 205. For an interesting suggestion that Daniel Webster was the type of American lawyer de Tocqueville admired, see R. Kent Newmyer, "Daniel Webster as Tocqueville's Lawyer," *American Journal of Legal History*, 11 (1967), 127–47.

50. De Tocqueville, *Democracy in America*, 206.

51. Id., 174.

52. Id., 207–8.

53. A strong collection of these facsimiles, pamphlets, and small books is housed at the New York Public Library.

54. Lerner, 1303–5, 1316. The way in which law in general may be fetishized is discussed in Hugh Collins, *Marxism and Law* (New York: Oxford University Press, 1982), 10–14. Wilbur Zelinsky, *Nation Into State: The Shifting Symbolic Foundations of American Nationalism* (Chapel Hill: University of North Carolina Press, 1988), 244, discusses the way all the major documents of the American civil religion—the Declaration of Independence, Washington's Farewell Address, Lincoln's major addresses, and the Constitution—might be fetishized.

55. Bertell Ollman, *The United States Constitution*, 4, delights in skewering Taft and Harding for their rabid reactions to Beard's work.

56. Kammen, xiv–xvii.

57. Karl Llewellyn, "The Constitution as an Institution," *Columbia Law Review*, 34 (1934), 23–24. Llewellyn added that many thought the Constitution began "when in the course of human events" or "We hold these truths to be self-

evident." Loyalty to the Constitution was really loyalty to "the Nation-As-It-Stands," including elections, the President, prosperity, the people, and national prestige. "All of which is somehow identified with the War of Independence and with a document, and conceived loosely as having existed, with minor aberrations, from the glorious beginning." Id., 24.

58. Studies of the transformation of criminal proceedings and criminal justice in general during the late nineteenth century include Lawrence M. Friedman and Robert V. Percival, *The Roots of Justice: Crime and Punishment in Alameda County, California, 1870–1910* (Chapel Hill: University of North Carolina Press, 1981) and Allen Steinberg, *The Transformation of Criminal Justice, Philadelphia, 1800–1880* (Chapel Hill: University of North Carolina Press, 1989). For a useful summary of changes in the criminal courts in the twentieth century, see Lawrence M. Friedman, *Crime and Punishment in American History* (New York: Basic Books, 1993), 383–418.

59. For a further explanation of the features and pervasiveness of the courtroom trial as cultural convention, see David Ray Papke, "The Courtroom Trial as American Cultural Convention," in David L. Gunn, ed., *The Lawyer and Popular Culture* (Littleton, Colo.: Fred B. Rothman, 1993), 103–10.

60. Quoted in Steven Weinstein, "Making a Case for Himself: Bochco's Replacement at 'L.A. Law' Dazzles a Jury of His Peers," *Milwaukee Journal*, October 21, 1990, T3.

61. Paul L. Murphy, *World War I and the Origin of Civil Liberties in the United States* (New York: W.W. Norton, 1979), 246–47, offers a different reaction, suggesting Americans of the Red Scare era did not turn their back on the rule of law but rather collapsed rational interest and moral ends into the admittedly open-ended concept.

62. Important treatments of the rule of law by twentieth-century European theorists include F. A. Hayek, *The Rule of Law* (1955; reprint Menlo Park, Calif.: Institute for Humane Studies, 1975) and Franz Neumann, *The Rule of Law: Political Theory and the Legal System in Modern Society* (Dover, N.H.: Berg Publishers, 1986). Among the dozens of articles on the rule of law in contemporary law reviews, three especially provocative ones are Francis J. Mootz, III, "Is the Rule of Law Possible in a Postmodern World?" *Washington Law Review*, 68 (1993), 249–305; Margaret Jane Radin, "Reconsidering the Rule of Law," *Boston University Law Review*, 69 (1989), 781–819; and J. Harvie Wilkinson, "The Rule of Reason in the Rule of Law," *University of Chicago Law Review*, 56 (1989), 779–809.

63. Antonin Scalia, "The Rule of Law as a Law of Rules," *University of Chicago Law Review*, 56 (1989), 1175–88.

64. Helle Porsdam, "Law as Soap Opera and Game Show: The Case of 'The People's Court,'" *Journal of Popular Culture*, 28 (1994), 2.

NOTES TO CHAPTER 2

1. As early as the late 1770s American newspapers included accounts of Fourth of July celebrations, and almanacs of the same years also cast the Fourth as the national birthday. David Waldstreicher, "Rites of Rebellion, Rites of Assent: Celebrations, Print Culture, and the Origins of American Nationalism," *Journal of American Culture*, 82:1 (1995), 50, 58. Works dealing with the emerging American civil religion are numerous and include Catherine L. Albanese, *Sons of the Fathers: The Civil Religion of the American Revolution* (Philadelphia: Temple University Press, 1976); Robert N. Bellah, "Civil Religion in America," *Daedalus*, 96 (1967), 1–19; Robert N. Bellah, *The Broken Covenant: Civil Religion in a Time of Trial* (New York: Seabury Press, 1975); Conrad Cherry, *God's New Israel: Religious Interpretations of American Destiny* (Englewood Cliffs, N.J.: Prentice-Hall, 1971); Wilbur Zelinsky, *Nation Into State: The Shifting Symbolic Foundations of American Nationalism* (Chapel Hill: University of North Carolina Press, 1988).

2. Staughton Lynd, *Intellectual Origins of American Radicalism* (New York: Pantheon Books), 140.

3. The speech itself was published in the *Liberator*, Garrison's weekly journal, 24:27, July 7, 1854, 106.

4. Garrison's Framingham performance, perhaps the most controversial of his career, is noted and interpreted in all studies of Garrison. Representative treatments include William E. Cain, *William Lloyd Garrison and the Fight against Slavery* (Boston: Bedford Books, 1995), 35–36; Walter M. Merrill, *Against the Tide: A Biography of William Lloyd Garrison* (Cambridge: Harvard University Press, 1963), 267–68; Russel B. Nye, *William Lloyd Garrison and the Humanitarian Reformers* (Boston: Little, Brown, 1955), 164; James Brewer Stewart, *William Lloyd Garrison and the Challenge of Emancipation* (Arlington Heights Ill.: Harland Davidson, 1992), 163–64; and John L. Thomas, *The Liberator: William Lloyd Garrison* (Boston: Little, Brown, 1963), 387.

5. See, for example, Stewart, 164–65 and Thomas, 387.

6. Walter M. Merrill, ed., *The Letters of William Lloyd Garrison*, vol. 1, *I Will Be Heard! 1822–1835* (Cambridge: Belknap Press, 1971), 5 [hereinafter *Letters*].

7. Samuel Sewall, a Boston friend and attorney, suggested that Garrison name the journal the *Safety Lamp* rather than the *Liberator* because the latter

name was too inflammatory, but in one of the best decisions of his early career Garrison kept the more provocative name. Cain, 4.

8. David Brion Davis, "The Emergence of Immediatism in British and American Antislavery Thought," *Mississippi Valley Historical Review*, 49, September, 1962, 220.

9. Merrill, *Against the Tide*, 31.

10. *Liberator*, 1:1, January 1, 1831, 1.

11. William Lloyd Garrison, *Thoughts on African Colonization: or An Impartial Exhibition of the Doctrines, Principles and Purposes of the American Colonization Society* (Boston: Garrison and Knapp, 1832), iii [hereinafter *African Colonization*].

12. William Lloyd Garrison, ed., *Speeches Delivered at the Anti-Colonization Meeting in Exeter Hall, London, July 13, 1833* (Boston: Garrison and Knapp, 1833), Garrison's own unpaginated speech, 7–8 [hereinafter *Exeter Hall*].

13. Lewis Perry, *Radical Abolitionism: Anarchy and the Government of God in Antislavery Thought* (Ithaca: Cornell University Press, 1973), 48.

14. Garrison, *African Colonization*, 80.

15. Thomas, 136–38.

16. Garrison, *African Colonization*, 80.

17. *Liberator*, 1:1, January 1, 1831, 1.

18. Garrison, *Exeter Hall*, 12.

19. Supra, note 11. An original copy of the booklike pamphlet is available in the Boston Public Library, Boston, Massachusetts.

20. Id., 3, 21–3.

21. Cain, 9–10.

22. Garrison, *Exeter Hall*, 8.

23. Garrison, *African Colonization*, 79–80.

24. Aileen S. Kraditor, *Means and Ends in American Abolitionism: Garrison and His Critics on Strategy and Tactics, 1834–1850* (New York: Vintage Books, 1967), 26–32.

25. Garrison, *After Colonization*, 80.

26. Davis, 226.

27. Stewart, 14.

28. Id., 39.

29. Wendell Phillips Garrison and Francis Jackson Garrison, *William Lloyd Garrison 1805–1879; The Story of His Life Told by His Children* (New York: Century, 1885–94), vol. 1, 163.

30. Quoted in Thomas, 108–9.

31. The indictment and other documents and pleadings relating to the trial are included in William Lloyd Garrison, *Brief Sketch of the Trial of William Lloyd Garrison, for an Alleged Libel on Francis Todd of Newburyport, Mass.* (Boston: Garrison and Knapp, 1834) [hereinafter *Brief Sketch*].

32. Norman L. Rosenberg, *Protecting the Best Men: An Interpretive History of the Law of Libel* (Chapel Hill: University of North Carolina Press, 1986), 121–29.

33. Additional accounts of the trial and sentencing are available in Merrill, *Against the Tide*, 34; Stewart, 44–45; and Thomas, 108–10.

34. Bertram Wyatt-Brown, *Lewis Tappan and the Evangelical War against Slavery* (Cleveland: Case Western University Press, 1969), 31–44. (Despite its title, this volume treats jointly the lives of Lewis and Arthur Tappan.)

35. Merrill, *Letters*, vol. 1, 94–95.

36. Garrison, *Brief Sketch*, supra, n. 31.

37. Id., 6, 14.

38. Id., 6, 1.

39. Rosenberg, 123. In the later antebellum years, in the face of hostile mobs and proposed censorship, other abolitionists would also wave vigorously the banner of free expression, id., 150–51.

40. Garrison and Garrison, vol. 1, 195.

41. Nye, 49.

42. *Liberator*, 3:9, March 2, 1833, 35.

43. Id.

44. *Liberator*, 3:25, June 22, 1833, 99.

45. Garrison and Garrison, vol. 1, 321; Merrill, *Against the Tide,* 190–92; Stewart, 61.

46. Merrill, *Letters*, vol. 1, 221.

47. Quoted in Garrison and Garrison, vol. 1, 320 (emphasis in original).

48. Thomas, 192–93.

49. *Crandall v. The State*, 10 Conn. 339 (1834), 366, 369.

50. Thomas, 192.

51. Merrill, *Letters*, vol. 1, 323.

52. Id., 311.

53. Id., 161.

54. Id., 155.

55. Id., 365.

56. Even with his youngster's hands rubbing his head, Garrison remained a self-conscious abolitionist. "You come to my incendiary head, my darling," he said, "to warm your cold hands." Fanny Garrison Villard, *William Lloyd Garri-*

son on Non-Resistance, Together with a Personal Sketch by His Daughter, and a Tribute by Leo Tolstoi (New York: Nation, 1924), 6–7.

57. Lawrence J. Friedman, *Gregarious Saints: Self and Community in American Abolitionism, 1830–1870* (New York: Cambridge University Press, 1982), 52–54.

58. Id., 49.

59. Merrill, *Letters*, vol. 1, 10–13.

60. Garrison's children thought later commentators might "find it hard to sympathize with Mr. Garrison's scriptural propaganda." Their father's efforts and the anti-slavery movement, in general, seemed to them probably the last great reform that the world is likely to see based upon the Bible and carried out with a millennial fervor." Garrison and Garrison, vol. 1, xiii.

61. Frederick B. Tolles, *Quakers and the Atlantic Culture* (New York: Macmillan, 1960), 107.

62. Mary Beth Norton, et al., *A People and a Nation* (Boston: Houghton Mifflin, 1986), vol. 1, 202.

63. Richard Ruland and Malcolm Bradbury, *From Puritanism to Postmodernism* (New York: Viking, 1991), 119.

64. Quoted in Nye, 34.

65. Merrill, *Letters*, vol. 2, 178.

66. The classic study of Noyes is Robert Allerton Parker, *A Yankee Saint: John Humphrey Noyes and the Oneida Community* (New York: Putnam's Sons, 1935). For a more modern commentary, see Spencer Klaw, *Without Sin: The Life and Death of the Oneida Community* (New York: Allen Lane, 1993).

67. Merrill, *Letters*, vol. 2, 258.

68. *Liberator*, 7:35, August 25, 1837, 140.

69. Stewart, 95–97.

70. *Liberator*, 7:26, June 23, 1837, 103.

71. *Liberator*, 7:51, December 15, 1837, 203.

72. *Liberator*, 8:39, September 28, 1838, 155.

73. Louis Filler, *The Crusade against Slavery, 1830–1860* (New York: Harper and Brothers, 1960), 156.

74. *Liberator*, 8:39, September 28, 1838, 154.

75. Lewis Perry, *Radical Abolitionism*, 76–78.

76. Id., 76.

77. Id.

78. Garrison, *African Colonization*, iii. The relevant part of the clause stated, "Representatives and direct taxes shall be apportioned among the several States which may be included within this Union, according to their respective

members, which shall be determined by adding the whole numbers of free persons, including those bound to service for a term of years and excluding Indians not taxed, three-fifths of all other persons."

79. Merrill, *Letters*, vol. 1, 249.

80. Kraditor, 5.

81. Thomas, 217.

82. Id., 218.

83. Lysander Spooner, *The Unconstitutionality of Slavery* (Boston: B. Marsh, 1845). Discussions of Spooner and other abolitionist treatments of the Constitution abound and include Kraditor, 191–95; Lynd, 153–84; and Perry, 194–98. See also Robert M. Cover, *Justice Accused: Antislavery and the Judicial Process* (New Haven: Yale University Press, 1975), 149–58 and William M. Wiecek, *The Sources of Antislavery Constitutionalism in America, 1760–1848* (Ithaca: Cornell University Press, 1977), 228–75.

84. Quoted in Kraditor, 195.

85. Kraditor, 196–97.

86. *Liberator*, 14:37, September 13, 1844, 146.

87. William Ingersoll Bowditch, *Slavery and the Constitution* (Boston: R. F. Wallcutt, 1849); Wendell Phillips, *The Constitution, a Pro-Slavery Compact* (New York: American Anti-Slavery Society, 1856). For a discussion of Bowditch and Phillips, see Kraditor, 208–11.

88. William S. McFeely, *Frederick Douglass* (New York: W.W. Norton, 1991), 84.

89. Preface to Frederick Douglass, *Narrative of the Life of Frederick Douglass, An American Slave* (1845; reprint Cambridge: Belknap Press, 1967), 4.

90. McFeely, 148.

91. Id., 149.

92. David W. Blight, *Frederick Douglass' Civil War: Keeping Faith in Jubilee* (Baton Rouge: Louisiana State University Press, 1989), 29–33.

93. *Liberator*, 23:50, December 16, 1853, 196.

94. *Liberator*, 12:18, May 6, 1842, 591.

95. Kraditor, 200.

96. Id., 207.

97. Wiecek, 238–39.

98. Garrison and Garrison, vol. 3, 117–18.

99. Thomas, 387.

100. *Liberator*, 33:17, April 24, 1863, 66.

101. William M. Wiecek points out the sad irony that Garrisonian constitu-

tionalism in its rigidity actually resembled that of Justice Taney in the infamous Dred Scott decision. *The Sources of Antislavery Constitutionalism*, 247.

NOTES TO CHAPTER 3

1. Wilbur Zelinsky, *Nation Into State: The Shifting Symbolic Foundations of American Nationalism* (Chapel Hill: University of North Carolina Press, 1988), 71.

2. For an interesting collection of essays on the pitfalls and rewards of psychobiography, see Geoffrey Cocks and Travis L. Crosby, eds., "Part II: The Psychology of the Individual in History," in *Psycho/History: Readings in the Method of Psychology, Psychoanalysis and History* (New Haven: Yale University Press, 1987), 83–222. For an extended and often searing critique of psychohistory in general, see David E. Stannard, *Shrinking History: On Freud and the Failure of Psychohistory* (New York: Oxford University Press, 1980). Hardly one to pull his punches, Stannard says individual works of psychohistory are characterized "by a cavalier attitude toward fact, a contorted attitude toward logic, an irresponsible attitude toward theory validation, and a myopic attitude toward cultural difference and anachronism." Id., 147.

3. Elizabeth Cady Stanton, *Eighty Years and More: Reminiscences, 1815–1897* (1898; reprint New York: Schocken Books, 1971), 4.

4. Id., 20.

5. Id., 21.

6. Lois W. Banner, *Elizabeth Cady Stanton: A Radical for Woman's Rights* (Boston: Little, Brown, 1980), 8.

7. For discussions of women's condition under the law in the early nineteenth century, see Norma Basch, *In the Eyes of the Law: Women, Marriage, and Property in Nineteenth-Century New York* (Ithaca: Cornell University Press, 1982), 15–41 and Joan Hoff, *Law, Gender and Injustice: A Legal History of U.S. Women* (New York: New York University Press, 1991), 117–50. On the subject of early nineteenth-century child custody law, see Michael Grossberg, *Governing the Hearth: Law and the Family in Nineteenth-Century America* (Chapel Hill: University of North Carolina Press, 1985), 234–53.

8. Ellen Carol DuBois, *Feminism and Suffrage: The Emergence of the Independent Women's Movement in America, 1848–1869* (Ithaca: Cornell University Press, 1978), 44.

9. Joan Hoff, "Women and the Constitution," in Bertell Ollman and Jonathan Birnbaum, eds., *The United States Constitution: 200 Years of Anti-Federalist,*

Abolitionist, Feminist, Muckraking, Progressive and Especially Socialist Criticism (New York: New York University Press, 1990), 233.

10. DuBois, *Feminism and Suffrage*, 44.

11. Stanton, *Eighty Years and More*, 41.

12. Ellen Carol DuBois, ed., *Elizabeth Cady Stanton, Susan B. Anthony: Correspondence, Writings, Speeches* (New York: Schocken Books, 1981), 9.

13. "Letter to Susan B. Anthony, September 10, 1855," in Theodore Stanton and Harriet Stanton Blatch, eds., *Elizabeth Cady Stanton*, vol. 2 (New York: Arno and The New York Times, 1969), 59–60.

14. Stanton, *Eighty Years and More*, 81.

15. Garrison's children delighted in recalling the impact their father had had on Cady Stanton: "Long before my father had quite freed himself from the trammels of orthodoxy, he was loosening the fetters of others. At the twenty-seventh anniversary of the American Anti-Slavery Society, Mrs. Elizabeth Cady Stanton remarked: "My own experience is, no doubt, that of many others. In the darkness and gloom of false theology, I was slowly sawing off the chains of my spiritual bondage when, for the first time, I met Garrison in London. A few bold strokes from the hammer of his truth, I was free!" Wendell Phillips Garrison and Francis Jackson Garrison, *William Lloyd Garrison, 1805–1879; the Story of His Life Told by His Children* (New York: Century, 1885–94), vol. 4, 336.

16. Banner, 39–40.

17. Anne M. Boylan, "Women and Politics in the Era Before Seneca Falls," *Journal of the Early Republic*, 10 (Fall, 1990), 363–82.

18. Carroll Smith-Rosenberg, "Beauty, the Beast and the Militant Woman: A Case Study in Sex Roles and Social Stress in Jacksonian America," in *Disorderly Conduct: Visions of Gender in Victorian America* (New York: Oxford University Press, 1985), 109–28.

19. One early chronicler of American feminists places Cady Stanton among the "Moral Crusader Feminists" rather than the "Enlightenment Feminists," but I take issue with this interpretation. Alice Rossi, ed., *The Feminist Papers from Adams to de Beauvoir* (New York: Columbia University Press, 1973), 246–50.

20. For a discussion of the power of natural rights philosophy in America, see John P. McWilliams, "Innocent Criminal or Criminal Innocence," in American Bar Association, ed., *Law and Literature: A Collection of Essays* (Chicago: American Bar Association, 1980), 6–11.

21. Sylvia D. Hoffert, *When Hens Crow: The Women's Rights Movement in Antebellum America* (Bloomington: Indiana University Press, 1995), 41–42.

22. Id., 45.

23. The "Declaration of Sentinents" is included in many texts and collections. For the version Cady Stanton herself preserved, see Elizabeth Cady Stanton, Susan B. Anthony, and Matilda Joslyn Gage, eds., *History of Woman Suffrage*, vol. 1 (New York: Fowler & Wells, 1881), 70–71.

24. Quoted in Banner, 41.

25. "Address Delivered at Seneca Falls, July 19, 1848," in DuBois, *Stanton/Anthony*, 27–35.

26. Stanton, Anthony, and Gage, *History of Woman Suffrage*, vol. 1, 72.

27. Elizabeth Cady Stanton, Susan B. Anthony, and Matilda Joslyn Gage, eds., *History of Woman Suffrage*, vol. 2 (New York: Fowler & Wells, 1882), 255–59. For an excellent discussion of the quasi-religious significance Cady Stanton attached to voting, the polling booth, and election day, see Mary D. Pellauer, *Toward a Tradition of Feminist Theology: The Religious Social Thought of Elizabeth Cady Stanton, Susan B. Anthony, and Anna Howard Shaw* (Brooklyn: Carlson Publishing, 1991), 77–88.

28. "Letter from Elizabeth Cady Stanton to the Salem, Ohio Convention, April 7, 1850," in Stanton, Anthony, and Gage, *History of Woman Suffrage*, vol. 1, 812 (emphasis in original).

29. Bennett's editorial is reprinted in Stanton, Anthony, and Gage, *History of Woman Suffrage*, vol. 1, 805. For comments on his campaign to mention underwear and, horrors, even legs in the *New York Herald*, see David Ray Papke, *Framing the Criminal: Crime, Cultural Work, and the Loss of Critical Perspective, 1830–1900* (Hamden, Conn.: Archon Books, 1987), 44.

30. For a review of Bennett's positions as well as those of other major newspapers, see Hoffert, 94–115.

31. Frederick Douglass, "Editorial from the North Star," in Miriam Scheir, ed., *Feminism: The Essential Historical Writings* (New York: Random House, 1972), 83–85.

32. For an account of the first Cady Stanton-Anthony meeting, see Alma Lutz, *Created Equal: A Biography of Elizabeth Cady Stanton* (1940; reprint New York: Octagon Books, 1974), 72.

33. For a full discussion and provocative analysis of American drinking in the early nineteenth century, see W. J. Rorabaugh, *The Alcoholic Republic: An American Tradition* (New York: Oxford University Press, 1979).

34. "Appeal for the Maine Law, Written by Mrs. Stanton and Read by Miss Anthony in the Assembly Chamber," in DuBois, *Stanton/Anthony*, 40–43.

35. "Letter to Susan B. Anthony, June 20, 1853," in Stanton and Blatch, *Elizabeth Cady Stanton*, vol. 2, 52.

36. Writing after the Civil War, Cady Stanton continued to demand divorce

reform, saying "It is the inalienable right of all to be happy." Quoted in William L. O'Neill, "Divorce as a Moral Issue: A Hundred Years of Controversy," in Carol V. R. George, ed., *"Remember the Ladies": New Perspectives on Women in American History* (Syracuse: Syracuse University Press, 1975), 134.

37. "Letter to Susan B. Anthony, April 2, 1859," in DuBois, *Stanton/Anthony*, 68.

38. "Letter to Susan B. Anthony, June 10, 1856," in Stanton and Blatch, *Elizabeth Cady Stanton*, vol. 2, 66.

39. Quoted in Banner, 59.

40. "Address to the Legislature of New York on Women's Rights, February 14, 1854," in Stanton, Anthony, and Gage, *History of Woman Suffrage*, vol. 1, 603–4.

41. "Speech to the Anniversary of the American Anti-Slavery Society, 1860," in DuBois, *Stanton/Anthony*, 82.

42. Quoted in Banner, 106.

43. "Speech to the McFarland-Richardson Protest Meeting, May, 1869" in DuBois, *Stanton/Anthony*, 125–30.

44. Quoted in Elisabeth Griffith, *In Her Own Right: The Life of Elizabeth Cady Stanton* (New York: Oxford University Press, 1984), 126.

45. Id., 119.

46. Quoted in Banner, 74.

47. "Gerrit Smith on Petitions, 1869," in DuBois, *Stanton/Anthony*, 122, 124.

48. Id., 32, 45.

49. Lutz, 178.

50. Quoted in Lutz, 180. For a good comparison of the two major arguments for women's suffrage in the late nineteenth century, see Aileen S. Kraditor, *The Ideas of the Woman Suffrage Movement, 1890–1920* (New York: Columbia University Press, 1965), 43–74.

51. Quoted in Griffith, 198.

52. "Address to the Founding Convention of the National American Woman Suffrage Association, 1890" in DuBois, *Stanton/Anthony*, 222–27.

53. Banner, 59.

54. Quoted in Banner, 118.

55. Griffith, 191.

56. Stanton and Blatch, *Elizabeth Cady Stanton*, vol. 2, 273.

57. Griffith, 207.

58. Quoted in Banner, 159.

59. Five other women (Phebe Hanaford, Ellen B. Dietrich, Ursula Gestafield, Louisa Southworth, and Frances E. Burr) were listed as co-authors of the work, but there is no doubt Stanton was the lead author. Published in two parts, the first volume of *The Women's Bible* was a bestseller, went through seven printings in only six months, and was translated into several foreign languages. Griffith, 211–12. In 1897, over Anthony's objections, Cady Stanton published a second volume of the work.

60. For representative treatments of this fabled last "address," see Banner, 172–73; DuBois, *Stanton/Anthony*, 265; and Griffith, 217.

61. "Diary Entry, January 18, 1892," in Stanton and Blatch, *Elizabeth Cady Stanton*, vol. 2, 281.

62. "Diary Entry, January 20, 1892," in Stanton and Blatch, *Elizabeth Cady Stanton*, vol. 2, 281–82.

63. "The Solitude of Self," in DuBois, *Stanton/Anthony*, 246–54.

64. Susan B. Anthony and Ida Husted Hayer, *History of Women's Suffrage*, vol. 4 (Rochester: Susan B. Anthony, 1902), 189.

NOTES TO CHAPTER 4

1. All three cartoons are initialed "HRH." *Chicago Tribune*, July 3–5, 1894.

2. Quoted in Nick Salvatore, *Eugene V. Debs: Citizen and Socialist* (Urbana: University of Illinois Press, 1982), 36–37.

3. For representative discussions of Debs's "Americanism," see Salvatore, 271–72 and 343–44, and David A. Shannon, *The Socialist Party of America* (New York: Macmillan, 1955), 12.

4. Eugene V. Debs, "How I Became a Socialist," in Jean Y. Tussey, ed., *Eugene V. Debs Speaks* (New York: Pathfinder Press, 1970), 48.

5. Salvatore, 125.

6. Some have suggested that "The Pioneer" was too large to have passed station platforms and that the claim it carried Lincoln was false advertising. Liston E. Leyendecker, *Palace Car Prince: A Biography of George Mortimer Pullman* (Niwot, Colo.: University Press of Colorado, 1992), 77–78, 121.

7. Barney Pace, "Three Cures for Gilded Age Chicago: Hull House, Pullman and the World's Fair of 1893," paper delivered at the American Culture Association Annual Convention, Louisville, April 24, 1984.

8. Stanley Buder, *Pullman: An Experiment in Industrial Order and Community Planning 1880–1930* (New York: Oxford University Press, 1967).

9. Arnold M. Paul, *Conservative Crisis and the Rule of Law: Attitudes of Bar and Bench, 1887–1895* (Ithaca: Cornell University Press, 1960), 133.

10. Ray Ginger, *The Bending Cross: A Biography of Eugene Victor Debs* (New Brunswick: Rutgers University Press, 1949), 112–13.

11. *Harper's Weekly*, 38:1959, July 14, 1894.

12. *Chicago Tribune*, June 30, 1894, 12.

13. Salvatore, 130–31.

14. Harold W. Currie, *Eugene V. Debs* (Boston: Twayne Publishers, 1976), 27; Charles White, "When a Trial Becomes a Political Circus," *Update on Law-Related Education*, 5 (Winter, 1981), 43–44.

15. The other directors of the ARU were sentenced to only three months. Salvatore, 138.

16. Barry F. Helfand, "Labor and the Courts: The Common-Law Doctrine of Criminal Conspiracy and its Application in the Buck's Stove Case," *Labor History*, 18 (1977), 91–114; Wythe Holt, "Labour Conspiracy Cases in the United States, 1805–1842: Bias and Legitimation in Common Law Adjudication," *Osgoode Hall Law Journal*, 22 (1984), 591–663; Leonard W. Levy, *The Law and the Commonwealth of Chief Justice Shaw* (Cambridge: Harvard University Press, 1957), 183–206.

17. Harry A. Millis and Royal E. Montgomery, *Organized Labor* (New York: McGraw-Hill, 1945), 505–6, 631. According to Harry H. Wellington, 118 labor injunction cases reached the federal courts between 1901 and 1928; in 70 of them the courts issued injunctions on the basis of *ex parte* proceedings. *Labor and the Legal Process* (New Haven: Yale University Press, 1968), 39.

18. William E. Forbath, *Law and the Shaping of the American Labor Movement* (Cambridge: Harvard University Press, 1991), 61.

19. Darrow and certain of his admirers made much of his switch to the side of labor, but Darrow's autobiography reveals some ambiguity on his part. "I had no feeling that the members of labor unions were better than employers," Darrow said. "I knew that like all other men they were selfish and unreasonable, but I believed that the distribution of wealth was grossly unjust, and I sympathized with almost all efforts to get higher wages. . . ." Even after leaving the Chicago and North-Western, Darrow continued to accept special assignments from his former employer. Clarence Darrow, *The Story of My Life* (New York: Charles Scribner's Sons, 1932), 58, 62.

20. Clarence S. Darrow, Brief and Arguments for Petitioners, Ex Parte Eugene V. Debs et al., Petitioners; October Term, 1894; 88.

21. Id., 74, 96.

22. *In re Debs*, 158 U.S. 564, and 598–99 (1895).

23. Eugene V. Debs to Jean Daniel Debs and Marguerite Bettrich Debs, January 8, 1895, and Eugene V. Debs to Jean Daniel Debs, January 14, 1895, in J. Robert Constantine, ed., *Letters of Eugene V. Debs*, vol. 1 (Urbana: University of Illinois Press, 1990), 81–82.

24. Iris Noble, *Labor's Advocate: Eugene V. Debs* (New York: Messner, 1966), 131–33.

25. The address is reprinted in excerpted form with the title "Liberty" in Stephen B. Presser and Jamil S. Zainaldin, eds., *Law and Jurisprudence in American History: Cases and Materials* (St. Paul: West Publishing, 1989), 696–701. For critiques of the "labor republicanism" scholarship, see Bryan D. Palmer, *Descent Into Discourse: The Reification of Language and the Writing of Social History* (Philadelphia: Temple University Press, 1990), 106–18 and Daniel T. Rodgers, "Republicanism: The Career of a Concept," *Journal of American History*, 79 (1992), 24–31.

26. Paul, 225; see also Leon Fink, "Labor, Liberty, and the Law: Trade Unionism and the Problem of the American Constitutional Order," *Journal of American History*, 74 (1987), 904, 913.

27. Debs, "How I Became a Socialist," 48.

28. Quoted in Currie, 31.

29. Id.

30. Salvatore, 150.

31. In the opinion of Arthur M. Schlesinger, Jr., the "sentimental hagiography" which Debs achieved during his lifetime seems in a later time "naive hero worship." "Introduction," *The Writings and Speeches of Eugene V. Debs* (New York: Hermitage Press, 1948), v.

32. Quoted in Salvatore, 175.

33. Salvatore, 149–50.

34. For a useful discussion of the ways "jurisprudence" is framed in the academic context, see Philip Soper, "Making Sense of Modern Jurisprudence: The Paradox of Positivism and the Challenge of Natural Law," *Creighton Law Review*, 22 (1988), 67.

35. Richard W. Fox also dubs Morris Hillquit a "catechist," but the subtheoretical implications of the label make it more appropriate for Debs. Fox, "The Paradox of Progressive Socialism: The Case of Morris Hillquit, 1901–1914," *American Quarterly* 26:2 (1974), 127.

36. Fink, 912.

37. George E. McNeill, ed., *The Labor Movement: The Problem of To-day* (Boston: A. M. Bridgman, 1887), 488.

38. David Ray Papke, *Framing the Criminal: Crime, Cultural Work and The*

Loss of Critical Perspective, 1830–1900 (Hamden, Conn.: Archon Books, 1987), 171.

39. Edward Bellamy, *Looking Backward* (1988; reprint New York: New American Library, 1960), 138–45.

40. Testimony of Eugene V. Debs, in United States Strike Commission, *Report on the Chicago Strike of June–July 1894* (1895), 170.

41. Karl Marx and Friedrich Engels, *Basic Writings on Politics and Philosophy*, (Garden City, N.Y.: Anchor Books, 1959), 24.

42. Karl Marx; *Capital; A Critique of Policial Economy* (New York: International Publishers, 1967), vol.1, 88.

43. Marx and Engels, *Basic Writings*, 43.

44. Alan Stone, "The Place of Law in the Marxian Structure-Superstructure Archetype," *Law and Society Review*, 19 (1985), 47.

45. Currie, 128. In defense of this imbalance, one might note the confidence of Debs and other Marxists in the process of historical evolution. As capitalism evolved into socialism, the proper socialist institutions—legal and others— would emerge.

46. Quoted in Currie, 124.

47. Eugene V. Debs, "The Role of the Courts," in Tussey, 51–52.

48. Id., 52.

49. Eugene V. Debs, "The Senate Nuisance—Abolish It," *Appeal to Reason*, February 27, 1915, 1.

50. Id.

51. Quoted in Ginger, 357.

52. Tussey, 294.

53. Eugene V. Debs, *Walls and Bars* (1927; reprint with a new introduction by Hans W. Mattick, Montclair, N.J.: Patterson Smith, 1973), 182.

54. Id., 36.

55. Id., 35–36 and 192.

56. Dianne Avery, "Images of Violence in Labor Jurisprudence: The Regulation of Picketing and Boycotts, 1894–1921," *Buffalo Law Review*, 37 (1988), 7.

57. Forbath, 127.

58. Altgeld had issued the pardons shortly after becoming governor of Illinois in early 1893, pausing in the process to criticize the earlier prosecutions. When the *Chicago Tribune* and other mainstream newspapers denounced Altgeld and the pardons, Debs, as editor of the *Magazine*, a publication of the Brotherhood of Locomotive Firemen, praised Altgeld. Ginger, 94.

59. Of the thirty-one telegrams later amended to the indictment for contempt, only the one of July 2, 1894, suggests violence. It reads in full: "The Gen-

eral Managers are weakening. If the strike is not settled in forty-eight hours, complete paralysis will follow. Potatoes and ice are out of sight. Save your money and buy a gun." The telegram was sent the day before the injunction was published in the Chicago newspapers and two days before Debs was formally served notice. A half dozen telegrams in the same packet urge non-violence. Parts of Information Heretofore Omitted in Printing, Ex Parte: In the Matter of Eugene V. Debs et al., Petitions, October Term, 1894, 1–9.

60. Ginger, 131.

61. *Chicago Tribune*, June 30, 1894, 1.

62. *Harper's Weekly*, 38: 1959, July 7, 1894, 627 and 38: 1961, July 21, 1894, cover.

63. Debs, "How I Became a Socialist," 47–48.

64. Debs, *Walls and Bars*, 61.

65. Id., 173.

66. Irving Howe, *Socialism in America* (San Diego: Harcourt, Brace, Jovanovich, 1985), 31.

67. H. Wayne Morgan, *Eugene V. Debs: Socialist for President* (Syracuse, N.Y.: Syracuse University Press, 1962), 24.

68. Bernard J. Brommel, "Eugene V. Debs: The Agitator as Speaker," *Central States Speech Journal*, 20 (1969), 202–14.

69. Quoted in Ronald Radosh, ed., *Debs* (Englewood Cliffs, N.J.: Prentice-Hall, 1971), 98.

70. Salvatore, 223.

71. Debs even suggested that when the party was close to winning, he would step aside as a candidate for President in favor of somebody who would be a more effective executive. Ginger, 271.

72. Rather then eat crow, Debs wrote, "We Socialists are making no apology for any word or deed of ours in the McNamara case, and as for myself personally I shall not denounce them. I condemn the crime, but I pity all the victims, all of them, the McNamaras included. . . ." Quoted in Currie, 71.

73. Quoted in Currie, 70.

74. Ginger, 247.

75. Quoted in Ginger, 251. Debs responded with an open letter in the *Toledo Socialist*, in which he called the President's pronouncements "cowardly." "Open Letter to President Roosevelt," in Tussey, 149–53.

76. Ginger, 258.

77. Quoted in Tussey, 15.

78. Currie, 43.

79. Ginger, 303.

80. Quoted in Currie, 82.

81. Eugene V. Debs, "Declaration of Revolt," *Appeal to Reason*, January 7, 1911, 1.

82. Ginger, 304.

83. Quoted in Ginger, 353.

84. In fact, the Justice Department stenographer had been rather overwhelmed by his assignment and managed to record only one-half of the speech. When the case went to trial, a better transcription was available from a second stenographer who had been hired by the Socialist Party. Max Eastman, *Heroes I Have Known, Twelve Who Lived Great Lives* (New York: Simon & Schuster, 1942), 50.

85. "The Canton, Ohio, Speech," in Tussey, 258.

86. Id., 266–68.

87. Id., 260 and 269.

88. Id., 253, 255 and 294.

89. Ginger, 359.

90. Id., 364.

91. Id.

92. Eastman, 55.

93. Debs, "Address to the Jury," in Tussey, 288.

94. Ginger, 375.

95. Brief for Plaintiff in Error, *Debs v. United States,* 249 U.S. 211 (1919), 32–71. For further discussion of Debs's briefs, see David M. Rabban, "The Emergence of Modern First Amendment Doctrine," *University of Chicago Law Review,* 50 (1983), 1205, 1248–52.

96. Brief for Defendant in Error, *Debs v. United States,* 249 U.S. 211 (1919), 69–91. For a useful treatment of the larger judicial context, see Paul L. Murphy, *World War I and the Origin of Civil Liberties in the United States* (New York: Norton, 1979), 179–247. For a further discussion of O'Brian's brief, see Rabban, 1252–57.

97. Alfred H. Kelley and Winfred A. Harbison, *The American Constitution; Its Origins and Development,* 4th ed. (New York: Norton, 1970), 210–22.

98. David M. Rabban, "The First Amendment in Its Forgotten Years," *Yale Law Journal,* 90 (1981), 520.

99. Fred D. Ragan, "Justice Oliver Wendell Holmes, Jr., Zechariah Chafee, Jr., and the Clear and Present Danger Test for Free Speech: The First Year, 1919," *Journal of American History,* 58 (1971), 25; G. Edward White, "Justice Holmes and the Modernization of Free Speech Jurisprudence: The Human Dimension," *California Law Review,* 80 (1992), 414–19. For an additional critique of

Holmes's insensitivity to the protection of political speech, see John Rawls, *Political Liberalism* (New York: Columbia University Press, 1993), 348–56.

100. *Debs v. United States,* 249 U.S. 211 (1919), 212–15.

101. Quoted in Ginger, 384.

102. Mark De Wolfe Howe, ed., *Holmes-Pollock Letters,* vol. 2 (Cambridge: Harvard University Press, 1941), 7; Howe, ed., *Holmes-Laski Letters,* vol. 1 (Cambridge: Harvard University Press, 1953), 197.

103. Debs served the first two months of his sentence in a federal prison in Moundsville, West Virginia, before being transferred to the federal prison in Atlanta. The kind words came from Joseph Z. Terrell, warden in Moundsville. Debs, Terrell felt, was a positive force in the prison. Ginger, 389.

104. Mary Beth Norton, et al., *A People and a Nation: A History of the United States,* vol. 2 (Boston: Houghton Mifflin Company, 1986), A-27. Although the number of votes exceeded the 900,672 received by Debs in 1912, the total was something of a disappointment. The Nineteenth Amendment had provided women's suffrage and thereby greatly expanded the electorate. Debs's 1920 vote was 3.4 percent of the total, but the 1912 total had constituted 6 percent.

105. Quoted in Ginger, 433.

106. Quoted in Currie, 126.

107. Maureen Cain and Alan Hunt, eds., *Marx and Engels on Law* (London: Academic Press, 1979), 63.

108. Stone, 40. "That simplistic perspective characterizes the worst work, which develops the image of an instrumentalist criminal law used by an elite to subjugate the masses. We may readily dispose of this perspective." Id.

109. Daniel F. Greenberg and Nancy Anderson, "Recent Marxisant Books on Law: A Review Essay," *Contemporary Crises,* 5 (1981), 295; Gary Young, "Marx on Bourgeois Law," *Research in Law & Society,* 2 (1979), 165. What is perhaps the most discussed recharacterization of law from a Marxist perspective sounds almost pre-Marxist: "Most men have a strong sense of justice at least with regard to their own interest. If the law is evidently partial and unjust, then it will mask nothing, legitimize nothing, contribute nothing to any class's hegemony. The essential precondition for the effectiveness of law, in its function as ideology, is that it shall display an independence from gross manipulation and shall seem to be just. It cannot seem to be so without upholding its own logic and criteria of equity, indeed, on occasion, by actually *being* just." E. P. Thompson, *Whigs and Hunters: The Origin of the Black Act* (New York: Pantheon Books, 1975), 263.

NOTES TO CHAPTER 5

1. Especially strong collections of essays, editorials, and broadsides by New-ton, Seale, Cleaver, and other Panther leaders are housed in "The Social Protest Collection" and "The Elizabeth and James Abajian Collection of Afro-Ameri-cana" in the Bancroft Library of the University of California at Berkeley. Ephemera without pagination cited in this chapter are housed in these collec-tions. Major autobiographical works include Huey P. Newton, *Revolutionary Suicide* (New York: Harcourt Brace Jovanovich, 1973); Bobby Seale, *A Lonely Rage: The Autobiography of Bobby Seale* (New York: Times Books, 1978) and *Seize the Time: The Story of the Black Panther Party and Huey P. Newton* (New York: Random House, 1970); Eldridge Cleaver, *Soul on Ice* (New York: Mc-Graw Hill, 1968) and *Soul on Fire* (Waco, Tex.: Word Books, 1978).

2. Technically speaking, David Hilliard became the party's formal leader when Newton and Seale were imprisoned, but Cleaver through his speaking and writing emerged as the party's most visible spokesman. Huey P. Newton, *To Die for the People: The Writings of Huey P. Newton* (New York: Vintage Books, 1972), 52. Hilliard did not write and speak as effectively as other party leaders of the 1960s, but for a later co-written memoir, see David Hilliard and Lewis Cole, *This Side of Glory: The Autobiography of David Hilliard and the Story of the Black Panther Party* (Boston: Little, Brown, 1993).

3. In dismissing Cleaver from the party, Newton said that Cleaver had overemphasized the importance of guns and armed resistance to the white power structure. Newton, *To Die for the People*, 49. Cleaver had also supported the New York 21, who had deplored Newton as merely "reformist" and whom Newton had expelled from the party. Elaine Brown, *A Taste of Power: A Black Woman's Story* (New York: Pantheon Books, 1992), 261.

4. Newton, *Revolutionary Suicide*, 13.

5. Id., 50.

6. Seale, *Seize the Time*, 5.

7. Id., 6.

8. Id., 11.

9. Cleaver, *Soul on Fire*, 64; Kathleen Rout, *Eldridge Cleaver* (Boston: Twayne Publishers, 1991), 6. Cleaver later wrote glowingly of Chris Lovdjieff, a teacher at San Quentin who taught him "Everything." Cleaver, *Soul on Ice*, 31.

10. Newton, *Revolutionary Suicide*, 59. For a nonautobiographical account of Newton's "street toughs," see Gilbert Moore, *A Special Rage* (New York: Harper & Row, 1971), 39.

11. Seale, *Seize the Time*, 12.

12. Cleaver, *Soul on Ice*, 3.

13. Id.

14. Sartre's prescription is discussed in Peter Brooks, *Reading for the Plot: Design and Intention in Narrative* (New York: Knopf, 1984), 114. Writing of fiction more than of autobiography, Brooks himself says, "Perhaps of greater interest than the concept of plot . . . is that of plotting, the moments where we seize the active work of structuring revealed or dramatized in the text." Id., 34–35.

15. Newton, *Revolutionary Suicide*, 11.

16. Cleaver, *Soul on Ice*, 13.

17. Id., 11–12.

18. Cleaver, *Soul on Ice*, 27.

19. Seale, *Seize the Time*, 155.

20. Huey P. Newton, *The Genius of Huey P. Newton* (San Francisco: Black Panther Party), 15.

21. Richard Hofstadter, *Anti-Intellectualism in American Life* (New York: Random House, 1962).

22. Seale, *Seize the Time*, 130.

23. Cleaver, *Soul on Ice*, 98–111. Cleaver says at one point that homosexuality is "a sickness, just as are baby-rape or wanting to become the head of General Motors." Id., 110.

24. Newton, *Revolutionary Suicide*, 111.

25. Eldridge Cleaver, *On the Ideology of the Black Panther Party* (San Francisco: Black Panther Party, 1969), 3.

26. Malcolm X, *The Autobiography of Malcolm X* (1964; reprint New York: Ballantine Books, 1973), "Epilogue," 384–85. C. Eric Lincoln, *The Black Muslims in America* (Boston: Beacon, 1961).

27. Seale, *Seize the Time*, 3–4. The son's full name was Malik Nkrumah Stagolee Seale. "Malik" came from Malcolm's Black Muslim name of El Hajj Malik Shabazz.

28. Cleaver, *Soul on Ice*, 50.

29. Gayraud S. Wilmore, *Black Religion and Black Radicalism* (1973; 2nd ed., Maryknoll, N.Y.: Orbis Books, 1983), 174.

30. Malcolm X, *The Autobiography*, 294.

31. Newton, *Revolutionary Suicide*, 3; Seale, *Seize the Time*, 240. Cleaver in fact saw Newton as having received the torch from Malcolm: "Huey's genius is that he took up where brother Malcolm left off when he was assassinated. Huey was successful in creating an organization unique in the history of Afro-Americans. A revolutionary political party with self-perpetuating machinery. This is

a historic achievement. And it is the thought of Huey P. Newton that holds the Black Panther Party together and constitutes its foundation." "Introduction," Newton, *The Genius of Huey P. Newton*, no pagination.

32. Cleaver, *Soul on Ice*, 61. The statement from Ossie Davis itself is reprinted as an appendix in Malcolm X, *The Autobiography*, 457–60.

33. Newton, *Revolutionary Suicide*, 113. For a discussion of how various other African American groups worked and used Malcolm, see Michael Eric Dyson, "X Marks the Spot: A Critical Reading of Malcolm's Readers," *Social Text*, 35 (1993), 25–55.

34. Eldridge Cleaver, "The Courage to Kill: Meeting the Panthers," in Robert Sheer, ed., *Eldridge Cleaver: Post-Prison Writings and Speeches* (New York: Random House, 1967), 39.

35. Newton, *Revolutionary Suicide*, 4. The volume begins with the following poem of the same title:

> By having no family,
> I inherited the family of humanity.
> By having no possessions,
> I have possessed all.
> By rejecting the love of one,
> I received the love of all.
> By surrendering my life to the revolution,
> I found eternal life.
> Revolutionary Suicide.

36. Seale, *Seize the Time*, 79–85.

37. Cleaver, *Soul on Ice*, 37.

38. W. J. Rorabaugh, *Berkeley at War: The 1960s* (New York: Oxford University Press, 1989), 76.

39. Cleaver, *Soul on Ice*, 12.

40. Newton, *To Die for the People*, 25.

41. Cleaver in fact stated that there is "much evidence that Marx and Engels were themselves racists—just like their White brothers and sisters of their era." *On the Ideology of the Black Panther Party*, 4.

42. Seale, *Seize the Time*, 48. In Moore, *A Special Rage*, 37, the author reports seeing the following volumes in Newton's 1969 prison cell: *The Economic and Philosophical Manuscripts of Karl Marx*, John Steinbeck's *The Grapes of Wrath*, Fred Smith's *The Warfare State*, John Eaton's *Socialism in the Nuclear Age*, and Ronald Segal's *The Race War*. Rout reports in *Eldridge Cleaver*, 50, that Cleaver held out the following as the most popular books among California

African American prison inmates: *The Autobiography of Malcolm X, Malcolm X Speaks*, Frantz Fanon's *The Wretched of the Earth*, LeRoi Jones's *Home*, Nat Hentoff's *Call the Keeper*, Robert F. Williams's *Negroes with Guns*, and Che Guevara's *On Guerilla Warfare*.

43. Cleaver, *Soul on Ice*, 13; Mikhail Alekandrovich Bakunin, *The Catechism of the Revolutionist*, Eldridge Cleaver, ed. (no city, publisher, or year of publication).

44. Cleaver, *On the Ideology of the Black Panther Party*, 5.

45. Seale, *Seize the Time*, 25.

46. Frantz Fanon, trans. Charles Lam Markmann, *Black Skins, White Masks* (1952; reprint New York: Grove Press, 1967), 83–110.

47. Frantz Fanon, trans. Constance Farrington, *The Wretched of the Earth* (1961; reprint New York: Grove Press, 1991).

48. The scholar Harold W. Cruse was one of the first to suggest the analogy. See his "Revolutionary Nationalism and the Afro-American," *Studies on the Left*, 2:3, 1962, 12–25.

49. Newton, *To Die for the People*, 83.

50. Cleaver, *On the Ideology of the Black Panther Party*, 6.

51. Newton, *To Die for the People*, 80.

52. Cleaver, "The Courage to Kill," 36–37. Perhaps needless to add, the situation of African Americans is not identical to that of colonized peoples. There are no mother countries and colonies or formal distinctions between colonizers and the colonized. However, the apparent exploitation of African Americans by outsiders led others to speak of domestic colonialism. Bob Blauner, "Internal Colonialism and Ghetto Revolt," in *Racial Oppression in America* (New York: Harper & Row, 1972), 51–111.

53. See, for example, Karl Marx, "The Eighteenth Brumaire of Louis Bonaparte," in Lewis S. Feuer, ed., *Marx and Engels: Basic Writings on Politics and Philosophy* (Garden City, N.Y.: Anchor Books, 1959), 345–58. In "Manifesto of the Communist Party," Marx describes the lumpenproletariat as "the social scum, that passively rotting mass thrown off by the lowest layers of old society." Id., 18.

54. Fanon, *The Wretched of the Earth*, 129.

55. Seale, *Seize the Time*, 30.

56. Cleaver, *On the Ideology of the Black Panther Party*, 7.

57. Brown, 135.

58. Various flyers for concerts featuring "The Lumpen" are preserved in "The Social Protest Collection," Bancroft Library, University of California at Berkeley. See, in particular, Carton 18, Folder 4.

59. Newton, *To Die for the People*, 26–30.

60. Seale, *Seize the Time*, ix.

61. Cleaver, *On the Ideology of the Black Panther Party*, 8.

62. This photograph appears on the original jacket cover of *Revolutionary Suicide*. Newton also chose for himself and then frequently used the title of "Minister of Defense."

63. Newton, *Revolutionary Suicide*, 78.

64. Id., 82.

65. Cleaver, *Soul on Ice*, 47.

66. Id., 19.

67. Lawrence M. Friedman, *The Republic of Choice: Law, Authority and Culture* (Cambridge: Harvard University Press, 1990) 40, 97–98.

68. Newton, *The Genius of Huey P. Newton*, 20.

69. Newton, *To Die for the People*, 82.

70. Huey P. Newton, "Toward a New Constitution" (flyer without pagination or year of publication).

71. Eldridge Cleaver, "The Black Man's Stake in Vietnam" (4-page flyer without pagination or year of publication).

72. This platform is reprinted in many places. One accessible version appears in Newton, *To Die for the People*, 3–6. Cleaver discussed the basic demands in an interview with journalist Nat Hentoff, "Playboy Interview: Eldridge Cleaver," *Playboy*, December 1968, 90–1. For the general commentary on "rights" in American culture, see David Ray Papke, "Understanding 'Rights' in Contemporary American Discourse," *Michigan Journal of Race & Law*, 2 (Spring, 1997), 521–36.

73. Seale, *Seize the Time*, 419.

74. "Trial of Bobby Seale" (Radio interview with Bobby Seale conducted at the beginning of the Chicago 8 Trial), Pacifica Radio Archives, 1986.

75. Seale, *Seize the Time*, 347.

76. Id., 329.

77. Eldridge Cleaver, *On the Constitution* (pamphlet with no city or publisher cited, 1970), no pagination.

78. Seale, *Seize the Time*, 86.

79. *Understand the Black Panther Party* (pamphlet with no city or publication cited, 1970), 13.

80. Quoted in "Huey Newton Shot Dead on Oakland Street," *San Francisco Chronicle*, August 13, 1989, A1.

81. "The Panthers, Still Untamed, Roar Back," *New York Times*, April 30, 1995, H17.

82. Seale, *Seize the Time*, 376.

83. Newton, *Revolutionary Suicide*, 122.

84. Id., 82.

85. Both Newton and Seale recall the same conversation. Newton, *Revolutionary Suicide*, 105–6; Seale, *Seize the Time*, 13–14.

86. Newton, *Revolutionary Suicide*, 146.

87. Cleaver, *Soul on Ice*, 129.

88. Prior to his arrest on October 28, 1967, Newton fumbled around for the right legal materials: "I picked up my law book from between the seats and started to get out. I thought it was my criminal evidence book, which covers laws dealing with reasonable cause for arrest and the search and seizure laws. If necessary, I intended to read the law to this policeman, as I had done so many times in the past. However, I had mistakingly picked up my criminal law book, which looks exactly like the other one." Newton, *Revolutionary Suicide*, 175–76.

89. James M. Nabrit, Jr., "Introduction," in Donald B. King and Charles W. Quick, eds., *Legal Aspects of the Civil Rights Movement* (Detroit: Wayne State University Press, 1965), 6.

90. Jill Norgren and Serena Nanda, *American Cultural Pluralism and Law* (New York: Praeger, 1988), 7.

91. Martin Luther King, Jr., "Letter from Birmingham Jail," in James M. Washington, ed., *A Testament of Hope: The Essential Writings of Martin Luther King, Jr.* (San Francisco: Harper San Francisco, 1986), 293–94. For a fascinating comparison of King's "Letter from Birmingham Jail" to jailhouse writings by Philip Berrigan and Jack Henry Abbott, see Teresa Godwin Phelps, "Voices from Within: Community and Law in Three Prison Narratives," *Journal of American Culture*, 15 (1992), 69–73.

92. Newton, *Revolutionary Suicide*, 106.

93. Quoted in Brown, 247.

94. Hentoff, "Playboy Interview," 108.

95. Newton, *Revolutionary Suicide*, 76–77.

96. Cleaver, *Soul on Ice*, 130.

97. Fanon, *The Wretched of the Earth*, 38.

98. Malcolm X, *The Autobiography*, 235.

99. Moore, *A Special Rage*, 196; Newton, *Revolutionary Suicide*, 114.

100. Newton, *Revolutionary Suicide*, 140.

101. "Executive Mandate Number One," in Newton, *To Die for the People*, 7–8.

102. Seale, *Seize the Time*, 77.

103. Robert L. Allen, *Black Awakening in Capitalist America* (Trenton, N.J.: Africa World Press, 1990), 82.

104. Rorabaugh, *Berkeley at War*, 78.

105. Seale, *Seize the Time*, 125.

106. Newton, *Revolutionary Suicide*, 120.

107. Id., 120.

108. Seale, *Seize the Time*, 420.

109. Sheer, *Eldridge Cleaver*, 198.

110. Robert L. Allen asserts, "The patrols were successful. A noticeable decrease was observed in the number of incidents of police harassment of the ghetto population at large." *Black Awakening*, 82.

111. Rorabaugh, *Berkeley at War*, 81.

112. Hentoff, "Playboy Interview," 104.

113. Newton, *Revolutionary Suicide*, 175–76.

114. Id., 188.

115. "Huey Newton's case is the showdown case. . . . We say that we have had enough of black men and women being shot down like dogs in the street." Eldridge Cleaver, "Conspiracy and Violence in White America," in Mona Bazaar, ed., *Free Huey . . . Or the Sky's the Limit!* (Oakland: Mona Bazaar, 1968), no pagination.

116. Cleaver claimed that after the police captured Hutton, they ordered Hutton to run and then gunned him down. Hentoff, "Playboy Interview," 106. Cleaver's thoughts as he fled the country are recorded in "Farewell Address," in Sheer, *Eldridge Cleaver*, 147–60.

117. A journalistic account of events in New Haven after the 1969 murder of Alex Rackley is Gail Sheehy, *Panthermania* (New York: Harper & Row, 1971).

118. Some found white lionizing of the Panthers nothing short of absurd. Tom Wolfe, *Radical Chic and Mau-Mauing the Flak Catchers* (New York: Farrar, Straus & Giroux, 1970).

119. *Black Panther*, February 21, 1990, 1.

120. "Police in Chicago Slay 2 Panthers," *New York Times*, December 5, 1969, 1; "Inquiry into Slaying of 2 Panthers Urged in Chicago," *New York Times*, December 6, 1969, 29; "Panthers Say an Autopsy Shows Party Official Was Murdered," *New York Times*, December 7, 1969, 68.

121. After protracted struggles scholars gained access to FBI files and documents, and the revealed record of domestic espionage on African American reformers and radicals is shocking. Ward Churchill, *Agents of Repression: The FBI's Secret Wars against the Black Panther Party and American Indian Movement*

(Boston: South End Press, 1990) and Kenneth O'Reilly, *Racial Matters: The FBI's File on Black America, 1960–72* (New York: The Free Press, 1989).

122. "Files Detail Years of Spying on Bernstein," *New York Times*, July 11, 1994, A1.

123. James S. Bowen, "Law, Legitimacy and Black Revolution," *Yale Journal of Law and Liberation*, 1 (1989), 150.

124. According to the distinguished historian Eugene Genovese, a system of domination may be gauged not by confrontations between oppressors and the oppressed but rather by the extent to which the system avoids such confrontations. *In Red and Black* (New York: Pantheon Books, 1971), 369.

NOTES TO CHAPTER 6

1. For a comment on Debs's effort to facilitate a lecture by Susan B. Anthony in Terre Haute, see Bruce Miroff, *Icons of Democracy: American Leaders as Heroes, Aristocrats, Dissenters, and Democrats* (New York: Basic Books, 1993), 224. Cleaver lionizes Debs and the abolitionists in *Soul on Ice* (New York: McGraw-Hill, 1968), 19 and 83. Debs's fondness for Hugo's *Les Misérables* began in his youth, and he read the novel time and again throughout his life. Ray Ginger, *The Bending Cross: A Biography of Eugene Victor Debs* (New Brunswick, N.J.: Rutgers University Press, 1949), 14. Newton speaks of his love of the novel in Huey P. Newton, *Revotionary Suicide* (New York: Harcourt Bruce Jovanovich, 1973), 81.

2. Sacvan Bercovitch, "Investigations of an Americanist," *Journal of American History*, 78:3 (December, 1991), 982.

3. Richard Hofstadter, *The Paranoid Style in American Politics and Other Essays* (New York: Alfred A. Knopf, 1966), 10–14.

4. James William Gibson, *Warrior Dreams: Paramilitary Culture in Post-Vietnam America* (New York: Hill and Wang, 1994), 7.

5. *McNeil-Lehrer News Hour*, April 26, 1995. Quoted in Richard Abanes, *American Militias: Rebellion, Racism and Religion* (Downers Grove, Ill.: Inter-Varsity Press, 1996), 18.

6. David Van Brima, "Militias," *Time*, 145:26 (June 26, 1995), 57.

7. Morris Dees, *Gathering Storm: America's Militia Threat* (New York: Harper Collins Publishers, 1996), 33–47.

8. Andrew Macdonald, *The Turner Diaries* (Hillsboro, W.Va.: National Vanguard Books, 1978; 2nd ed., 1980), 2

9. Id., 207.

10. Id., 206–8.

11. Published in 1888, Edward Bellamy's *Looking Backward* was immensely popular and led to the founding of Bellamy Clubs and a Nationalist Party. The novel imagines an American future in which economic chaos and inequality has given way to a democratic form of state capitalism.

12. For a treatment of the Militia of Montana and its various publications, see Dees, 83.

13. James Brooke, "Matchmaker for Lonely Heart Opponents of 'New World Order,'" *New York Times*, Feb. 12, 1997, A10.

14. However, they ultimately did not like the militia cells they visited and also were not well liked by the militiamen. Kenneth S. Stern, *A Force upon the Plain: The American Militia Movement and the Politics of Hate* (New York: Simon & Schuster, 1996), 197.

15. Peter Applebome, "An Unlikely Legacy of the 60's: The Violent Right," *New York Times*, May 7, 1995, A1.

16. Abanes, 37.

17. Id., 38.

18. Carey Goldberg, "The Freemen Go to Court, But Not Without a Struggle," *New York Times*, June 14, 1996, A7.

19. Stern, 196.

20. Marcus is quoted in Paul Glastris, "Patriot Games," *Washington Monthly*, June 1995, 23–26. For a discussion of the Nichols proceedings, see Abanes 35–36.

21. Abanes, 31.

22. Id., 27.

23. Jill Smolowe, "Enemies of the State," *Time*, 145:19, May 8, 1995, 63.

24. Mark Koernke, "A Call to Arms" (Real World Productions, 1993). The video is quoted in Abanes, 2.

25. Quoted without citation in Dees, 80.

26. Abanes, 29.

27. Abanes, 30–32.

28. Quoted without citation in Dees, 85. According to Fitzhugh MacCrae, leader of New Hampshire's Hillsborough County Dragons, the Second Amendment "is the only amendment that empowers the rest of them." Quoted in Smolowe, 62.

29. This sentiment can translate into a variety of insurrectionist theory. Stern, 111–15.

30. Joelle E. Polesky, "The Rise of Private Militia: A First and Second Amendment Analysis of the Right to Organize and the Right to Train," *University of Pennsylvania Law Review*, 144 (1996), 1593–1642; David C. Williams,

"The Militia Movement and Second Amendment Revolution," *Cornell Law Review*, 81 (1996), 879–952.

31. Dallas A. Blanchard, *The Anti-Abortion Movement and the Rise of the Religious Right* (New York: Twayne Publishers, 1994), 37.

32. For a useful summary of abortion-related attitudes among various religious groups, see Joseph B. Tamney, Stephen D. Johnson, and Ronald Burton, "The Abortion Controversy: Conflicting Beliefs and Values in American Society and within Religious Subgroups," in Ted G. Jelen and Marthe A. Chandler, eds., *Abortion Politics in the United States and Canada* (Westport, Conn.: Praeger, 1994), 41–56.

33. For a review of anti-abortion stances prompted by various political persuasions, see Malcolm L. Groggin, "Introduction," in Groggin, ed., *Understanding the New Politics of Abortion* (Newbury Park, Calif.: Sage Publications, 1993), 10–15.

34. The United States Supreme Court lead opinion in the case locates the right to abortion within the right of privacy. However, the opinion itself acknowledges that there is disagreement as to just where the right of privacy is located within the Constitution. *Roe v. Wade*, 410 U.S. 113 (1973), at 153.

35. These included a ban on using public facilities for abortions, mandatory viability testing before abortions are performed, and even a declaration that life begins at conception. *Webster v. Reproductive Health Services*, 492 U.S. 490 (1989).

36. Quoted in Marian Faux, *Crusades: Voices From the Abortion Front* (New York: Birch Lane Press, 1990), 117.

37. Frustrated with the majority opinion, Scalia said, "It thus appears that the mansion of constitutional abortion law, constructed overnight in *Roe v. Wade*, must be disassembled doorjamb by doorjamb, and never entirely brought down, no matter how wrong it may be. *Webster*, 537.

38. The Court upheld the statute's requirements that women be told of fetal development and alternatives to ending their pregnancies, that women wait twenty-four hours after receiving the information, that doctors keep detailed records on all abortions and that unmarried girls under eighteen obtain the consent of one parent or a state judge before receiving an abortion. *Planned Parenthood of S.E. Pennsylvania v. Casey*, 505 U.S. 833 (1992)

39. Quoted in Harriet Chiang, "Court Upholds Right to Abortion," *San Francisco Chronicle*, June 30, 1992, A1.

40. Blanchard, 86.

41. Karen O'Connor, *No Neutral Ground? Abortion Politics in an Age of Absolutes* (Boulder, Colo.: Westview Press, 1996), 172.

42. Quoted in "Gunman Kills 2 at Florida Abortion Clinic," *Stamford Advocate,* July 30, 1994, A11.

43. Mark Curriden, "An Unusual Theory Tested and Rejected," *American Bar Association Journal* December 1994, 26.

44. For useful history of the Pro-Life Action League, see Blanchard, 69–70.

45. For a useful history of Operation Rescue, see Blanchard, 64–67.

46. Blanchard, 90.

47. Joseph M. Scheidler, *Closed: 99 Ways to Stop Abortion* (Rockford, Ill.: Tan Books and Publishers, 1985; revised ed., 1993).

48. Id., 17.

49. Id., 18.

50. Id., 256.

51. Id., 308.

52. Faux, 53.

53. Blanchard, 67.

54. Faux, 131–38.

55. For a discussion of Christian Reconstructionism, see Blanchard, 49–50.

56. For a mocking account of Terry's conduct in his Los Angeles and Atlanta trials, see Faux, 151–72.

57. Charles Hersch makes this argument in "Five Tellings of Abortion Clinic Protest: *Madsen v. Women's Health Center* and the Limits of Narrative," *Legal Studies Forum,* 29:4 (1995), 400–401.

58. Randall Terry, *Operation Rescue* (Springdale, Pa.: Whitaker House, 1988), 22.

59. Id., 129.

60. Richard Lacayo, "Crusading against the Pro-Choice Movement," *Time,* 138:15, October 21, 1991, 26–28.

61. Lois Romano and Tom Kenworthy, "Oklahoma City Bombing Trial Set to Begin," *Indianapolis Star,* March 30, 1997; D5.

62. Blanchard, 148.

63. Reports growing out of Congressional investigations include Subcommittee of Terrorism, Technology and Government Information of the Committee on the Judiciary, "The Militia Movement in the United States" (1995); House Committee on the Judiciary, "Clinic Blockades" (1992); and House Committee on the Judiciary, "Abortion Clinic Violence" (1993).

64. Abanes, 29.

65. Blanchard, 89.

66. For an explanation of the role anti-abortion activism can play in one's personal makeup, see Carol J. C. Maxwell, "'Where's the Land of Happy?' In-

dividual Meaning and Collective Antiabortion Activism," in Jelen and Chandler, 89–106.

67. Raymond Williams has developed the notions of "dominant," "residual," and "emergent" as ways to distinguish trends and developments within larger cultural formations. However, he also acknowledges how difficult it is to distinguish between new phases of the dominant culture and developments which are substantially oppositional to it, that is, developments which are merely novel versus those that are truly emergent. In the dominant culture of advanced capitalism, he says, "Again and again what we have to observe is in effect a 'pre-emergence,' active and pressing but not yet fully articulated, rather than the evident emergence which could be more confidently named." *Marxism and Literature* (New York: Oxford University Press, 1977), 126.

68. This is the opposite of what one frequently hears from American political leaders, e.g., President George Bush. When he addressed Americans at the beginning of the 1991 Gulf War, the President spoke of the opportunity to forge a "new world order" in which "the rule of law, not the law of the jungle" would govern. "Transcript of the Comments of Bush on the Air Strikes against the Iraquis," *New York Times*, January 17, 1991, A14.

Bibliographical Essay

CHAPTER I

The legal faith—or law-related ideology, if one prefers that characterization—may be thought of as part of the even larger and more complex civil religion that developed in the early decades of the Republic. Robert N. Bellah's "Civil Religion in America," *Daedalus*, 96 (1967): 1–19, is a particularly influential essay on the topic, but many other scholars have followed his lead. Relevant works include Catherine L. Albanese, *Sons of the Father: The Civil Religion of the American Revolution* (Philadelphia: Temple University Press, 1976); Conrad Cherry, *God's New Israel: Religious Interpretations of American Destiny* (Englewood Cliffs, N.J.: Prentice-Hall, 1971); and Wilbur Zelinsky, *Nation Into State: The Shifting Symbolic Foundations of American Nationalism* (Chapel Hill: University of North Carolina Press, 1988). Bellah explored the relevance of "civil religion" in the late twentieth century in *The Broken Covenant: Civil Religion in a Time of Trial* (New York: Seabury Press, 1975).

As for just the legal faith, two excellent works contemplate the symbolic identity of the United States Constitution through the full sweep of the nation's history. Michael Kammen's *A Machine That Would Go of Itself: The Constitution in American Culture* (New York: Alfred A. Knopf, 1986) offers comments on the document from American politicians and critics. Sanford Levinson's *Constitutional Faith* (Princeton: Princeton University Press, 1988) is enamored with the ways various assumptions regarding the Constitution parallel certain traditional religious assumptions.

I have in my own writings attempted to dissect and analyze the courtroom trial as a motif in American culture. See David Ray Papke, "The Courtroom Trial as American Cultural Convention," in David L. Gunn, ed., *The Lawyer and Popular Culture* (Littleton, Colo.: Fred B. Rothman, 1993). Milner S. Ball treats the American courtroom trial as a variety of theater in "The Play's the Thing: An Unscientific Reflection on the Courts Under the Rubric of Theater," *Stanford Law Review*, 28 (1975): 81–115.

A well-written and provocative work on legalism in the Early Republic is Robert A. Ferguson, *Law and Letters in American Culture* (Cambridge: Harvard University Press, 1984). A contrasting work, one not grounded in American history or culture but rather Marxism, is Hugh Collins, *Marxism and Law* (New York: Oxford University Press, 1982).

CHAPTER 2

The two most important sets of primary materials relating to William Lloyd Garrison are well compiled and widely available. Walter M. Merrill and Louis Ruchames's *The Letters of William Lloyd Garrison,* 6 vols. (Cambridge: Harvard University Press, 1971–1981) is comprehensive and nicely indexed. All thirty-five volumes of the *Liberator* (1831–65) are available on microfilm, and although hours at a microfilm reader are draining, Garrison's journal is never less than amazing.

Biographies of Garrison are numerous and include two early works by his children Wendell Phillips Garrison and Francis Jackson Garrison, *William Lloyd Garrison 1805–1879; The Story of His Life Told by His Children,* 4 vols. (New York: Century, 1885–94) and Fanny Garrison Villard, *William Lloyd Garrison on Non-Resistance, Together with a Personal Sketch by His Daughter, and a Tribute by Leo Tolstoi* (New York: Nation, 1924). Neither work musters a negative word about a beloved father, but the former is a goldmine of primary documents and quotations.

Twentieth-century scholars have time and again been drawn to Garrison. Biographies from the 1950s and 1960s include: Russell B. Nye, *William Lloyd Garrison and the Humanitarian Reformers* (Boston: Little, Brown, 1955); Walter M. Merrill, *Against the Tide: A Biography of William Lloyd Garrison* (Cambridge: Harvard University Press, 1963); and John L. Thomas, *The Liberator: William Lloyd Garrison* (Boston: Little, Brown, 1963). A fine recent study is James Brewer Stewart, *William Lloyd Garrison and the Challenge of Emancipation* (Arlington Heights, Ill.: Harland Davidson, 1992). William E. Cain's *William Lloyd Garrison and the Fight against Slavery* (Boston: Bedford Books, 1995) is primarily a collection of selections from the *Liberator,* but it also includes a lengthy biographical essay and useful notes regarding various specific essays and editorials.

The secondary literature on American abolitionism is of course immense, but three especially insightful works regarding Garrison's evolving views on law are Aileen S. Kraditor, *Means and Ends in American Abolitionism: Garrison and His Critics on Strategy and Tactics, 1834–1850* (New York: Vintage Books, 1967); Lewis Perry, *Radical Abolitionism: Anarchy and the Government of God in Anti-*

slavery Thought (Ithaca: Cornell University Press, 1973); and William M. Wiecek, *The Sources of Antislavery Constitutionalism in America, 1760–1848* (Ithaca: Cornell University Press, 1977).

CHAPTER 3

Several widely available and extremely interesting collections of primary works exist for Elizabeth Cady Stanton. Her own *Eighty Years and More: Reminiscences, 1815–1897* (1898; reprint New York: Schocken Books, 1971) both re-captures and reimagines the major experiences of her life. In a dogged effort to preserve the experiences and texts of the nineteenth-century women's movement, Cady Stanton and others collected materials from the years 1848–1883: Elizabeth Cady Stanton, Susan B. Anthony, Matilda Joslyn Gage, eds., *History of Woman Suffrage,* 3 vols. (New York: Fowler & Wells, 1881–87). In subsequent years, Susan B. Anthony and Ida Husted Harper collected, edited, and published similar materials up until 1920. For a superbly well-edited modern collection, see Ellen Carol DuBois, ed., *Elizabeth Cady Stanton, Susan B. Anthony: Correspondence, Writings, Speeches* (New York: Schocken Books, 1981).

Modern biographies of Elizabeth Cady Stanton begin with Alma Lutz, *Created Equal: A Biography of Elizabeth Cady Stanton* (1940; reprint New York: Octagon Books, 1974). Two more recent and highly readable works are Lois W. Banner, *Elizabeth Cady Stanton: A Radical for Woman's Rights* (Boston: Little, Brown, 1980) and Elisabeth Griffith, *In Her Own Right: The Life of Elizabeth Cady Stanton* (New York: Oxford University Press, 1984).

Two works which are rich in insight regarding women's legal condition in the nineteenth century are Norma Basch, *In the Eyes of the Law: Women, Marriage, and Property in Nineteenth-Century New York* (Ithaca: Cornell University Press, 1982) and Joan Hoff, *Law, Gender and Injustice: A Legal History of U.S. Women* (New York: New York University Press, 1991). For a more general treatment of many of the legal issues that most agitated Cady Stanton, see Michael Grossberg, *Governing the Hearth: Law and the Family in Nineteenth-Century America* (Chapel Hill: University of North Carolina Press, 1985).

CHAPTER 4

Anyone interested in Eugene Debs should stop in Terre Haute, Indiana. Large collections of Debs's papers and memorabilia are housed there by Indiana State University and by the Debs Foundation. Indeed, the very home to which Debs returned time and again after labor actions and political campaigns is preserved and open to the public. The scholar J. Robert Constantine has edited a superb collection of Debs's letters, *Letters of Eugene V. Debs*, 3 vols. (Urbana: University of Illinois Press, 1990).

Debs has been blessed by two wonderful biographers of two different eras. Ray Ginger's *The Bending Cross: A Biography of Eugene Victor Debs* (New Brunswick : Rutgers University Press, 1949) lionizes Debs with both warmth and great thoroughness. Nick Salvatore's equally impressive *Eugene V. Debs: Citizen and Socialist* (Urbana: University of Illinois Press, 1982) acknowledges more of Debs's weaknesses but nevertheless offers an endorsement of Debs's commitment to indigenous democratic traditions. Also useful is Harold W. Currie, *Eugene V. Debs* (Boston: Twayne Publishers, 1976), which attempts to synthesize Debs's thought in various areas, and H. Wayne Morgan, *Eugene V. Debs: Socialist for President* (Syracuse, N.Y.: Syracuse University Press, 1962).

The literature on socialism in American history is almost as large as the literature on either abolitionism or the women's movement. The older David A. Shannon, *The Socialist Party of America* (New York: Macmillan, 1955) is a still useful overview of Debs's party. A more personal and literary account is Irving Howe, *Socialism in America* (San Diego: Harcourt, Brace, Jovanovich, 1985).

On the subject of injunctions against labor actions and the more general treatment of labor in turn-of-the-century courts, see William E. Forbath, *Law and the Shaping of the American Labor Movement* (Cambridge: Harvard University Press, 1991). Other interesting books concerning the same general subject include Gerald G. Eggert, *Railway Labor Disputes: The Beginnings of Federal Strike Policy* (Ann Arbor: University of Michigan Press, 1967); Victoria Hattam, *Labor Visions and State Power: The Origins of Business Unionism in the United States* (Princeton: Princeton University Press, 1993); Arnold M. Paul, *Conservative Crisis and the Rule of Law: Attitudes of Bar and Bench, 1887–1895* (Ithaca: Cornell University Press, 1960); and Christopher L. Tomlins, *The State and the Unions: Labor Relations, Law, and the Organized Labor Movement in America, 1880–1960* (New York: Cambridge University Press, 1985).

Those interested in the Marxist understanding of law might begin with Maureen Cain and Alan Hunt, eds., *Marx and Engels on Law* (London: Academic Press, 1979). A succinct but nevertheless provocative overview of the subject is the previously mentioned Hugh Collins, *Marxism and Law* (New York: Oxford University Press, 1982).

CHAPTER 5

In a burst of remarkable foresight, archivists at the University of California-Berkeley saved essays, editorials, broadsides, and other ephemera from their community in the turbulent 1960s and early 1970s. Great stores of materials by and about the Black Panthers are, as a result, available in "The Social Protest Collection" and "The Elizabeth and James Abajian Collection of Afro-Americana" in the University's Bancroft Library.

I was pleasantly surprised in my own research to realize how many autobiographical works had been published by leading Black Panthers. They include Huey Newton, *Revolutionary Suicide* (New York: Harcourt Brace Jovanovich, 1973) and *To Die for the People: The Writings of Huey P. Newton* (New York: Vintage Books, 1972); Bobby Seale, *A Lonely Rage: The Autobiography of Bobby Seale* (New York: Times Books, 1978) and *Seize the Time: The Story of the Black Panther Party and Huey P. Newton* (New York: Random House, 1970); and Eldridge Cleaver, *Soul on Ice* (New York: McGraw Hill, 1968) and *Soul on Fire* (Waco, Tex.: World Books, 1978).

In more recent years, other Black Panthers have brought their reflections into print. Worth noting are Elaine Brown, *A Taste of Power: A Black Woman's Story* (New York: Pantheon Books, 1992) and David Hilliard and Lewis Cole, *This Side of Glory: The Autobiography of David Hilliard and the Story of the Black Panther Party* (Boston: Little, Brown, 1993).

Books on the Black Panthers are a scattered, uneven lot. See Gilbert Moore, *A Special Rage* (New York: Harper & Row, 1971); Kathleen Rout, *Eldridge Cleaver* (Boston: Twayne Publishers, 1991); Gail Sheehy, *Panthermania* (New York: Harper & Row, 1971); and Tom Wolfe, *Radical Chic and Mau-Mauing the Flak Catchers* (New York: Farrar, Straus & Giroux, 1970). A recent indictment of the Black Panthers is Hugh Pearson, *The Shadow of the Panther: Huey Newton and the Price of Black Power in America* (Reading, Mass.: Addison-Wesley, 1994).

CHAPTER 6

For a safe peek at the militia, one might consult various chat boxes or bulletin boards on the Internet. Book-length studies, for the most part hostile, include Richard Abanes, *American Militias: Rebellion, Racism and Religion* (Downers Grove, Ill.: InterVarsity Press, 1996); Morris Dees, *Gathering Storm: America's Militia Threat* (New York: Harper Collins Publishers, 1996); and Kenneth S. Stern, *A Force upon the Plain: The American Militia Movement and the*

Politics of Hate (New York: Simon & Schuster, 1996). James William Gibson's *Warrior Dreams: Paramilitary Culture in Post-Vietnam America* (New York: Hill and Wang, 1994) offers an interesting cultural backdrop for the militia movement.

Less secretive than the leaders of the militia, leaders of the anti-abortion movement have themselves published books. Two works by prominent anti-abortionists are Joseph M. Scheidler, *Closed: 99 Ways to Stop Abortion* (Rockford, Ill.: Tan Books and Publishers, 1985; revised ed., 1993) and Randall Terry, *Operation Rescue* (Springdale, Pa.: Whitaker House, 1988).

The secondary literature on the anti-abortion movement is much more diverse and balanced than is the literature on the militia movement. Books and collections providing useful overviews include Dallas A. Blanchard, *The Anti-Abortion Movement and the Rise of the Religious Right* (New York: Twayne Publishers, 1994); Malcolm L. Groggin, ed., *Understanding the New Politics of Abortion* (Newbury Park, Calif.: Sage Publications, 1992); Ted G. Jelen and Marthe A. Chandler, ed., *Abortion Politics in the United States and Canada* (Westport, Conn.: Praeger, 1994); and Karen O'Connor, *No Neutral Ground: Abortion Politics in an Age of Absolutes* (Boulder, Colo.: Westview Press, 1996). A more specialized work bringing to life individual voices on both sides of the abortion debate is Marian Faux, *Crusades: Voices From the Abortion Front* (New York: Birch Lane Press, 1990).

Index

About the Author

David Ray Papke is the R. Bruce Townsend Professor of Law at the Indiana University School of Law-Indianapolis, and he is the first professor on his campus to hold a joint appointment in the Schools of Law and Liberal Arts. He earned his undergraduate degree at Harvard College, his law degree at the Yale Law School, and his Ph.D. in American Studies at the University of Michigan.

Professor Papke is internationally recognized for his research and writing on law in American history and culture. He is the author of *Framing the Criminal: Crime, Cultural Work, and the Loss of Critical Perspective, 1830–1900* (1987) and *Narrative and the Legal Discourse* (1991). In 1995 he was awarded the Bryant Spann Memorial Prize for his study of Eugene Debs. At present, he is at work on a book-length study of the 1895 Pullman strike and litigation.